Corporate Social Responsibility

Corporate Social Responsibility

Doing the Most Good for
Your Company and Your Cause

PHILIP KOTLER
and
NANCY LEE

WILEY

John Wiley & Sons, Inc.

Published by John Wiley & Sons, Inc., Hoboken, New Jersey.
Published simultaneously in Canada.

For general information on our other products and services, or technical support, please contact our Customer Care Department within the United States at (800) 762-2974, outside the United States at (317) 572-3993, or fax (317) 572-4002.

Wiley also publishes its books in a variety of electronic formats. Some content that appears in print may not be available in electronic books. For more information about Wiley products, visit our web site at www.wiley.com.

Designations used by companies to distinguish their products are often claimed by trademarks. In all instances where the author or publisher is aware of a claim, the product names appear in Initial Capital letters. Readers, however, should contact the appropriate companies for more complete information regarding trademarks and registration.

Library of Congress Cataloging-in-Publication Data:
Kotler, Philip.
    Corporate social responsibility : doing the most good for your company and your cause / Philip Kotler and Nancy Lee.
      p. cm.
    ISBN 0-471-47611-0 (cloth)
  1. Social responsibility of business. 2. Social marketing. 3. Corporations—Charitable contributions. 4. Corporate image. I. Lee, Nancy, 1932– II. Title.
  HD60.K67 2005
  658.4'08—dc22   2004020375

Printed in the United States of America.

10 9 8 7 6 5 4 3 2

CONTENTS

Contents

ACKNOWLEDGMENTS

The authors want to acknowledge the following people for sharing their stories and perspectives regarding corporate social initiatives, and in many cases, taking the time and effort to complete surveys, confer with other colleagues and partners involved in these initiatives, research historical files and proof copy. We thank you.

Aleve, Rich Ehrmann at Aleve and Kelly Gifford at the Arthritis Foundation
American Express, Anthony Mitchell
AT&T Broadband/Comcast, Liz Castells-Heard at Castells & Asociados
AT&T Wireless, Richard Brown
Athena Water, Trish May
Avon, Laura Castellano
Ben & Jerry's, Chrystie Heimert
Best Buy, Linda Wilkinson at Best Buy and Tricia Conroy at e4partners
Body Shop, Steve McIver
British Airways, Kate Walton at UNICEF UK
Chiquita, Michael Mitchell
Cisco Systems, Nayeem Sheikh
Coca-Cola, Carol Martel
ConAgra Foods, Nancy Peck-Todd
Cone Inc., Carol Cone
Costco, Sheri Flies
Crest, Tricia Montgomery
Dell, Bryant Hilton
Dole, Amy Myrdal and Marcy Reed
Fannie Mae, Lesia Bullock
FedEx, Pam Roberson and Ron Wong
Ford, Kristen Kinley and Andy Acho
General Electric, Debra Wexler
General Mills, Chris Shea and Marybeth Thorsgaard

General Motors, David Jerome and Ann Kihn

Hewlett-Packard, Maureen Conway

Home Depot, Park Howell at Park and Company

IBM, Stanley Litow and Robin Willner

Intel, Gary Niekerk

Johnson & Johnson, Andrea Higham

Kenneth Cole Productions, Kristin Hoppmann

Kraft, Sally Maier and Michael Mudd

LensCrafters, Susan Knobler and Pam Kraemer

Levi Strauss & Co., Jeff Beckman and Stuart Burden

Lysol, Ruth Apgar at Reckitt Benckiser

McDonald's, Joanne Jacobs

Microsoft, Joanna Fuller

Motorola, Rich Guimond

Mustang Survival, Elizabeth Bennett at Seattle Children's Hospital & Regional Medical Center

New York Times Company Foundation, Rita Wnuk

Nike, Jill Zanger

Nordstrom, Deniz Anders

Northwest Airlines, Carol Hollen

Pampers, May Stoeckle at P&G and Andrea Furia at the National Institute of Child Health and Human Development

PARADE, Christie Emden

PETsMART, Jennifer Pflugfelder

Premera Blue Cross, Dana Hurley

QVC, Patricia McLaughlin at the American Legacy Foundation

REI, David Jayo

Safeco, Rose Lincoln and Wendy Stauff

7-Eleven, Margaret Chabris

Share Our Strength, Bill Shore

Shell, Debbie Breazeale at Shell and Garry Snowden at Conservation Volunteers Australia

Silk, David Kargas for White Wave

Starbucks, Sue Mecklenburg

Subway, Libby Puckett at North Carolina Heart and Stroke Prevention and Steve Hanhauser at MarketSmart Advertising

Target, Diane Carlson

Timberland, Kate King and Celina Adams

Wal-Mart, Wendy Sept, Chad Graham, and Karen Wess

Washington Mutual, Sheri Pollock and Deanna Oppenheimer

INTRODUCTION

If you are reading this introduction, chances are you work in your company's department for community relations, corporate communications, public affairs, public relations, environmental stewardship, corporate responsibility, or corporate citizenship. But it is just as likely that you are a marketing manager or a product manager, have responsibility for some aspect of corporate philanthropy, or are on staff at a corporate foundation. On the other hand, you may work at an advertising, public relations, or public affairs firm and be looked to for advice by your corporate clients in the area of corporate social initiatives. And you may be the CEO.

If you are like others in any of these roles, we think it's also quite possible that you feel challenged and pulled by the demands and expectations surrounding the buzz for corporate social responsibility. It may be as fundamental as deciding what social issues and causes to support and making recommendations on which ones to reject. It may involve the grace and finesse often required for screening potential community partners and figuring out how much or what to give. It most likely requires rigor in selling your ideas internally, setting appealing yet realistic expectations for outcomes, and then building cross-functional support for implementation plans. You may be concerned with how to integrate a new initiative into current strategies and to handle the extra workload. Or perhaps you are currently on the hot seat to evaluate and report what happened with all that money you gave last time to a cause, or gave as a result of retooling practices implemented to save the planet last year.

If so, we have written this book for you. More than 25 of your colleagues in firms including Ben & Jerry's, IBM, Washington Mutual, Johnson & Johnson, Timberland, Microsoft, The Body Shop, American Express, and Starbucks have taken time to share their stories and their recommendations for how to do the most good for your company as well as for a cause. You'll read about their hard lessons learned and perceived keys to success.

We have a common agenda. We all want a better world and are convinced that communities need corporate support and partnerships to help make that happen. A key to bringing about this support is for corporations to recognize and realize opportunities for bottom-line benefits, including corporate goodwill.

Even though this book has been written primarily for those in for-profit corporations and their communication agencies and foundations, it can also be beneficial to those in nonprofit organizations and public sector agencies seeking corporate support and partners for social initiatives. It offers a unique opportunity for you to gain insight into a corporation's wants and needs and can better prepare you to decide what companies to approach and how to listen before you ask. The final chapter, just for you, presents 10 recommendations that will increase your chances they will say yes. When you recognize and practice the marketing role inherent in this process, your target markets will appreciate it.

Our sincere hope is that this book will leave corporate managers and staff better prepared to choose the most appropriate issues, best partners, and highly leveraged initiatives. We want it to help you engender internal enthusiasm for your recommendations and inspire you to develop blue ribbon initiatives. And, perhaps most important, we imagine it increasing the chances that your final report on what happened is both credible and incredibly good news for your company and the cause.

Corporate Social Responsibility

The Case for Doing
at Least Some Good

*For many years, community development goals were philanthropic activ-
ities that were seen as separate from business objectives, not fundamental
to them; doing well and doing good were seen as separate pursuits. But I
think that is changing. What many of the organizations that are represented here today are learning is that cutting-edge innovation and competitive advantage can result from weaving social and environmental
considerations into business strategy from the beginning. And in that
process, we can help develop the next generation of ideas and markets and
employees.[1]*

—Carly Fiorina, Hewlett-Packard, at the
Business for Social Responsibility
Annual Conference, November 12, 2003

This is a practical book. It is intended to help guide the decision
making of corporate managers, executives, and their staff, be-
sieged on a daily basis with requests and proposals for support of
social causes. These requests seem to come from everywhere and
everyone for everything: from nonprofit organizations, public sector
agencies, special interest groups, suppliers, potential investors, stockholders, politicians, even colleagues and board members; for issues
ranging from health to public safety to education to community

development to protecting animal rights to sustaining the environment. And the pressures to respond *strategically* seem to be building, with increased internal and external expectations to address economic responsibilities as well as social ones—to do good for the corporation as well as the cause. This book is also intended to help guide evaluation of program outcomes, as there are similar increased pressures to prove the business and social value of allocations of scarce resources.

The book distinguishes six major types of corporate social initiatives and offers perspectives from professionals in the field on strengths and weaknesses of each in terms of benefits to the cause and benefits to the company. These initiatives include ones that are marketing related (i.e., cause promotions, cause-related marketing, and corporate social marketing) as well as ones that are outside the typical functions of marketing departments (i.e., employee volunteering and socially responsible business practices). The focus is on assimilating recommended best practices for choosing among the varied potential social issues that could be addressed by a corporation; selecting an initiative that will do the most good for the social issue as well as the corporation; developing and implementing successful program plans; and evaluating program efforts. An underlying assumption of this book is that most for-profit corporations will do some good, for some cause, at least some of the time.

This opening chapter sets the stage with a few definitions to establish a common language for discussions in future chapters. It highlights trends and statistics that support the assumption that corporations have an increased focus on social responsibility; describes the various perceived factors experts identify as fueling these trends; and concludes with current challenges and criticisms facing those attempting to do the most good.

WHAT IS GOOD?

A quick browse of web sites for the Fortune 500 reveals that *good* goes by many names, including corporate social responsibility, corporate citizenship, corporate philanthropy, corporate giving, corporate community involvement, community relations, community affairs, community development, corporate responsibility, global citizenship, and corporate societal marketing.

For purposes of focused discussion and applications for best practices, the authors prefer the use of the term *corporate social responsibility* and offer the following definition:

> *Corporate social responsibility is a commitment to improve community well-being through discretionary business practices and contributions of corporate resources.*

A key element of this definition is the word *discretionary*. We are not referring here to business activities that are mandated by law or that are moral or ethical in nature and perhaps therefore expected. Rather, we are referring to a *voluntary* commitment a business makes in choosing and implementing these practices and making these contributions. Such a commitment must be demonstrated in order for a company to be described as socially responsible and will be fulfilled through the adoption of new business practices and/or contributions, either monetary or nonmonetary. The term *community well-being* in this definition includes human conditions as well as environmental issues.

Others have offered several distinct definitions of corporate social responsibility (CSR). One from the World Business Council for Sustainable Development reflects the council's focus on economic development in describing CSR as "business' commitment to contribute to sustainable economic development, working with employees, their families, the local community, and society at large to improve their quality of life."[2] The organization Business for Social Responsibility defines CSR as "operating a business in a manner that meets or exceeds the ethical, legal, commercial, and public expectations that society has of business." This definition is somewhat broader as it encompasses business decision making related to "ethical values, legal requirements, as well as respect for people, communities, and the environment."[3]

We also use the term *corporate social initiatives* to describe major efforts under the corporate social responsibility umbrella and offer the following definition:

> *Corporate social initiatives are major activities undertaken by a corporation to support social causes and to fulfill commitments to corporate social responsibility.*

Causes most often supported through these initiatives are those that contribute to community health (i.e., AIDS prevention, early detection for breast cancer, timely immunizations), safety (designated driver programs, crime prevention, use of car safety restraints), education (literacy, computers for schools, special needs education), and employment (job training, hiring practices, plant locations); the environment (recycling, elimination of the use of harmful chemicals, reduced packaging); community and economic development (low-interest housing loans); and other basic human needs and desires (hunger, homelessness, animal rights, voting privileges, antidiscrimination efforts).

Support from corporations may take many forms, including cash contributions, grants, paid advertising, publicity, promotional sponsorships, technical expertise, in-kind contributions (i.e., donations of products such as computer equipment or services such as printing), employee volunteers, and access to distribution channels. Cash contributions may come directly through a corporation or indirectly through a foundation it has established to focus on corporate giving on behalf of the corporation.

Corporations may be sponsoring these initiatives on their own (such as the New York Times Company Foundation support for journalism and journalists) or in partnership with others (as with ConAgra Foods and America's Second Harvest). They may be conceived of and managed by one department within the corporation, or by a team representing multiple business units.

As noted earlier, we have identified six major types of corporate social initiatives, which are the focus of this book, with a chapter dedicated to a detailed review of each initiative. An overview of these initiatives is presented in Chapter 2.

WHAT ARE THE TRENDS?

In the last decade, directional signals point to increased corporate giving, increased corporate reporting on social responsibility initiatives, the establishment of a corporate social norm to do good, and an apparent transition from giving as an obligation to giving as a strategy.

Increased Giving

According to Giving USA, charitable giving by for-profit corporations has risen from an estimated $9.6 billion in 1999 to $12.19 billion in 2002.[4]

Cone/Roper's Executive Study in 2000, exploring cause initiatives from the corporate perspective, found that 69 percent of companies planned to increase future commitments to social issues.[5] (For more than 10 years, the well-known Cone/Roper tracking studies have been instrumental in providing ongoing research on attitudes toward corporate involvement in cause initiatives. Their research includes surveys of consumers, employees, and executives. Their benchmark study of consumer attitudes, conducted in 1993, as well as results from subsequent studies, is described later in this chapter.[6])

Increased Reporting

According to KPMG, a U.S. professional services firm, a 2002 survey of the Global Fortune Top 250 companies indicated a continued increase in the number of American companies reporting on corporate responsibility. In 2002, 45 percent of these companies issued environmental, social, or sustainability reports, compared with 35 percent in their 1999 survey.[7]

Major avenues for this reporting include corporate annual reports with special sections on community giving and, increasingly, the publication of a separate annual community giving report. Starbucks, for example, in 2003 published its second annual *Report on Corporate Social Responsibility* and, in an opening letter from the Chairman and CEO, emphasized that this report is a way "to provide transparency on our business practices, measurements of our performance, and benchmarks for future reports." It further explains that Starbucks took additional measures in the second year of reporting "to assure our stakeholders that the information in this report is accurate by engaging an independent third party to verify its contents."[8]

A review of Fortune 500 web sites also indicates that a majority now have special reports on giving, with sections typically labeled "Corporate Social Responsibility," "Corporate Citizenship," "Community Development," "Community Giving," or "Community Involvement." Many of these sections provide lengthy detail on topics like annual giving amounts, philanthropic priorities, major initiatives, employee volunteerism, and sustainable business practices.

Establishment of a Corporate Social Norm to Do Good

Within these annual reports and on these web sites, there are also consistent and similar messages from CEOs, signaling that commitments to corporate social responsibility have entered the mainstream of corporate dialogue as a must-do, as indicated in the following examples:

- American Express: "Good Works = Good Business. . . . Not only is it appropriate for the company to give back to the communities in which it operates, it is also smart business. Healthy communities are important to the well-being of society and the overall economy. They also provide an environment that helps companies such as American Express grow, innovate, and attract outstanding talent." (Harvey Golub, Chairman and CEO, and Kenneth Chenault, President and Chief Operating Officer, 2000)[9]

- Dell: "Dell is a global company that delivers products and services to more than 190 countries. We have more than 40,000 employees who live and work on six continents. That's why it's important that we provide technology to all communities that we call home." (Michael Dell, Chairman and CEO, July 2003)[10]

- Fannie Mae: "Fannie Mae and the Greenlining Institute share a common mission. We are both devoted to improving the quality of life in underserved communities. We both are working to bring more opportunities to people and places inside the old red lines. And we both believe in the power of housing." (Franklin D. Raines, Chairman and CEO, April 2003)[11]

- Ford Motor Company: "There is a difference between a good company and a great company. A good company offers excellent products and services. A great company also offers excellent products and services but also strives to make the world a better place." (William Clay Ford, Jr., Chairman of the Board and CEO)[12]

- Kellogg: "There are many measures of a company's success. The most obvious, of course, are profitability and share value. A company may also be measured by its ability to change with the times, or develop innovative products. These elements are all vital to Kellogg Company. But there is another important measure that we hold ourselves accountable for—our social responsibility." (Carlos M. Gutierrez, Chairman and CEO, 2003)[13]

- Hewlett-Packard: "I honestly believe that the winning companies of this century will be those who prove with their actions that they can be profitable and increase social value—companies that both do well and do good. . . . Increasingly, shareowners, customers, partners, and employees are going to vote with their feet—rewarding those companies that fuel social change through business. This is simply the new reality of business—one that we should and must embrace." (Carly Fiorina, Chairman and Chief Executive Officer, November 2003)[14]

- McDonald's: "Social responsibility is not a program that begins and ends. Acting responsibly has always been a part of who we are and will continue to be the way McDonald's does business. It's an ongoing commitment." (McDonald's CEO, Jim Cantalupo, CEO, 2003)[15]

- Nike: "The performance of Nike and every other global company in the twenty-first century will be measured as much by our impact on quality of life as it is by revenue growth and profit margins. We hope to have a head start." (Phil Knight, Chairman and CEO, 2001)[16]

A Shift from Obligation to Strategy

In a seminal article in the *Harvard Business Review* in 1994, Craig Smith identified "The New Corporate Philanthropy," describing it as a shift to making long-term commitments to specific social issues and initiatives; providing more than cash contributions; sourcing funds from business units as well as philanthropic budgets; forming strategic alliances; and doing all of this in a way that also advances business goals.

One milestone Smith identified that contributed to this evolution was a Supreme Court decision in the 1950s that removed legal restrictions and unwritten codes which up to that time had restricted, or at least limited, corporate contributions and involvement in social issues. Subsequently, by the 1960s most U.S. companies began to feel pressures to demonstrate their social responsibility and established in-house foundations and giving programs.[17]

One of the next milestones Smith cited was the *Exxon Valdez* oil spill in 1989, which brought into serious question the philanthropy of the 1970s and 1980s, where corporations tended to support social issues least associated with their line of business, give to a variety of causes, and turn over management of their giving to separate foundations. When Exxon then needed access to environmentalists for expertise and support, management was "without ties to environmental leaders nurtured by the foundation."[18] A final milestone that Smith identified was the emergence and visibility of models in the 1990s such as one used at AT&T that proposed a new view of the role of a corporate foundation and its relationship to the for-profit arm. Its perspective was that not only should philanthropic initiatives of the foundation support business objectives but that business units, in return, should provide support for philanthropic activities in the form of resources such as marketing expertise, technical assistance, and employee volunteers.[19]

David Hess, Nikolai Rogovsky, and Thomas W. Dunfee suggest that another force driving this shift is the new "moral marketplace factor," creating an increased importance of perceived corporate morality in choices made by consumers, investors, and employees. They point to several examples of marketplace morality, including "investors choosing socially screened investment funds, consumers boycotting Shell Oil because of its decision to sink the Brent Spar oil rig, and employees' desires to work for socially responsible firms."[20]

The following section contrasts the more traditional approach to corporate philanthropy with the new strategic approach in terms of best-practice issues of selecting, developing, implementing, and evaluating corporate social initiatives.

The Traditional Approach: Fulfilling an Obligation

Prior to the 1990s, decisions regarding the selection of social issues to support tended to be made based on themes reflecting emerging pressures for "doing good to look good." Corporations would commonly establish, follow, and report on a fixed annual budget for giving, sometimes tied to revenues or pretax earnings. Funds were allocated to as many organizations as possible, reflecting a perception that this would satisfy the most constituent groups and create the most visibility for philanthropic efforts. Commitments were more short-term, allowing the organization to spread the wealth over a variety of organizations and issues through the years. Interestingly (given where we are today), there was more of a tendency to avoid issues that might be associated with core business products, which might be perceived as self-serving, and to steer clear of major and often controversial social issues such as AIDS, judging that these were best handled by those with expertise in governmental or nonprofit organizations. Decisions regarding issues to support and organizations to sponsor were also more heavily influenced by preferences (and wishes) of senior management and directors of boards than by needs to support strategic business goals and objectives.

When developing and implementing specific initiatives, the rule of thumb might have been described as to "do good as easily as possible," resulting in a tendency to simply write a check. Most donors were satisfied with being one of many corporate sponsors, as visibility for efforts was not a goal or concern. And because it would require extra effort, few attempts were made to integrate and coordinate giving programs with other corporate strategies and business units such as marketing, human resources, and operations.

In terms of evaluation, it appears little was done (or asked for) to establish quantifiable outcomes for the business or the social cause; the approach was simply to trust that good happened.

The New Approach: Supporting Corporate Objectives as Well

As noted earlier, Craig Smith described how in the early 1990s, many turned to a new model of corporate giving, a strategic approach that ultimately impacted what issues corporations supported, how they designed and implemented their programs, and how they were evaluated.

Decision making now reflects an increased desire for "doing well and doing good." We see more corporations picking a few strategic areas of focus that fit with corporate values; selecting initiatives that support business goals; choosing issues related to core products and core markets; supporting issues that provide opportunities to meet marketing objectives, such as increased market share, market penetration, or building a desired brand identity; evaluating issues based on their potential for positive support in times of corporate crisis or national policy making; involving more than one department in the selection process, so as to lay a foundation of support for implementation of programs; and taking on issues the community, customers, and employees care most about.

Developing and implementing programs in this new model looks more like "doing all we can to do the most good, not just some good." It is more common for managers to make long-term commitments and to offer in-kind contributions such as corporate expertise, technological support, access to services, and donation of retired equipment. We see more efforts to share distribution channels with cause partners; to volunteer employee time; to integrate the issue into marketing, corporate communications, human resources, community relations, and operations; to form strategic alliances with one or more external partners (private, public, nonprofit); and to have funding come from additional business units such as marketing and human resources.

Evaluation now has increased importance, perceived as critical to answering the question "What good did we do?" Trusting is not good enough. This input is valued as a part of a strategic framework that then uses this feedback for course correction and credible public reporting. As a result, we see increased pressures for setting campaign goals, measuring outcomes for the corporation, and measuring impact for the cause.

Amid these increased pressures for evaluation of outcomes, program partners are challenged with determining methodologies and securing resources to make this happen.

WHY DO GOOD?

Most health care professionals promise that if we engage in regular physical activity we'll look better, feel better, do better, and live longer. There are many who say that participation in corporate social initiatives has similar potential benefits. It appears that such participation *looks good* to potential consumers, investors, financial analysts, business colleagues, in annual reports, in the news, and maybe even in Congress and the courtroom. It is reported that it *feels good* to employees, current customers, stockholders, and board members. There is growing evidence that it *does good* for the brand and the bottom line as well as for the community. And there are some who claim that corporations with a strong reputation for corporate social responsibility actually *last longer*.

Let's examine the existing evidence that participation in corporate social initiatives can impact key performance factors, which could then support these claims.

Business for Social Responsibility is a leading nonprofit global organization providing businesses with information, tools, training, and advisory services related to integrating corporate social responsibility in their business operations and strategies. Their research and experience concludes that companies have experienced a range of bottom-line benefits, including reference to several of the following:[21]

- Increased sales and market share.
- Strengthened brand positioning.

- Enhanced corporate image and clout.
- Increased ability to attract, motivate, and retain employees.
- Decreased operating costs.
- Increased appeal to investors and financial analysts.

Increased Sales and Market Share

Surveys conducted by Cone/Roper, mentioned earlier in this chapter, have provided strong evidence that companies can benefit significantly from connecting themselves to a cause, as illustrated in the following (now often quoted) findings from their benchmark survey of consumers in 1993/1994:

- "Eighty-four percent said they have a more positive image of companies that do something to make the world better."
- "Seventy-eight percent of adults said they would be more likely to buy a product associated with a cause they cared about."
- "Sixty-six percent said they would switch brands to support a cause they cared about."
- "Sixty-two percent said they would switch retail stores to support a cause."
- "Sixty-four percent believe that cause-related marketing should be a standard part of a company's activities."[22]

Further, it was found that cause marketing activities had the strongest impact on people in higher education and income categories—those who attended college and earn more than $30,000 a year.

Evidently, these attitudes were strengthened after 9/11, as evidenced by the 2001 Cone/Roper Corporate Citizenship Study, which indicated an increased importance for corporate involvement in social issues. In March 2001, an estimated 65 percent of Americans surveyed believed companies should support causes. By November, that number had increased to 79 percent. "The atmosphere since September 11 has accelerated and intensified a trend that our Cone/Roper research has documented since 1993," said Carol Cone, CEO of Cone. "We are seeing extraordinary jumps of 20 to 50 percent in public opinion. Corporate citizenship should now become a critical component of business planning as Americans are promising increased support for companies that share their values and take action."[23]

In 2002, there appeared to be no letup. The 2002 Cone Corporate Citizenship Study reported that 84 percent of Americans said they would be likely to switch brands to one associated with a good cause, if price and quality are similar.[24]

Others have similar contentions and present strong evidence that involvement in social causes increases brand preference:

- Paul Bloom, Steve Hoeffler, Kevin Keller, and Carlos Basurto contend that "consumers these days monitor and pay attention to how brands are marketed, and if they like the way that marketing is done because they have some type of positive feelings about or affinity toward the social cause being supported in the marketing program, then consumers will weigh the brand's marketing approach more heavily and positively compared to how they would weigh a brand's marketing program if it were supporting a nonsocial cause (e.g., commercial sponsorship) in forming preferences."[25]

- In an article by Minette Drumwright in the *Journal of Marketing*, entitled "Socially Responsible Organizational Buying: Environmental Concern as a Noneconomic Buying Criterion," the case is made that "as the earth becomes more populous and more resource depleted, noneconomic criteria are likely to play more prominent roles in organizational buying processes." She quotes several studies: "In surveys, 75 percent of consumers have said their purchasing decisions are influenced by a company's reputation with respect to the environment, and eight in ten have said they would pay more for products that are environmentally friendly (Klein 1990). One survey notes that 85 percent have said they believe that U.S. companies should be doing more to become environmentally responsible (Chase and Smith 1992)."[26]

- As summarized by Business for Social Responsibility, a 1999 study conducted by Environics International Ltd., The Prince of Wales Business Leaders Forum, and The Conference Board surveyed 25,000 citizens in 23 countries regarding corporate social responsibility. Highlights of findings included the following:

  - Ninety percent of respondents want companies to focus on more than profitability.

- Sixty percent said they form an impression of a company based on perceptions of social responsibility.
- Forty percent said they either responded negatively to or said negative things about companies they perceive as not being socially responsible.
- Seventeen percent reported they had actually avoided the products of companies if they perceived them as not being socially responsible.[27]

Clearly, one of the best examples of a corporate social initiative that increased sales and market share was the American Express campaign for the restoration of the Statue of Liberty in the early 1980s. Featured in Chapter 4, American Express is an inspiring example of the potential for cause-related marketing. Instead of just writing a check to help with the cause, American Express tried a new approach, and the marketing world was watching. They pledged that every time cardholders used their cards, the company would make a contribution to a fund to restore the Statue of Liberty, as well as an additional contribution for every new card application. The campaign generated $1.7 million in funds for "the lady," a 27 percent increase in card usage, and a 10 percent jump in new card member applications.[28]

Strengthened Brand Positioning

In their book *Brand Spirit*, Hamish Pringle and Marjorie Thompson make a strong case for the contribution that linking a company or brand to a relevant charity or cause can make to the "spirit of the brand." They contend that consumers are going beyond "the practical issues of functional product performance or rational product benefits and further than the emotional and psychological aspects of brand personality and image. Consumers are moving towards the top of Maslow's Hierarchy of Needs and seeking 'self-realization.' "[29] What they are asking for and are drawn to now are demonstrations of good. "In an anthropomorphic sense, if consumers know how a brand functions and how it 'thinks' and 'feels.' then the new question that has to be answered is 'What does it believe in?' "[30]

Bloom, Hoeffler, Keller, and Basurto see "marketing initiatives containing a larger amount of social content having a more positive effect on brand judgments and feelings than initiatives that are similar in size and scope but contain less social content. By 'social content' we mean activities in the marketing initiative that are meant to make tangible improvements to social welfare. Thus a program that would make a donation to an environmental organization every time a purchase was made would be higher in social content than a program that gave a consumer a free toy every time a purchase was made."[31]

Consider, for example, the spirit that participation in corporate social initiatives has given to the Ben & Jerry's brand. Most of us, when we see or hear the words "Ben & Jerry's," think of a philanthropic company that promotes and supports positive social change. We may know about their PartnerShops program that waives standard franchise fees for nonprofit organizations in order to offer supportive employment; or we may know about their commitment to promoting world peace, including a list of 50 ways to promote peace in the world posted on their corporate web site, www.benjerry.com; or we may know about their "Coffee For A Change" program, which pays a premium for coffee beans from farmers committed to sustainable farming practices. In the end, when we see the lineup of ice creams in the freezer section of our favorite grocer, many of us have a unique image and positive feeling for the Ben & Jerry's label.

Improved Corporate Image and Clout

Several existing and respected reports cover standards and assessment of performance in the area of corporate social responsibility, including the following:

- The Council on Economic Priorities is a public service research firm that evaluates company performance on a range of social dimensions and publishes *Shopping for a Better World* to influence consumers' purchase decisions.[32]
- *Fortune* publishes an annual list of "America's Most Admired Companies," based on a survey of 10,000 executives and securities analysts conducted by HayGroup, a global consultancy firm. Respondents are asked to rate companies, using a scale from 0 to 10, on eight attributes: innovation, financial soundness, employee talent, use of corporate assets, long-term investment value, quality of management, quality of products/services, and social responsibility. These eight attributes were determined more than 20 years ago through research that uncovered strong opinions that social responsibility—defined simply as "responsibility to the community

and/or the environment"—should be one of the eight attributes. In 2004, those on the top 10 list for the social responsibility subcategory in the United States were United Parcel Service, Alcoa, Washington Mutual, BP, McDonald's, Procter & Gamble, Fortune Brands, Altria, Vulcan Materials, and American Express.[33]

- *Business Ethics* publishes a list of "100 Best Corporate Citizens," recognizing companies' corporate social responsibility toward stakeholders, including the environment and the community. In 2002, the top five Best Corporate Citizens were IBM, Hewlett-Packard, Fannie Mae, St. Paul Companies, and Procter & Gamble.[34]

- Other external reports and standards covering corporate social responsibility include the Global Reporting Initiative, the Global Sullivan Principles, Social Accountability 8000, the Caux Round Table, the Interfaith Center on Corporate Responsibility, Sunshine Standards for Corporate Reporting to Stakeholders, and the Keidanren Charter for Good Corporate Behavior.[35]

In addition to positive press from reports such as these, according to Business for Social Responsibility, "companies that demonstrate they are engaging in practices that satisfy and go beyond regulatory compliance requirements are being given less scrutiny and more free rein by both national and local government entities."[36]

A strong reputation in the community can be a real asset in times of crisis. Hess, Rogovsky, and Dunfee describe a dramatic example of this, in which a good reputation protected McDonald's during the 1992 South Central Los Angeles riots. "The company's efforts in developing community relations through its Ronald McDonald Houses and its involvement in developing employee opportunities gave the company such a strong reputation, McDonald's executives stated, that rioters refused to harm their outlets. While vandalism caused tremendous damage to businesses in the area, all 60 of McDonald's franchises were spared harm."[37]

And finally, this positive corporate image may also influence policy makers as well. Craig Smith, in the article mentioned earlier, "The New Corporate Philanthropy," cites an example for AT&T in the early 1990s. The AT&T Foundation, the principal instrument for AT&T philanthropy, supports various education and art programs for children. As a result, "in the postelection (Clinton/Gore) economic summit in Little Rock, Arkansas . . . [AT&T CEO Robert] Allen was able to comment on the link between economic performance and the well-being of children. Then, as if to thank Allen for addressing a crucial issue on the policy agenda, President Clinton called on Allen to speak about the information superhighway. In front of the nation, the CEO of AT&T was able to make a point crucial to the company's government relations strategy: the superhighway should be a private rather than a public initiative."[38]

Increased Ability to Attract, Motivate, and Retain Employees

Cone/Roper studies also indicate that a company's participation in social initiatives can have a positive impact on prospective and current employees, as well as citizens and executives. According to their March 2001 survey, employees working in companies reported to have cause-related programs were 38 percent more likely to say they are proud of their company's values than were employees in companies not reported to have these programs. Even before 9/11, 48 percent of respondents indicated that a company's commitment to causes is important when deciding where to work. After 9/11, that percentage rose to 76.[39] And in their 2002 Citizenship Study with a national cross section of 1,040 adults, 80 percent of respondents said they would be likely to refuse to work at a company if they were to find out about negative corporate citizenship practices.[40]

Similarly, one noteworthy study conducted by Net Impact found that more than half of the 2,100 MBA students surveyed indicated they would accept a lower salary in order to work for a socially responsible company. Two additional studies conducted by the World Resources Institute and the Initiative for Social Innovation Through Business, also focused on MBAs, reported that these graduates look for the right corporate culture, as well as the right salary, job description, and opportunities for promotion.[41]

At Timberland, for example, full-time U.S. employees are given 40 hours of paid time off to perform community service; part-time employees get 16 hours per year. This program, called Path of Service, began in 1992, and by the year 2000, nearly 95 percent of Timberland's U.S. employees were participating in the program. The program has been recognized by many, including *Fortune*, which for the past three years has rated Timberland as one of its "100 Best Companies to Work For." This service program was cited as a factor in its selection.[42]

Decreased Operating Costs

Several business functions can cite decreased operating costs and increased revenue from grants and incentives as a result of the implementation of corporate social initiatives. One arena easy to point to includes companies who adopt environmental initiatives to reduce waste, reuse materials, recycle, and conserve water and electricity.

At Cisco Systems, for example, an energy conservation initiative called "Cleaner Air and Millions in Savings" is expected to save the company about $4.5 million per year in operating costs. In addition, these energy savings will eventually qualify the company for an estimated $5.7 million in rebates from the local energy supplier, Pacific Gas & Electric.[43]

Another area for potential reduced costs is in advertising expenditures, especially as a result of increased free publicity. The Body Shop, for example, is noted for its campaign against using animals for cosmetic testing. According to an article by the World Business Council for Sustainable Development, "The Body Shop was launched on the basis of fair prices for fairly produced cosmetics. Anita Roddick, its founder, generated so much favorable publicity that the company did not need to advertise: a win-win on the cost-benefit front, leaving aside the do-gooding."[44]

Increased Appeal to Investors and Financial Analysts

Some argue that involvement in corporate social initiatives can even increase stock value. They point to the ability to attract new investors and reduce exposure to risk in the event of corporate or management crises:

- In an article appearing in the *Financial Times* in July 2003, Jane Fuller wrote: "It pains me to say this, but I am becoming less cynical about Corporate Social Responsibility. This is not because of the weight of words expended on this subject by companies, lobbyists, and politicians. It is because companies that are less exposed to social, environmental, and ethical risks are more highly valued by the market . . . In other words, investors are already pricing in social, environmental, and ethical factors. This is not sentimental behavior. It represents a cool appraisal of various costs."[45]

- Praveen Sinha, Chekitan Dev, and Tania Salas suggest that demand for investments in firms deemed socially responsible can be enhanced "as some mutual funds and large pension funds are mandated to make investments in only those companies deemed socially responsible (for instance, CREF's Social Choice Fund)."[46]

- Business for Social Responsibility agrees that companies that address ethical, social, and environmental responsibilities have "rapidly growing access to capital that might not otherwise have been available." They cite a Social Investment Forum report that estimates that assets under management in portfolios using screens linked to ethics, the environment, and corporate social responsibility have grown from "$639 billion in 1995 to $1.185 trillion in 1997, to $2.16 trillion in 1999."[47]

- An often-quoted study by the University of Southwestern Louisiana, "The Effect of Published Reports on Unethical Conduct on Stock Prices," demonstrated that publicity about unethical corporate behavior lowers stock prices for a minimum of six months.[48]

- According to an article posted by SocialFunds.com in April 2002, an academic study conducted at DePaul University concluded that the 100 companies making *Business Ethics'* list of 100 Best Corporate Citizens had a better financial performance than the remaining companies on the S&P 500. *Business Ethics* editor and publisher Marjorie Kelly was quoted as saying, "These top companies perform substantially better than their S&P 500 peers, in strictly financial terms."[49]

WHAT ARE THE MAJOR CURRENT CHALLENGES TO DOING GOOD?

Managers and program planners are challenged at each of the fundamental decision points identified throughout this book—decisions related to choosing a social issue, selecting an initiative to support this issue, developing and implementing program plans, and evaluating outcomes.

Choosing a Social Issue

Challenges are perhaps the greatest in this very first step, as experience has shown that some social issues are a better fit than others, and this first decision has the greatest impact on subsequent programs and outcomes. Those making the recommendations will end up juggling competing priorities and publics. They will be faced with tough questions, including these:

- How does this support our business goals?
- How big of a social problem is this?
- Isn't the government or someone else handling this?
- What will our stockholders think of our involvement in this issue?
- Is this something our employees can get excited about?
- Won't this encourage others involved in this cause to approach us (bug us) for funds?
- How do we know this isn't the "cause du jour"?
- Will this cause backfire on us and create a scandal?
- Is this something our competitors are involved in and own already?

In February 2003, a feature article in *Business2.0* entitled "The Selling of Breast Cancer" described one of the pitfalls in this decision making in real terms. In the summer of 2000, Dreyer's had apparently decided it wanted to support the cause of fighting breast cancer. "It had watched other companies conduct campaigns backing the search for a cure—and had seen their logos displayed at well-attended rallies and their products festooned with the cause's signature pink ribbons." When Dreyer's approached the Komen Foundation, however, they found that Yoplait had an exclusive contract to be the only yogurt manufacturer involved in this cause.[50]

Selecting an Initiative to Address the Issue

Once an issue has been chosen, managers will be challenged regarding recommendations on what initiative or initiatives among the six identified in Chapter 2 should be selected to support the issue. Again, they will need to be prepared to answer tough questions:

- How can we do this without distracting us from our core business?
- How will this initiative give visibility to this company?
- Do these promotions really work? Who pays attention to them?
- What if we tie our funding commitment to sales and end up writing them a check for only $100? How will that look?

- What if consumers find out that the amount of the sale that actually goes to the cause is minuscule?
- Have we calculated the productivity cost for giving our employees time off for volunteering?
- Giving visibility, especially shelf space in our stores, for this cause doesn't pencil out. Shouldn't we just write a check or give a grant?

Developing and Implementing Program Plans

Key decisions at this point include whether to partner with others and, if so, with whom; determining key strategies, including communications and distribution channels; assigning roles and responsibilities; developing timetables; and determining budget allocations and funding sources. The questions continue, especially around issues of time and money:

- How can we do this when money is needed for increased performance?
- What do we say to stockholders who see this as money that belongs to them?
- Why is our department being asked to fund this?
- Will having partners bog down the decision-making process and therefore take more of our staff time?
- Will we be doing enough good for the cause to justify the expense?
- Isn't this just brand advertising in disguise?
- What is our exit strategy?
- How do we keep from looking hypocritical?

Philip Morris began a social marketing initiative in 1999 with the slogan, "Talk to your kids about not smoking. They'll listen." This mass media campaign included print ads in magazines, a free 16-page, four-color brochure, and a web site with tips and lists of additional resources for parents. For some, this initiative probably rang hollow, with people perhaps questioning the authenticity of a claim that a member of the tobacco industry is not interested in a market representing an estimated one billion packs of cigarettes a year.[51]

Evaluation

Ongoing measurement of marketing activities and financial investments for corporations has a long record, with decades of experience in building sophisticated tracking systems and databases that provide analysis of returns on investments and compare current activities to benchmarks and "gold standards." By contrast, the science of measuring return on investments in corporate social initiatives is very young, with little historic data and expertise. Marketing professionals and academic experts in the field confirm this challenge.

- Sinha, Dev, and Salas report that "Since the benefits related to CSR are not directly measurable, and most firms do not disclose expenses related to such activities, it is difficult to directly assess the return on CSR investment."[52]

- McDonald's reports that even measuring a major event is challenging. "Most of our current goals and measurements are related to processes, systems development, and standard setting. . . . We are 70 percent franchised around the world: Currently, we do not have systems to collect and aggregate what some 5,500 independent owner/operators do for their community, people, and environment at the local level."[53]

- John Gourville and Kash Rangan confirm this difficulty: "Rarely do firms fully assess a cause marketing alliance and its potential impact on both the for-profit and the nonprofit entities. Yes, there are several stunning success stories . . . but most for-profit businesses would be hard-pressed to document the long-term business impact of their cause marketing campaigns and most nonprofits would have trouble pinpointing the value they bring to the partnership."[54]

And yet, as Bloom, Hoeffler, Keller, and Basurto conclude, "showing that the program was a more financially productive promotional tool than other possible promotional tools is becoming increasingly necessary."[55]

Subsequent chapters, especially our summary chapter on best practices (Chapter 9), is intended to help answer these questions and prepare managers for these challenges.

CHAPTER

2

Corporate Social Initiatives: Six Options for Doing Good

Since its founding in 1889, Washington Mutual has made giving back to the communities in which it operates a top priority, not simply because it's good for business, but because it's the right thing for responsible corporate citizens to do. And make no mistake, the results are tangible.
—Kerry Killinger, Chairman, President, and CEO of Washington Mutual, in the 2001 Community Annual Report[1]

I n Chapter 1 we defined corporate social initiatives as major activities undertaken by a corporation to support social causes and to fulfill commitments to corporate social responsibility. We have identified six major initiatives under which most social responsibility–related activities fall, and this chapter gives brief descriptions of each. In subsequent chapters, each initiative is presented in more detail, including typical programs, potential benefits, potential concerns, keys to success, when to consider the initiative, and steps in developing program plans. The final chapters of the book summarize these perspectives to present best practices for choosing, implementing, and evaluating corporate social initiatives.

The six social initiatives explored are as follows:

1. Cause Promotions: A corporation provides funds, in-kind contributions, or other corporate resources to increase awareness and concern about a social cause or to support fundraising, participation, or volunteer recruitment for a cause. The corporation may initiate and manage the promotion on its own (i.e., The Body Shop promoting a ban on the use of animals to test cosmetics); it may be a major partner in an effort (Aleve sponsoring the Arthritis Foundation's fundraising walk); or it may be one of several sponsors (Keep America Beautiful 2003 sponsors for the "Great American Cleanup" included Lysol, PepsiCo, and Firestone Tire & Service Centers, among others).

2. Cause-Related Marketing: A corporation commits to making a contribution or donating a percentage of revenues to a specific cause based on product sales. Most commonly this offer is for an announced period of time, for a specific product, and for a specified charity. In this scenario, a corporation is most often partnered with a nonprofit organization, creating a mutually beneficial relationship designed to increase sales of a particular product and to generate financial support for the charity (for example, Comcast donates $4.95 of installation fees for its high-speed Internet service to Ronald McDonald House Charities through the end of a given month). Many think of this as a win-win-win, as it provides consumers an opportunity to contribute for free to their favorite charities as well.

3. Corporate Social Marketing: A corporation supports the development and/or implementation of a behavior change campaign intended to improve public health, safety, the environment, or community well-being. The distinguishing feature is the *behavior change* focus, which differentiates it from cause promotions that focus on supporting awareness, fundraising, and volunteer recruitment for a cause. A corporation may develop and implement a behavior change campaign on its own (i.e., Philip Morris encouraging parents to talk with their kids about tobacco use), but more often it involves partners in public sector agencies (Home Depot and a utility promoting water conservation tips) and/or nonprofit organizations (Pampers and the SIDS Foundation encouraging caretakers to put infants on their backs to sleep).

4. Corporate Philanthropy: A corporation makes a direct contribution to a charity or cause, most often in the form of cash grants, donations, and/or inkind services. This initiative is perhaps the most traditional of all corporate social initiatives and for many decades was approached in a responsive, even ad hoc manner. As mentioned in Chapter 1, more corporations are now experiencing pressures, both internally and externally, to move to a more strategic approach, choosing a focus and tying philanthropic activities to the company's business goals and objectives.

5. Community Volunteering: A corporation supports and encourages employees, retail partners, and/or franchise members to volunteer their time to support local community organizations and causes. This activity may be a stand-alone effort (i.e., employees of a high tech company tutoring youth in middle schools on computer skills) or it may be done in partnership with a nonprofit organization (Shell employees working with The Ocean Conservancy on a beach cleanup). Volunteer activities may be organized by the corporation, or employees may choose their own activities and receive support from the company through such means as paid time off and volunteer database matching programs.

6. Socially Responsible Business Practices: A corporation adopts and conducts discretionary business practices and investments that support social causes to improve community well-being and protect the environment. Initiatives may be conceived of and implemented by the organization (i.e., Kraft deciding to eliminate all in-school marketing) or they may be in partnership with others (Starbucks working with Conservation International to support farmers to minimize impact on their local environments).

To further illustrate and bring to life these distinctions, three case examples follow: Washington Mutual, Dell Inc., and McDonald's. In each case, background information on the corporation's focus for social initiatives is briefly described, followed by an example of a social initiative in each of the six areas.

WASHINGTON MUTUAL, INC.

With a history dating back to 1889, Washington Mutual, Inc.—or WaMu, as it is known—is a national financial institution with a 115-year legacy of contributing to the communities where it does business. As reported in its 2003 Community Annual Report, total combined

Table 2.1 Examples of Washington Mutual's Corporate Social Initiatives

	Cause Promotions	Cause-Related Marketing	Corporate Social Marketing	Corporate Philanthropy	Community Volunteering	Socially Responsible Business Practices
Description	Supporting social causes through promotional sponsorships	Making a contribution or donating a percentage of revenues to a specific cause based on product sales or usage	Supporting behavior change campaigns	Making direct contributions to a charity or cause	Providing volunteer services in the community	Adopting and conducting discretionary business practices and investments that support social causes
Example	WaMu sponsors teacher recruitment programs	The *WaMoola for Schools®* program ties support for local schools to Visa® Check Card usage.	WaMu sponsors bank days at elementary schools where parent and team volunteers work with students to open savings accounts and make regular deposits	WaMu awards cash grants to fund professional development of teachers	WaMu supports employees to volunteer in classrooms and spruce up school grounds	WaMu provides on-the-job training for high school interns

charitable giving by Washington Mutual, Inc. and its subsidiaries equaled $94.0 million for the year, up from $72.0 million in 2002.

WaMu has a strategic focus for giving, with a top priority since 1927 placed on improving K-12 education. In 2003 alone, it gave $15.7 million in cash grants to education initiatives. Its customer research and community needs assessment findings consistently identify education as a key community concern. Contributions to this effort are primarily achieved through cash grants, innovative programs, and employee volunteerism. (See Table 2.1.)

The banks in the Washington Mutual family of companies have a standard practice to involve its branch network in support of education initiatives and to make strong efforts to connect those initiatives to its product offerings, to feature them in new market launches, and to create visibility for its contributions and initiatives in its advertising, publicity, and collateral and special events. Research indicates that the results of these initiatives are an increase in business, goodwill in the community, and customer loyalty. WaMu advises other corporate managers to stick with a few good ideas, develop long-term equity, and take special, even bold measures to ensure that messages regarding giving do not get lost among other efforts.[2]

Note that the theme of education is reflected in each example of WaMu's social initiatives in this summary list. A detailed description of the programs follows.

Cause Promotions: Teacher Recruitment

WaMu supports a variety of programs and efforts to attract and keep talent in the classroom. Spurred by the U.S. Department of Education's prediction that our nation will need more than two million new teachers over the next decade, WaMu focuses on programs targeting recent college graduates as well as mid-career professionals.

As an example of a local program, financial centers in Miami, Florida, helped Washington Mutual sponsor a May 2003 town hall meeting that facilitated community discussions around teacher recruitment, induction, and retention. In attendance were more than 200 community members, including local businesspeople, elected officials, parents, administrators, and teachers. One activity of support included the distribution of 197,000 fliers publicizing the event to parents and Washington Mutual's banking customers (see Figure 2.1). The meeting aired on

Figure 2.1 Washington Mutual was a sponsor of a town hall meeting on teacher recruitment, induction, and retention. (Courtesy of KCNC-TV.)

WFOR-TV, CBS4, a local television station, with a reported 40,000 households tuned in and more than 10.4 million audience impressions garnered by this airing and related coverage.

Cause-Related Marketing: The WaMoola for Schools® Program

In a time when educational budgets are tighter than ever, every dollar counts when it comes to school funding. This is especially true for unrestricted funds, in which schools can decide for themselves how to use the money—whether it's for teacher training, special assemblies, school supplies, playground equipment, field trips, or musical instruments. WaMu found every school has a wish list, and wants to help fulfill them.

The *WaMoola for Schools®* program was specifically created to support K-12 schools. For years under this program the banks in the Washington Mutual family of companies gave $1 per checking account to a public K-12 school. This year (2004), it relaunched this program to support both public and private K-12 schools. It is believed to be the first program of its kind to tie support for local schools to Visa® Check Card purchases once the customer enrolls, and in turn allows schools to accumulate points that will be converted to cash at the end of each year.

The program was designed to be simple and flexible. There's no enrollment fee, and Washington Mutual does not charge customers for using its check cards for purchases (though merchants might). Under the program, customers enroll by selecting a school to benefit and begin by simply using their check cards when making everyday purchases. The designated public or private school will receive a point currently equivalent to 5 cents for each purchase made using the card. At the end of the year, the points will be converted into cash and schools receive a check from Washington Mutual (see Figure 2.2).

Corporate Social Marketing: School Savings® Program

Since 1923, the *School Savings®* program has provided students with hands-on lessons about handling money responsibly. Professionals from local Washington Mutual financial centers work with elementary schools and parent volunteers to teach students positive savings habits. At participating schools across the country, students are encouraged to open a Washington Mutual savings account and then to bring their allowance,

Figure 2.2 The WaMoola for Schools® program awards points to designated schools for each purchase made using a Washington Mutual VISA® Check Card by a customer enrolled in the program. At the end of the year, the points are converted to cash and Washington Mutual mails checks to the local schools. (Reprinted courtesy of Washington Mutual.)

birthday checks, and odd-job money on weekly school Bank Days to give to the volunteer to deposit at the bank.

The *School Savings* program is primarily promoted through a grass-roots effort. Resource materials and training classes are provided for financial center employees so they can learn about the program and present it to local schools. Marketing materials such as a kid-oriented, fun program guide, brochure, and calendar are used at PTA meetings and other local events to promote the program (see Figure 2.3). Nearly

Figure 2.3   Materials used in classrooms to teach students positive savings habits. (Reprinted courtesy of Washington Mutual.)

200,000 students at more than 1,000 elementary schools around the country now participate in the *School Savings* program.

Corporate Philanthropy: Cash Grants for Education

WaMu also gives millions of dollars each year to fund the professional development of teachers, leadership training for principals, organizational development for schools, and programs that provide information about school performance to parents. Special emphasis is placed on grants to education programs benefiting K-12 public schools in low- to moderate-income communities.

When choosing among applications, WaMu looks for those with clearly measurable results and ones providing opportunities for teachers to grow professionally, learn from experience, and work with their peers to improve performance.[3]

An example is WaMu's funding of professional development opportunities for teachers. Through its Teacher Scholarship Fund, WaMu provides assistance for educators seeking certification by the National Board for Professional Teaching Standards. At year-end 2003, WaMu provided scholarship assistance to more than 2,400 teachers nationwide.[4]

Community Volunteering: CAN! (Committed Active Neighbors)™

In 2003, WaMu employees volunteered 44,000 times for a total of 184,000 hours of community service. Many employees volunteer for schools, organizing projects ranging from helping teachers in the classroom and sprucing up school grounds to conducting school supply drives. Employees worked on the projects either solo or as teams.[5]

The company provides management support for eligible employees to volunteer up to four hours of paid time off per month, and incentives that include company donations to the nonprofits employees serve.

One financial education activity is the *Classroom Presentations* program, consisting of free, one-hour courses introducing young students to the concept of money and teenagers to the concept of credit management. As an example, in Pasadena, California, WaMu volunteers arrived at Eugene Field Elementary wearing CAN! shirts, visors, and handmade medallions shaped like giant coins, and made their presentation on financial literacy fun through rap songs (see Figure 2.4).[6]

Figure 2.4 WaMu employees volunteering in a classroom.
(Photo: Jeff Braverman.)

WaMu also offers financial education classes for adults. *Your Money Matters* is a four-part curriculum specifically designed for adults who have little or no banking experience. Classes are available in both English and Spanish and include *Checking and Savings, Budgeting and Your Credit, Lending Basics,* and *Credit Card Basics.* In 2003, more than 8,500 consumers participated in *Your Money Matters* classes.

Socially Responsible Business Practices: High School Intern Program

Washington Mutual's *High School Intern Program (HIP)* reflects the company's commitment to preparing a workforce for the future and giving students the opportunity to gain extensive job training and valuable work experience. Likewise, the program enables Washington Mutual to recruit and mentor new talent. Washington Mutual works with local schools to recruit interns for such positions as financial representatives, support specialists, and other administrative jobs.

This training gives HIP interns work experience, transferable job skills, and, in some cases, academic credit. Some interns become regular Washington Mutual employees. In 2003, nearly 800 high school students across the country graduated from the two-year program.[7]

Among the company's top priorities in support of its commitment to socially responsible business practices is the development of a workforce responsive to the needs of the diverse communities in which Washington Mutual does business. In 2003, WaMu ranked 4th in the nation in *Working Woman* magazine's "Top 25 Companies for Executive Women" and once again ranked among *Fortune*'s "Best Companies for Minorities."[8]

DELL INC.

Dell is a global company that delivers products and services in more than 190 countries and has more than 40,000 employees who live and work on six continents.[9] Major products include enterprise computing products, desktops, monitors, printers, notebooks, handhelds, software, and peripherals.

Dell has a focus on fully integrating improved environmental performance into business practices and marketing efforts, as well as corporate giving. In a letter on Dell's commitment to the environment, Chairman and CEO Michael Dell wrote: "Dell is fully committed to products and practices that minimize risk to the environment, working to reduce—and eventually eliminate—environmentally sensitive substances and to keep materials out of landfills."[10] This is further articulated through an environmental policy that includes designing products with the environment in mind, preventing waste and pollution, and achieving an environmentally focused culture.[11]

In the summary list, note the theme of environmental stewardship in each of the major initiatives. A more detailed description of each of the programs follows.

Cause Promotions: Dell Recycle

Electronic equipment is a fast-growing portion of America's potential trash, with 250 million computers predicted to become obsolete by

Table 2.2 Examples of Corporate Social Initiatives for Dell

	Cause Promotions	Cause-Related Marketing	Corporate Social Marketing	Corporate Philanthropy	Community Volunteering	Socially Responsible Business Practices
Description	Supporting social causes through promotions to increase awareness, fundraising, volunteers	Donating a percentage of revenues to a specific cause based on product sales	Supporting behavior change campaigns	Making direct contributions to a charity or cause	Providing volunteer services in the community	Adopting and conducting discretionary business practices and investments that support social causes
Example	Dell sponsors efforts to collect used computers for donations to local nonprofits and public agencies	Dell offers 10 percent off selected new products when up to three used products are recycled online	Dell offers free and convenient return of used printers for recycling or reuse	Through Dell's "Direct Giving" program with employees, employee donations are made to Earth Share, which supports multiple environmental projects	Dell employees around the globe participate in "Global Community Involvement Week" each September, including activities such as park cleanup	Dell creates product design programs with specific environmental guidelines, policies, and goals

2005.[12] Through Dell's partnership with the National Cristina Foundation (NCF), customers can donate computer equipment to charity, do their part to reduce landfills, and possibly receive a tax deduction. The National Cristina Foundation is a nonprofit organization that places used computers and other technology with local nonprofit organizations and public agencies that serve disabled and economically disadvantaged children and adults.[13]

In December 2001, Dell and NCF marked the one-year anniversary of this partnership through which hundreds of computers had been donated and reused by organizations worldwide. A special holiday promotion encouraged consumers to donate their used computers at no cost through Dell Recycling at www.dell4me.com/recycling, where consumers would enter information about their system online and NCF would search for partner agencies to match the donation in the donor's area. The local organization would then work with the consumer to arrange pickup or drop-off.[14] Figure 2.5 shows Dell's recycling logo.

Cause-Related Marketing: Discounts for Recycling Online

In another effort to encourage recycling of used equipment, Dell offered a deal in the summer of 2003 (see Figure 2.6): Recycle up to three items of select equipment, such as desktops, monitors, or notebooks, and get 50 percent off the regular recycling price per unit. Any brand of computer, keyboard, mouse, monitor, printer, fax machine, scanner, or

No computer should go to waste.

Figure 2.5   Logo used for Dell's recycling messages. (Reprinted courtesy of Dell.)

Figure 2.6   A promotional offer by Dell to stimulate recycling. (Reprinted courtesy of Dell.)

speakers were accepted for recycling. The offer also included a coupon for 10 percent off any online purchases of software and peripheral products. Preliminary results suggested as much as a 200 percent increase in orders per day.

Corporate Social Marketing: Printer Recycling

In March 2003, Dell began offering a new product line, printers, and as part of this launch, promoted their new printer-recycling program.

When customers purchase a Dell printer, they can now recycle their outdated printers at no additional cost and without leaving home. They can put it in the box their new Dell printer comes in, attach the prepaid shipping label supplied by Dell, and then go online to arrange for free pickup by Airborne at home or office.[15]

Corporate Philanthropy: Direct Giving

Dell's "Direct Giving" program gives employees a chance to contribute to the nonprofit of their choice through payroll deduction. One of the key beneficiaries of employees' generosity over the past few years is Earth Share of Texas. Earth Share in turn is a funding source for a variety of environmental projects and organizations.

Community Volunteering: Eco-Efficiency Team

Dell's "Eco-efficiency Team" is a forum for employees to bring ideas for environmentally oriented projects for Dell to consider and to then give employees volunteer opportunities in the community. Employees volunteering at recycling events in Nashville and Austin not only added to the productivity of the event, but also gave staff exposure to the company's commitment to sustainable activities.

Socially Responsible Business Practices: Design for Environment Program[16]

Dell's 2003 Environmental Report articulates their "Design for Environment" program, giving examples of measures they take in product design to (a) extend product life span; (b) reduce energy consumption; (c) avoid environmentally sensitive materials, particularly those that may have an adverse impact on the environment at product end-of-life; (d) promote dematerialization (reduced volume of materials in a product); and (e) use parts that are capable of being recycled at the highest level.

Dell participates in the U.S. Environmental Protection Agency (EPA) ENERGY STAR program to reduce power consumption of office equipment. The program allows manufacturers to partner with the EPA to design and certify products that meet or exceed federal government guidelines for low power consumption. Dell has actively participated in the program since 1993.

Currently, more than 50 substances and compounds are restricted for use in the manufacture of Dell products and in the finished products themselves. Dell has set a goal for 2003–2005 to, at a minimum, maintain a 20 percent reduction in the amount of lead shipped in displays when compared to 2002 levels. In addition, Dell has transitioned from cathode-ray tube (CRT) monitors to the liquid crystal display (LCD) technology used in flat-panel displays, resulting in a reduction in lead content. Dell is also actively working with resin suppliers to increase the usage of post-consumer recycled-content plastics.[17]

McDONALD'S CORPORATION

McDonald's Corporation is among *Fortune's* "Most Admired Companies" for social responsibility (2000–2002, 2004) and in 2001 was ranked in the *Wall Street Journal* as number five in reputation for corporate social responsibility.[18]

In April 2002, McDonald's issued its first Social Responsibility Report, in which Chairman and CEO Jim Cantalupo wrote: "McDonald's has the honor of serving more customers around the world than anyone else. With this privilege comes a responsibility to be a good neighbor, employer, and steward of the environment, and a unique opportunity to be a leader and a catalyst for positive change. We recognize the challenges and the obstacles, but believe strongly in the importance of social responsibility."[19]

The report suggests a renewed and perhaps even more accountable commitment to being a socially responsible leader and states that it is a " beginning and a template by which we will measure our progress in the area of social responsibility."[20] The report then details a wide range of initiatives in the areas of community, environment, people, and marketplace, and outlines related goals and plans, at the same time acknowledging the challenges McDonald's faces in gathering information and measuring progress.[21]

In the summary list, note the themes of the well-being of families and children and giving back to the local communities in which they do business. A more detailed description of each of the programs follows.

Cause Promotion: International Youth Camp

In 2000, McDonald's was a major sponsor of the Olympic Youth Camp, a program that brought more than 400 young men and women from around the globe to Sydney, Australia, where they participated in a variety of arts, sports, and cross-cultural activities. The Youth Camp was inaugurated at the 1912 Olympic Games in Stockholm, Sweden.

McDonald's was the first global company to sponsor the National Olympic Committee (NOC) selection of the 2000 Sydney Youth Camp participants from nearly 200 countries around the world. Participating McDonald's restaurants and NOCs worldwide worked together to select two McDonald's Olympic Achievers from each country to attend the Sydney 2000 Olympic Youth Camp.[22] Once on site, McDonald's honored these outstanding young corporate citizens through an international news event in their honor. McDonald's reached out to media to help communicate the importance of supporting young people who support their communities with such good works.

Cause-Related Marketing: World Children's Day

On November 20, 2002, a worldwide fundraising effort involved McDonald's restaurants from New York to New Zealand in more than 100

Table 2.3 Examples of Corporate Social Initiatives for McDonald's

	Cause Promotions	Cause-Related Marketing	Social Marketing	Corporate Philanthropy	Community Volunteering	Socially Responsible Business Practices
Description	Supporting social causes through promotions to increase awareness, fundraising, volunteers	Donating a percentage of revenues to a specific cause based on product sales	Supporting behavior change campaigns	Making direct contributions to a charity or cause	Providing volunteer services in the community	Adapting and conducting discretionary business practices and investments that support social causes
Example	McDonald's sponsored the Olympic Youth Camp program held in 2000 in Sydney, Australia	McDonald's earmarked $1 for children's causes from the sale of Big Macs and other items on World Children's Day, November 20, 2002	McDonald's promotes timely childhood immunizations	Ronald McDonald House offers places for families to stay for families with seriously ill children	McDonald's provided meals for professionals and volunteers at September 11 disaster sites	McDonald's changed to recycled-content packaging and reduced packaging materials

countries worldwide (see Figure 2.7).[23] All activities were intended to raise funds and awareness for Ronald McDonald House Charities and other local children's causes.[24]

Promotional messages promised that at every participating McDonald's restaurant, a donation would be made to children's charities based on sales of specific items. In the United States, for example, a donation of $1 was made to children's charities for every Big Mac, Egg McMuffin, Happy Meal, and Mighty Kids Meal sold. This offer was publicized via all major communication vehicles, including the Internet, e-mail, television, radio, and point-of-purchase in restaurants.

Additional activities included special events around the globe on November 20, with a launch in the New York Times Square McDonald's Restaurant, where famous celebrities and athletes performed the "World Children's Day" song and worked behind counters, and a concert was given with celebrities including Celine Dion.[25]

More than $12 million was raised in 24 hours, and sales increases varied from 5 percent in some countries to as much as 300 percent in others. These results did not go without challenges. Managers involved in the event coordination reported unique issues, including finding an appropriate date and managing 100-plus countries with varying fundraising laws and cultures.

Figure 2.7 McDonald's logos used to promote World Children's Day. (Used with permission from McDonald's Corporation.)

Social Marketing: Immunize for Healthy Lives®

Vaccine-preventable diseases like measles, chicken pox, polio, and hepatitis B are still a threat to children, according to the American Academy of Pediatrics (AAP), so it's important to immunize children on time. To help children and families, Ronald McDonald House Charities has teamed up with the AAP and health care providers around the United States on "Immunize for Healthy Lives," an immunization education program in existence since 1994.

August is the back-to-school vaccination time period, when most parents take their school-aged children to be immunized before returning to the classroom. But health professionals also recommend that vaccinations begin at infancy to protect against meningitis and pneumonia. By age two, children can be protected from more than 11 preventable diseases.

Ronald McDonald House Charities is committed to the health and well-being of children and families. By working with health care providers around the country, the "Immunize for Healthy Lives" program educates parents on the importance of timely immunizations so they can help their children stay healthy. Figure 2.8 shows a tray liner created for use in McDonald's restaurants to provide parents with helpful information.

Local communities around the United States have taken on special activities to promote the "Immunize for Healthy Lives" campaign:

- In North Carolina, immunization schedules are distributed through nearly 300 McDonald's restaurants throughout the state, with the campaign reaching up to 13 million customers in a month.
- In Harrisburg, Pennsylvania, Health Department nurses visit participating McDonald's restaurants to review children's immunization records. Nurses also give free McDonald's coupons for ice cream to parents asking, "Do my kids need shots?"

Corporate Philanthropy: Ronald McDonald House Charities

The relationship between McDonald's Corporation and Ronald McDonald House Charities and its programs dates back to the inception of the charitable organization. Today, one can find support and participation from McDonald's Corporation, its franchisees, crew members, suppliers, and business partners at every level of the charity's activity—United States, international, corporate, regional, and local. Members

Figure 2.8   McDonald's tray liner encouraging timely immunizations for children. (Used with permission from McDonald's Corporation.)

of the McDonald's family serve as volunteers on the boards and committees of the local chapters, working alongside other members of their community. Together they tackle the challenges of operating a public charity—raising necessary funds and awareness and delivering program services to children and their families.

Ronald McDonald House Charities creates, finds, and supports programs that directly improve the health and well-being of children worldwide. It is a nonprofit, 501(c)(3) organization with more than 181 local chapters currently operating in 48 countries. Each local Ronald McDonald House Charities chapter is a separate public charity, operated by a local board of directors.

The cornerstone of Ronald McDonald House Charities is the Ronald McDonald House program, which provides a home away from home for families of seriously ill children undergoing treatment at hospitals far from their own homes. The first Ronald McDonald House was established in Philadelphia in 1974. Today, there are more than 235 Ronald McDonald Houses in more than 25 countries (see Figure 2.9).

In addition to its cornerstone program, Ronald McDonald House Charities supports a variety of other programs, which include Ronald McDonald Family Rooms, Ronald McDonald Care Mobiles, and scholarships. The charity also awards grants to other organizations that directly improve the health and well-being of children. To date, Ronald McDonald House Charities' national body and global network of local chapters have awarded more than $400 million in grants to children's programs worldwide.

Community Volunteering: Disaster Relief

McDonald's, working through owner/operators, employees, and suppliers, has a longtime record of helping communities hit by tornadoes,

Figure 2.9 Ronald McDonald House programs provide a home away from home for families of seriously ill children. (Used with permission from McDonald's Corporation.)

hurricanes, floods, earthquakes, riots, or other disasters. McDonald's has partnered with American Red Cross and its International Red Cross network to provide food and other support to disaster victims, meals for the professionals and volunteers on the scene to aid them, and a haven of safety for others in the community.[26]

On 9/11 and in the weeks that followed, McDonald's provided more than 750,000 free meals around the clock at McDonald's mobile restaurants set up near the disaster sites in New York City, at the Pentagon, and in Pennsylvania (see Figure 2.10). At each location, 45-foot-long portable units served McDonald's Quarter Pounders, Chicken Mc-Nuggets, bottled water, and soft drinks to feed recovery workforces.[27]

Socially Responsible Business Practices: Recycling

Several activities represent a commitment to progress in reducing packaging volume and adding recycled content:

- In the early 1990s, in most parts of the world, McDonald's changed its carryout bags from bleached, 100 percent virgin paper

Figure 2.10   McDonald's provided free meals near 9/11 disaster sites in New York City. (Used with permission from McDonald's Corporation.)

fiber to unbleached, recycled content. During that same period, McDonald's purchased more than $4 billion worth of products made from recycled materials for use in the construction and operation of restaurants worldwide. McDonald's USA recently switched to a 40 percent recycled-content white bag, while making other packaging changes to offset the increased environmental impact.

- In 2002, McDonald's purchased more than $460 million in recycled packaging materials and reduced its packaging materials by an additional 35 million pounds (see Figure 2.11).

Although a process is in place to work with suppliers to find ways to streamline packaging and minimize use of resources, broad-based solutions are challenged by differences around the world in safe food requirements, local supplier availability, cultural differences, waste management practices, and infrastructure.[28]

To support McDonald's goal of sustainability, a Global Environmental Council (GEC) was formed in 2002 to identify global priorities,

Figure 2.11 In 2002, McDonald's reduced packaging materials by 35 million pounds. (Used with permission from McDonald's Corporation.)

initiatives, and projects. It reports to the Social Responsibility Steering Committee established by the board of directors.[29]

SUMMARY

Most corporate social initiatives under the corporate social responsibility umbrella fall within one of the following distinct categories: cause promotions, cause-related marketing, corporate social marketing, corporate philanthropy, community volunteering, and socially responsible business practices.

Though there are commonalities among these initiatives (i.e., similar causes they are supporting, partnerships that are formed, and communication channels that are used), each has a characteristic that makes it distinct. Cause promotions are distinguished by the fact that they are supporting a cause by increasing community awareness and contributions to the cause. Cause-related marketing is unique in that donations to a cause are tied to the corporation's product sales volume. Corporate social marketing is always focused on a goal of influencing a behavior change. Community volunteering involves employee and related franchise and retail partners' donation of their time in support of a local cause. Corporate philanthropy entails writing a check or making a direct, in-kind contribution of corporate services and resources. And corporate socially responsible business practices, as implied, relate to the adoption of discretionary business practices and investments that then contribute to improved environmental and community well-being.

Why is it important to develop these distinctions? As with most disciplines, awareness and familiarity with tools in the toolbox increases the chances they will be considered and then used. As noted in Chapter 1, traditional corporate giving and citizenship focused primarily on one of these initiatives, philanthropy. As we have seen in the examples presented in this chapter, a more strategic and disciplined approach involves selecting an issue for focus and then considering each of the six potential options for contributing to the cause.

Based on the in-depth examples for Washington Mutual, Dell, and McDonald's, a few observations are noteworthy at this point:

- A corporate theme for social responsibility can be expressed in all six of the initiatives. Washington Mutual's K-12 education focus is reflected in each of the initiatives described. Based on reviews of many corporate social responsibility programs, this model can be very effective for connecting the corporation to a cause, as will be described in Chapter 9 concerning best practices. It is, however, currently quite unusual.

- It is more common for a corporation to have several themes, and for themes to be reflected by only a few initiatives. Examples presented for McDonald's covered several themes: children's health, children and families with special needs, disaster relief, and environmental stewardship.

- One campaign may integrate several initiatives. For example, Starbucks has a program called "Starbucks Make Your Mark" that recruits volunteers for assistance with local community and nonprofit projects such as cleanup of trails and parks. This campaign has an element of cause promotion (i.e., recruiting customers in their stores to sign up for projects by visiting Starbucks.com). It also has an element of cause-related marketing, as it promises to make a contribution to the nonprofit sponsor based on the number of volunteer hours given to the project. And it has a community volunteer component, as staff in the Starbucks partner stores are also encouraged to show up for the event.

Finally, it is useful to note other terms that are used to label these initiatives, to underscore the distinctions. Cause promotions may be most similar to programs sometimes described as cause marketing, cause sponsorships, cause advertising, co-branding, or corporate sponsorships. Cause-related marketing is included by some when describing cause marketing or co-branding programs. Corporate social marketing may be considered a subset of cause marketing. Corporate philanthropy may be expressed as corporate giving, community giving, community development, community involvement, corporate social investing, or community outreach. Community volunteering is often covered when referring to community service, community development, community relations, community involvement, community outreach, community partnerships, and corporate citizenship programs. And the term socially responsible business practices is for some synonymous with corporate social responsibility, corporate citizenship, and corporate commitment.

As noted earlier, the delineation of these distinct subcategories may help increase consideration of these initiatives and may make understanding and application of the keys to success for a particular initiative more likely. The following six chapters outline each initiative's unique and recommended circumstances for consideration and keys for successful development and implementation.

Corporate Cause Promotions: Increasing Awareness and Concern for Social Causes

We're all in it together. We're an eclectic collective of environmental ad-
vocates along with some innovative ice cream and music makers, working
in concert to tackle the man-made problem of global warming.[1]
> —Introduction to the "One Sweet Whirled"
> campaign created by Ben & Jerry's,
> SaveOurEnvironment.org, and the
> Dave Matthews Band

In a cause promotion a corporation provides funds, in-kind contributions, or other corporate resources to increase awareness and concern about a social cause or to support fundraising, participation, or volunteer recruitment for a cause.

Persuasive communications are the major focus for this initiative, with an intention to create awareness and concern relative to a social issue and/or to persuade potential donors and volunteers to contribute to the cause or participate in activities to support the cause. Successful campaigns utilize effective communication principles, developing motivating messages, creating persuasive executional elements, and selecting efficient and effective media channels. Campaign plans are based on clear definitions of target audiences, communication objectives and goals, support for promised benefits, opportune communication channels, and desired positioning.

Cause promotion is distinguished from other corporate social initiatives primarily by the emphasis on promotional strategies.

- It differs from cause-related marketing in that contributions and support are not tied to company sales of specified products.
- It differs from social marketing in that the focus is not on influencing individual behavior change. Although cause promotion campaigns have calls to action, they are most commonly in the areas of contributing, such as by donating money or time or by signing petitions.
- It differs from philanthropy in that it involves more from the company than simply writing a check, as promotional campaigns will most often require involvement in the development and distribution of materials and participation in public relations activities, and will include visibility for the corporation's sponsorship.
- Although a cause promotion may include employee volunteerism, it goes beyond this to participating as well in the development and implementation of promotional materials.
- It differs from socially responsible business practices in that the focus is primarily on external communications, as opposed to internal operations, and the target audiences for the promotions are primarily outside the organization.

Historically, cause promotion has been a common form of corporate giving, along with philanthropy and employee volunteerism. It has involved everything from putting company logos on special events and advertisements for causes to contributing retail store space for promotional materials.

Most commonly, corporations are approached to contribute to a cause promotion being developed by a nonprofit organization or consortium of agencies. In some cases, the corporation decides to support a social cause and then reaches out to partner with organizations in the community associated with the cause. In a few cases, the corporation may go it alone, developing and managing the campaign internally.

TYPICAL CAUSE PROMOTIONS

Corporate cause promotions most commonly focus on the following communication objectives. Examples of each will be explored in the remainder of this chapter.

- *Building awareness and concern* about a cause by presenting motivating statistics and facts, such as publicizing the number of children who go to sleep hungry in America each night or the number of dogs that are euthanized each year; by sharing real stories of people or organizations in need or who have been helped by the cause, such as one about a middle-aged man in a developing country who gets much-needed eyeglasses for the first time in his life, or a local hospital reporting they don't have the number of critical nurses they need to serve their community; or by presenting educational information, such as a brochure on warning signs for youth suicide.

- *Persuading people to find out more* about the cause by visiting a special web site (e.g., one with information on nursing schools in the nation) or by requesting an informational brochure or tool kit (e.g., for tips on conducting a bake sale to raise money for food banks in their community).

- *Persuading people to donate their time* to help those in need (e.g., employees in a retail store delivering eyeglasses, or citizens in a community hosting a bake sale to benefit local charities).

- *Persuading people to donate money* that will benefit a cause (e.g., hosting a section of a corporate web site where visitors can donate to animal welfare charities).

- *Persuading people to donate nonmonetary resources*, such as unwanted cell phones and used clothing (e.g., for women's shelters).

- *Persuading people to participate in events*, such as attending an art show featuring minority professional photographers, participating in a fundraising walk, or signing a petition to ban animal testing.

As outlined in Table 3.1, corporations participating in cause promotions include manufacturers, retailers, service providers, and many others. Issues supported are varied as well and include environmental causes, hunger, housing, needs for health care and medical services, human rights, animal welfare, education, medical research, and diversity.

By their very nature, cause promotion activities have a common theme of *communications*. They utilize publicity, printed materials, special events, web sites, and advertising, featuring the logo and key messages of the company as well as those representing the cause. In addition, however, cause promotion campaigns may also include employee involvement, messages on product labeling, and utilization of retail shelf space.

Corporations most often partner with nonprofit organizations whose mission is related to the cause, as well as media partners, professional associations, and special interest groups. Table 3.1 summarizes causes supported by 10 major corporations featured in this chapter.

POTENTIAL CORPORATE BENEFITS

Not surprisingly, many of the corporate benefits associated with cause promotions are marketing related: strengthened brand positioning and brand preference, increased traffic, and customer loyalty. In addition, further benefits flow from providing customers and employees opportunities and convenient ways to contribute to causes, and are created by forging new and strong partnerships with community organizations.

Strengthens Brand Positioning
Notice in the following example from Ben & Jerry's the role that brand position played in guiding the choice of a social issue, selecting an initiative, and forming partnerships.

Table 3.1 Examples of Cause Promotion Initiatives

Corporation	Cause	Target Audiences	Sample Activities	Major Partners
Ben & Jerry's	Global warming	Anyone who loves ice cream and cares about the environment Current customers	New flavor of ice cream Concert tour CD Web site Public Relations	Dave Matthews Band SaveOurEnvironment.org
PETsMART®	Animal adoption	Customers in stores Potential dog and cat pet owners	Raising money in stores and on web site Offering retail space for pet adoption	PETsMART Charities Animal shelters
Aleve	Arthritis	People with arthritis Those wanting to contribute to the cause	Arthritis Walk promotion: Printed materials Publicity Web site T-shirts, banners, and booths at event	Arthritis Foundation
British Airways	Children in need around the world	Travelers on British Airways flights	Providing envelopes for collecting change Flight crew promotions Web site	UNICEF
Wal-Mart	Children's hospitals	Customers in stores	Employee promotions in stores	Children's Miracle Network

(Continued)

53

Table 3.1 *(Continued)*

Corporation	Cause	Target Audiences	Sample Activities	Major Partners
PARADE magazine	Hunger	PARADE readers	Feature articles "Great American Bake Sale" fundraising event Web site	Share Our Strength Local food charities ABC TV
Nordstrom	Diversity	Customers	Art show in select stores Public relations	Professional black photographers
The Body Shop	Animal testing for cosmetics	Policy makers Cosmetics industry Customers	In-store signage Printed materials Badges Petitions Labeling on packages Public relations Web site	Animal rights and advocacy groups
Johnson & Johnson	Nursing shortages	High school students College students Counselors Health care systems	Advertising Recruitment materials Special events Public relations Web site	Professional nursing associations Colleges and universities Health care systems
LensCrafters	Eyeglasses and eye care for those in need	People in North America and developing countries in need of eyeglasses and eye care	Eyeglass collection Employee volunteerism Printed materials Web site	Lions Club International

Example: Ben & Jerry's and Global Warming

Ben & Jerry's mission statement is consistent with the creative approach taken in most of what they do. It has three parts, all considered essential and equal by the company: product and economic and social missions. Notice the words we have italicized in the product and social mission statements that follow, language that sets the stage for their brand positioning:

> "Product Mission: to make, distribute and sell the *finest quality, all natural* ice cream and *euphoric concoctions* with a continued commitment to incorporating *wholesome, natural ingredients* and promoting business practices that respect the *Earth* and the *environment*."

> "Social Mission: to operate the company in a way that actively recognizes the central role that business plays in society by initiating *innovative ways* to improve the *quality of life* locally, nationally, and internationally."[2]

This positioning must have made the decision to support awareness of global warming and to launch a cause promotion initiative easy. In April 2002, Ben & Jerry's teamed up with the Dave Matthews Band and SaveOurEnvironment.org to help fight global warming. Together, they created the "One Sweet Whirled" global warming campaign, intended to increase awareness of the reality of the threats from global warming and to learn more about what can be done.[3]

Campaign elements include a new flavor of ice cream, One Sweet Whirled (see Figure 3.1); a concert tour; a CD; a web site with related links; and public relations efforts to increase awareness and concern about global warming and to promote actions that individuals can take to make a difference (a social marketing element of the campaign).

In 2002 alone, the campaign generated 53,236 pledges to reduce carbon pollution, representing a potential reduction of 187,486,501 total pounds; 63,967 letters sent to Congress; and 12,570 new SaveOurEnvironment.org members.

Figure 3.1   Ben & Jerry's supports awareness of global warming with a special ice cream flavor and more. (Reprinted courtesy of Ben & Jerry's.)

Builds Traffic and Customer Loyalty

In the following example, the corporation benefits from a creative and natural donation of abundant resources—its store space—and the appeal of abandoned and homeless pets.

Example: PETsMART® and Pet Adoption

PETsMART Charities® creates and supports programs that save the lives of homeless pets (see Figure 3.2).[4] They have a vision of "a lifelong, loving home for EVERY pet." Several initiatives support this goal, including in-store adoption centers, in-store campaigns to encourage customer donations, and online fundraising.[5]

With more than four million homeless pets euthanized every year, PETsMART, Inc. made the conscious decision not to sell cats and dogs. Instead, the company created their in-store PETs-MART Charities Adoption Centers, donating space to local animal welfare organizations so they can make homeless pets more visible and accessible to potential families.[6] PETsMART, Inc. donates more than $5 million annually in space and supplies for the adoption centers, and the charity works with more than 2,700 animal welfare organizations across North America. These organizations keep 100 percent of their adoption fees and there is no cost to them to use the in-store Centers.

The store and the PETsMART Charities also work together to implement a biannual "Just A Buck, Change Their Luck" fundraising campaign to help homeless pets. This event is held for three weeks in the spring and again in the fall. Customers are asked if they'd like to donate "just a buck" (or more) when they make a purchase. Customers who donate $10 or more receive a commemorative T-shirt. Those who donate $15 or more receive a limited edition tote bag. All of the more than 650 stores nationwide and in Canada participate in the campaign. Donations can also be made online, where the T-shirts and tote bags are also offered for donations of $15 and $20 respectively.

Between 1994 and 2003, this program has saved the lives of more than 1.7 million homeless pets through the in-store adoption areas alone, and continues to save lives today. Consider as well the benefit to PETsMART in terms of the thousands, if not millions, of customers exposed to the effort, and, for those adopting a pet, their likelihood of returning to a PETsMART store for food, needed supplies, and grooming services.[7]

Figure 3.2 PETsMART provides space for in-store adoption centers for homeless pets. (Printed with permission from PETsMART, Inc.)

Creates Brand Preference with Target Markets

Direct competitors of the Aleve brand might find this selection of an initiative and partnership enviable.

Example: Aleve and Arthritis Foundation

In 2002, Aleve began to market more stringently to consumers with arthritis. In order to generate brand awareness among these consumers, Aleve developed a partnership with the Arthritis Foundation and became the National Presenting Sponsor of the Arthritis Foundation's nationwide Arthritis Walk event. This relationship has helped Aleve to disseminate its key messages of strength and efficacy to the more than 70 million Americans who have arthritis. Upon initial discussions, Aleve and the Arthritis Foundation quickly realized that they had the same goal at heart: to help consumers relieve their arthritis pain and restore their mobility so they can get back to doing the things they love to do. The sponsorship of the Arthritis Walk and the partnership have provided benefits to both Aleve and the Arthritis Foundation, a true win-win proposition.

The 2003 Arthritis Walk, held in May in support of National Arthritis Month, attracted 24,767 participants, with men, women, and children with arthritis "leading the way wearing special shirts and blue hero hats to show they are taking control of their arthritis."[8] Aleve was able to further leverage this relationship by integrating the Aleve logo into the overall Arthritis Walk logo appearing on all recruitment materials and promotional materials, including TV ads, T-shirts, banners, and web sites (see Figure 3.3).

In addition to sponsoring the Arthritis Walk, Aleve has been able to incorporate this relationship into other elements of the marketing mix. Aleve has worked with the foundation in everything from advertising, where Aleve added a five-second tag to their commercials during May to publicize the Arthritis Walk, to packaging, where Aleve received the Arthritis Foundation's Ease-of-Use Commendation for its Easy Open Arthritis Cap bottles. Also, Aleve was able to utilize the relationship in a cause-related marketing initiative. In 2003, Aleve offered a copy of the Arthritis Foundation's *Walk With Ease* book (an $11.95 value) for free when the consumer sent in a proof-of-purchase seal from a package of Aleve Easy Open Arthritis Cap.

Overall, Aleve's relationship with the Arthritis Foundation and the full integration of that relationship into all elements of the marketing mix has allowed Aleve to generate greater brand awareness and establish its authority in arthritis pain relief. The value of this relationship and the trust it has helped Aleve to establish with consumers is immeasurable.

The Arthritis Foundation has also greatly benefited from this relationship by increasing awareness, increasing participation in the Arthritis Walk events, and driving consumers to their 800 number and web site for helpful information on arthritis.

Figure 3.3 Aleve increases awareness and participation in Arthritis Walk events. (Reprinted courtesy of Arthritis Foundation.)

Figure 3.4   British Airways provides an envelope to make it easy for customers to donate onboard to UNICEF. (Reprinted courtesy of British Airways.)

Provides Customers Convenient Ways to Contribute and Participate in Causes

The corporate sponsor in the following example makes it easy for the customer to say yes and perhaps even difficult to say no.

Example: British Airways and Change for Good

An estimated 16 million Americans travel to Europe each year, and chances are they arrive home with foreign currency in their pockets and purses. In 1994, British Airways began offering promotional support to the United Nations Children's Fund (UNICEF) by collecting currency from customers on board British Airways flights.

Through this program called "Change for Good," passengers can donate unwanted foreign coins and notes at any time during the flight, using envelopes they find at their seat or by requesting one from the cabin crew (see Figure 3.4). It is reported that many of the crew members are enthusiastic enough about the program to also make voluntary announcements during flights and move through the cabins to collect the envelopes. British Airways then works with UNICEF in decision making regarding which countries will be recipients of donations.[9]

The conversion to the euro by 12 European countries in 2002 created a new promotional opportunity for the partners, solving the problem of what to do with currencies no longer usable in 12 European countries.[10] Promotional messages stressed that UNICEF will still be able to convert these currencies.[11]

By the year 2002, British Airways had raised over $31 million (U. S. dollars) for UNICEF programs, helping with projects in over 50 countries around the world. Funds raised by British Airways represented an estimated half of the total amount raised by UNICEF "Change for Good" programs, in part due to the fact that this program runs year-round on all routes.[12]

Provides Opportunities for Employees to Get Involved in Something They Care About

Imagine the following cause promotion, which raises money in retail stores for local children's hospitals, if it were undertaken without the participation and enthusiasm of employees. Consider, as well, that participation is voluntary and the enthusiasm apparently spontaneous.

Example: Wal-Mart and Children's Miracle Network

The Wal-Mart Foundation makes it clear in its mission statement that its emphasis is on its associates, their children, families, and local community. Wal-Mart believes this grassroots style of giving provides opportunities for its associates to identify and then support causes that will improve the quality of life right in their own communities (see Figure 3.5). It further explains that its priority funding areas include children. "Children are the heart, soul, and future of any community, so we're proud to be involved at the local level in programs that benefit children. It is our fondest wish that each and every child has the opportunity to lead a healthy, happy, and fulfilling childhood."[13]

Corporate sponsorship of Children's Miracle Network (CMN) then is not surprising, and the direct involvement of associates is apparently key to the more than $250 million raised for 170 children's hospitals since 1988. In 2002 alone, associates nation-wide raised more than $34 million for CMN.[14]

Children's Miracle Network says, "Wal-Mart associates love to reach impossible goals, especially when it comes to helping kids." For example, one store created a "crazy hat" campaign where associates wore "goofy-looking hats," persuaded cus-tomers to donate dollar bills, and then attached them to their hats. In two months, this store raised $6,000 through crazy hats alone. A store manager reported that they had fun com-peting with each other, making comments such as, "I raised one hundred and two dollars last Saturday with my crazy hat." They are evidently engaging the customers as well; one associ-ate overheard a customer shout, "That dollar on that hat is mine!"[15]

In 2002, Wal-Mart received the Ron Brown Award, the highest Presidential Award recognizing achievement in employee rela-tions and community initiatives.

Creates Partnerships

Any nonprofit organization or cause is fortunate when a strong media partner joins the promotional effort. In the following example, it would appear *Parade* magazine reaped the rewards as well.

Figure 3.5   Logo used for Wal-Mart Foundation's community involvement program. (Reprinted courtesy of Wal-Mart.)

Example: *Parade* Magazine and Hunger

In the spring of 2003, *Parade* magazine and Share Our Strength, a leading antihunger organization, launched "The Great American Bake Sale," a cause promotion to raise awareness of childhood hunger in this country and funds for hunger relief. The campaign, which launched in April 2003 and ran through July, encouraged anyone and everyone across the country to host a bake sale in their community and/or to buy items from a Great American Bake Sale event. Proceeds were sent to Share Our Strength, which granted 75 percent of the net funds to local hunger-relief organizations in the states where the funds were collected. The remaining funds were targeted for high-risk areas and populations and for public policy advocacy. Sponsors included ABC Television Network, Betty Crocker, Tyson Foods, Inc., Reynolds Consumer Products, and numerous prominent American chefs.[16]

The event was launched with a cover story in *Parade* magazine, which included the statistic that "Tonight 13 million children in the United States may go to bed hungry." (See Figure 3.6.) As of January 2004, *Parade* distributed by more than 335 Sunday newspapers, has a circulation of 35.7 million and an estimated readership of more than 78 million.[17] Other activities to promote the Great American Bake Sale included mention in select corporate sponsors' advertising as well as on sponsor web sites. ABC integrated the bake sale plot into an episode of its hit series *Eight Simple Rules for Dating My Teenage Daughter*. The cast, including the late John Ritter, appeared at bake sale events around the nation and recorded public service announcements to further promote the program.

In their October 5, 2003, issue, *Parade* reported that the Great American Bake Sale had raised $1.1 million to fight childhood hunger in the Untied States. An estimated 375,000 people participated by baking or buying goods. More than 500 companies contributed resources.[18] The partners have already planned a repeat in 2004, adding additional elements, including a free kit for to those who register to help plan and produce bake sales.

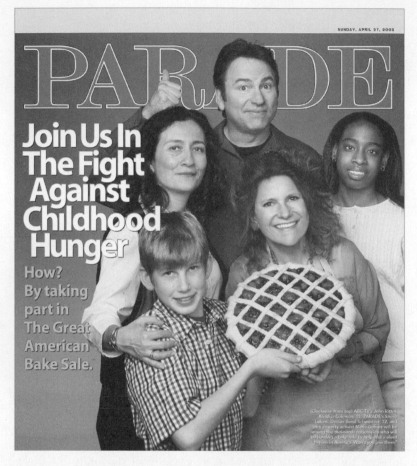

Figure 3.6   *Parade* magazine helps raise awareness and funds for hunger relief. (Reprinted courtesy of Parade Publications.)

Strengthens Corporate Image

Nordstrom is well known for its customer service, and its commitment to diversity is one factor that has contributed to this strong reputation.

Example: Nordstrom and Diversity

One of the main sections listed on Nordstrom's home page under "About Nordstrom"—right up there with "Store Locations" and

"Investor Relations"—is "Diversity Affairs." A visit to this section is reminiscent of many other corporations' entire corporate social responsibility section, with separate write-ups on their "Diversity Affairs Mission Statement," "Employment Statistics," "Minority Recruitment and Support," "Diversity in Advertising," "Supplier Diversity Program." "Community Service" is a subset within this section.

An introduction in this section sets the background for an apparently strong commitment: "There is something unique about Nordstrom that goes beyond our merchandise, our stores, and even our renowned services. It's our people. Our employees make Nordstrom the nation's premier retailer—and diversity is a key component of that winning combination. . . ."[19]

A cause promotion hosted by Nordstrom in February 2003 and again in 2004 is representative of this value and commitment. A press release announced that in celebration of Black History Month, Nordstrom would be showcasing during the month of February the work of African-American photographers in a premiere exhibit titled "Love Now," with works of "photographers' interpretation of love in our times." The exhibit was displayed in select Nordstrom stores and was considered "a public tribute to the art and talent of black professional photographers."

It is also consistent with this commitment that Nordstrom "regularly advertises in both local and national minority publications including *Essence, Minority Business News USA, Hispanic Business, Hispanic, Catalina, Minority Business Entrepreneur, Black Enterprise* and *Ability* magazine. In its mainstream advertising, Nordstrom has long been committed to featuring models of color and models with disabilities in at least one-third of its advertisements."[20] (See Figure 3.7.)

Since 1993, Nordstrom has been named by *Hispanic* magazine as one of the 100 best companies offering employment opportunities for Hispanics. In 2003, *Fortune* magazine named Nordstrom to its "100 Best Companies to Work for in America" list, for the seventh year in a row. Fortune magazine also named Nordstrom to its "Best Companies for Minorities" list four out of the five years since it began the list. *Asian Enterprise* magazine selected Nordstrom as one of the "Best Companies for Asian Pacific Americans."

POTENTIAL CONCERNS

As with most campaigns and programs that are promotional in nature, several potential downsides for the corporation should be kept in mind during the decision-making and planning process.

Visibility for the corporation can get lost. Most managers considering major sponsorship of a social issue are interested in ensuring visibility for

Figure 3.7 Nordstrom's advertising represents their corporate commitment to diversity. (Reprinted courtesy of Nordstrom.)

their company on promotional materials in return for the investment of corporate resources, often funded by the marketing department. One could argue that otherwise, it is a philanthropic initiative ("just writing a check"). Many would consider the placement of Aleve's logo on the Arthritis Walk materials an ideal model. This strategy, a co-branding approach, positions the company as a partner in the cause. Contrast this with the perceived commitment of an organization that is in a lineup of three to five corporate logos across the bottom of promotional materials.

Most promotional materials are not sustainable. Brochures, fliers, public service announcements, news articles, special events, even another T-shirt, water bottle, or baseball cap can be here today and gone tomorrow. Managers are encouraged to consider a sustainable component in the campaign, one such as the new flavor of ice cream developed by Ben & Jerry's, an element that provides campaign messaging opportunities as well.

Tracking total investments and return on promotional investments is especially difficult. Many report that not only is it difficult to track results for the company from the promotional effort, it is also difficult to track the actual expenditure of corporate resources, especially nonmonetary contributions (e.g., employee time, retail store space). As stated early in the chapter, the intention of a cause promotion is often just to increase awareness and concern regarding a cause, frequently without a call to action. This is harder and more expensive to measure than changes in behavior or redemption of coupons, for example, which can be accomplished through internal tracking systems. Changes in awareness and levels of concern typically require more quantitative research, adding to the costs of the effort. How, for example, would Nordstrom track the benefit of the art show to the organization (or to the cause, for that matter)?

You may get swamped with requests for contributions from other organizations connected to the cause. As you will read in the next section on Johnson & Johnson's Campaign for Nursing's Future, this highly visible campaign that was focused on nurse recruitment and retention generated inquiries from numerous related organizations. Responding to requests then adds even more to the expenditure of effort and time.

This approach requires more time and involvement than writing a check. PETsMART, for example, spends time and effort coordinating and supporting its in-store adoption programs, hosting sections of its corporate web site for donations from the general public, and collecting donations at checkout stands.

Promotions are often easy to replicate, removing any competitive advantage. As will be described in the next section, The Body Shop has been advocating against animal testing for cosmetics for more than 10 years. There are few entry barriers for other cosmetic brands to also take "no animal testing" positions, even though it may be with lower levels of commitment. The consumer, however, has a hard time discriminating between claims.

KEYS TO SUCCESS

The following three cases offer perspectives from managers at The Body Shop, Johnson & Johnson, and LensCrafters in terms of keys to successful cause promotion initiatives. Their common themes reflect recommendations to carefully select an issue (up front) that can be tied to a business's products and company values. They say it should be a cause that management can commit to long-term, is a concern for customers and target markets, motivates employees, and has the most chance for media exposure. When developing cause promotion plans, take care to develop strong partnerships, incorporate and ensure visibility for your brand, and figure out a way to measure and track results.

The Body Shop "Against Animal Testing" Initiative

The Body Shop opened its first store in 1976 and is now a well-respected international retailer offering high-quality skin and body care products in 50 countries around the world through more than 1,900 outlets. The company is known by many for its values-driven business practices and cause promotion campaigns, including ones against animal testing within the cosmetics and toiletries industry. The following perspective from their head of communications and campaigns highlights the importance of a long-term commitment and a willingness to stay the course in order for a campaign to achieve a win-win result.

In 1990, The Body Shop launched the first in a series of public aware-ness campaigns against animal testing (AAT) in the cosmetic industry. We elected to campaign on this issue for a number of reasons: It was core to our beliefs as a business that animal testing was unacceptable in order to create a new cosmetic or toiletry product or ingredient; the issue was highly relevant to both our industry and the consumer; and it was an issue on which we could realistically make a difference. It was estimated in 2002 that over 35,000 animals were used in cosmetics tests every year throughout the European Union alone.[21]

This campaign was originally managed by Corporate Communi-cations and subsequently by the Values and Vision Department, working in partnership across the globe with campaign partners from the animal welfare movement. A particular emphasis was placed on the United Kingdom and European Union, with a focus on amend-ing proposed legislation relating to the sale and marketing of cosmet-ics in order to bring about a cosmetic animal test ban.

Funding for this campaign is provided from our Communica-tions and Values departments, our franchisee network, and our char-itable Foundation.

Promotional vehicles have included in-store and out-of-store communications and campaign materials, with considerable use of Anita Roddick in the early years, as a business leader calling on the cosmetic industry to take action to end animal testing. In-store cam-paigns included window posters, leaflets, the sale of badges and bags, and the collection of signatures on a campaign petition, promoted through our stores and by partner animal welfare groups to their sup-porters. Product labels state clearly that we are "Against Animal Testing" (see Figure 3.8) and in terms of business practices, we were

Figure 3.8   The Body Shop's logo used for advocacy efforts. (Reprinted courtesy of The Body Shop.)

the first cosmetic company to have supplier-monitoring systems independently audited and certified.

In terms of outcomes, we are proud to have helped reduce and to bring an end to cosmetic animal testing in countries such as the United Kingdom and the Netherlands and to have played a significant role in the European Union agreeing to a test ban that is due to come into force in 2009. In November 1996, The Body Shop presented the European Union (EU) the largest petition against animal testing in history—signed by over four million people calling on the EU to honor a commitment to stop the testing and sale of animal-tested cosmetic products. In November 2002, The Body Shop welcomed the news that Europe will ban cosmetics animal testing, due to come into force in stages over the next few years.

As a result, The Body Shop is closely aligned with the issue of no animal testing for cosmetic purposes wherever you go in the world. The issue and the campaign have contributed to generating significant media coverage for The Body Shop and our ethics. In 1998, a survey of international chief executives that was reported in the *Financial Times* ranked The Body Shop the 27th most respected company in the world. And we were the first international cosmetics retailer to be endorsed by leading animal protection groups under their Humane Cosmetic Standard.

We offer others the following thoughts when aligning with a social issue and developing campaign plans:

- Select an issue that is extremely engaging for your customers and relevant to your industry and your products.
- Choose initiatives that align with your company mission and business objectives, so that they are not seen to be peripheral by your internal and external publics.
- Take on causes that will be motivating for your employees, recognizing that they will enjoy the opportunity to go beyond retailing to making a real difference on social issues.
- Select issues that have the most chance to become mainstream, ones that are "winnable" enough to be popular with the media, public, and politicians but controversial enough to generate debate.

- Once selected, commit wholeheartedly. Avoid short-term solutions, promises you can't fulfill, and ensure this is not viewed simply as a marketing exercise.
- Recognize that you will be expected to demonstrate your commitments in your own corporate behavior, policies, and practices.
- Develop campaign goals with tangible outcomes that demonstrate sustainable solutions, ones that provide the best return for business and society.
- Ensure that key stakeholders are engaged in your social initiatives. Be clear about the level of commitment to a particular initiative, effectively manage expectations of all relevant stakeholders, and remember to communicate campaign successes with them and acknowledge their role in helping to bring about change.[22]

Johnson & Johnson's "Campaign for Nursing's Future" Initiative

In 1943, Robert Wood Johnson wrote a credo for the company, a one-page document that outlined responsibilities to customers, employees, the community, and shareholders. Fulfillment of that credo is evident in the following description of their "Campaign for Nursing's Future." Provided by the executive director for the campaign, this summary highlights key components of this cause promotion initiative and measurable outcomes for their effort.

Johnson & Johnson has a long history of working with nurses. In fact, the first line of our credo says, "We believe our first responsibility is to the doctors, nurses, and patients, to mothers and fathers and all others who use our products and services." Recognizing that our country was experiencing the most severe nursing shortage in our history, we launched the Johnson & Johnson "Campaign for Nursing's Future" in February 2002, a multiyear, nationwide effort to enhance the image of the nursing profession, recruit new nurses, and retain nurses currently in the system (see Figure 3.9). We knew we had the marketing skills to make a difference. When we created this program, which is managed by a corporate marketing executive, we made a commitment to invest at least $25 million towards this campaign.

Figure 3.9   Johnson & Johnson's logo used for a multimedia campaign to support the nursing profession. (Reprinted courtesy of Johnson & Johnson.)

Campaign elements have included a *national television, print, and interactive advertising campaign* in English and Spanish, celebrating nursing professionals and their contributions to health care; a very visible *public relations component* with press releases, video news releases, and satellite radio tours, available to hundreds of media outlets across the country; *recruitment materials* including brochures, pins, posters, and videos, also in English and Spanish, distributed free of charge to hospitals, high schools, nursing schools, and nursing organizations; *fundraising* for student scholarships, faculty fellowships, and grants to nursing schools to expand their program capacity; *celebrations at regional nursing events* to excite and empower the local nursing community; a *web site* (www.discovernursing.com) about the benefits of a nursing career, featuring searchable links to hundreds of nursing scholarships and more than 1,000 accredited nursing educational programs; and activities to *create and fund retention programs* designed to improve the nursing work environment.

In terms of outcome for the cause, a Harris Poll in October 2002 reported that 46 percent of 18- to 24-year-olds recalled the advertising; 62 percent had discussed a nursing career for themselves or a friend; and among this group 24 percent said the commercials were a factor in their consideration. The discovernursing.com web site traffic tallied 800,000 unique visitors, who spent an average of 15 minutes exploring the site. As of April 2003, the site has had more than nine million page views. Surveys showed that recruitment materials were being used by 97 percent of high schools and 73 percent of nursing schools. More important, 84 percent of nursing schools that received the materials reported an increase in applications/enrollment for the fall 2003 semester. Overall, the American Association of Colleges of Nursing reported that baccalaureate nursing school enrollments were up 8 percent.[23] In 2002, when the National Research Center for College and University Admissions surveyed over a million college-bound students, nursing and related careers ranked ninth among all professions. This year (2003) nursing has moved into fourth place! More than 90,000 students ranked nursing as their first choice.

We are especially pleased with the response, acknowledgment, and support of nurses and health care organizations around the world. Through the Johnson & Johnson Internet site alone, we have received more than 1,700 messages—the largest response to any single topic received by the web site. This is especially significant when you consider that the call to action in the commercials is for discovernursing.com and not Johnson & Johnson's web site. Many of the messages have come from nurses to thank us for recognizing and telling others about the importance of their profession. We continue to receive thousands of e-mails and letters every month. And we have been honored by numerous organizations, including American Organization of Nurse Executives, National Student Nurses Association, American Nurses Association, and *NurseWeek*.

We think these successes can be attributed to several fundamental strategies:

- We chose an issue that mattered to our key publics, one of concern for leaders in the industry we serve as well as for our customers and the community at large.
- We chose an issue consistent with our credo.
- We developed relationships with others to support the campaign, organizations including health care systems, nursing schools, and professional associations around the country, organizations important to our core business strategy as well.
- We used a multimedia strategy with consistent messages in broadcast, print, publicity, special events, printed materials, videos, and on our web site.

And we want to acknowledge (and pass on) our challenges. It has been time-consuming dealing with the volume of requests we receive for funding from a variety of nursing constituencies who see the campaign and assume (perhaps) that Johnson & Johnson has unlimited resources. It is difficult to disappoint them. We also underestimated the amount of time and resources it would take to manage an initiative of this complexity, as we have only two full-time employees working on this campaign.[24]

LensCrafters' "Give the Gift of Sight" Initiative

Established in 1988, "Give the Gift of Sight" is a family of charitable vision care programs providing free eye care and glasses to people in need in North American communities and in developing countries. All Gift of Sight programs are sponsored by Luxottica Retail (LensCrafters' parent company) and LensCrafters Foundation, in partnership with Lions Clubs International and other charities throughout North America.

Two of these programs exemplify cause promotion initiatives. Their "Give New Life to Your Old Glasses" campaign encourages customers to donate their used glasses to those in need. Promotional materials (print and web site) ask customers to "Please help us continue our international missions by donating your old eyeglasses and sunglasses. Often the glasses people receive on our missions are the only glasses they will ever receive." (See Figure 3.10 for a sample brochure.) Since 1988, 1,160,000 pairs of glasses have been collected, recycled, and hand-delivered on international missions. In addition, they also encourage and accept cash donations to their Gift of Sight programs through their 501(c)(3) LensCrafters Foundation, online or through the mail, stressing the fact that LensCrafters Inc. covers more than 90 percent of LensCrafters Foundation overhead, so donations go directly to deliver glasses to needy people.[25]

The vice president of the LensCrafters Foundation offers the following perspective on the real key to success of the Gift of Sight program, and the true value and benefit to the company.

Gift of Sight (GOS) requires the direct participation of LensCrafters employees. Because each person's eyeglass prescription and fit is unique, glasses must be hand-delivered by trained volunteers, capturing the energy and expertise of our people. This is what makes this

Figure 3.10　Brochure used to promote donation of used glasses to those in need. (Reprinted courtesy of LensCrafters.)

program unique. A majority of LensCrafters' 18,000 employees participate in GOS in one form or another (assisting recipients in our stores, on our two Vision Vans, in community outreach programs, and on international optical missions to developing countries). Through GOS, our employees develop an emotional alignment with our company that's crucial to our competitive context.

LensCrafters has chosen to differentiate itself from optical competitors with similar products through superior service. While we created GOS for its social benefits, we maintain and grow it because it helps us build a *service-minded culture*. Employees involved in GOS feel proud of the company and remain with it longer. We continue to expand GOS programs because we're convinced they provide terrific teambuilding and leadership training opportunities. What better way to teach teamwork, flexibility, creativity, and the power of a positive attitude than to take 25 like-minded adults to a developing country for two weeks and challenge them to deliver exams and recycled glasses to 25,000 local people—knowing they will face electrical outages, equipment held up in customs, unfamiliar food, and strange accommodations. On 86 missions to 25 developing countries our teams have figured out how to work together to overcome obstacles. This learning is transferable to their stores and their lives. What better way to teach diversity than to challenge every store and home office department to partner up with local schools, senior centers, nursing homes, and shelters to help deliver free eye care to more than 500,000 people annually.

For LensCrafters, building more dedicated employees is a competitive benefit. Through GOS, we give a higher level of meaning to our jobs so that no employee ever feels he or she is "just selling glasses." Delivering glasses to someone who's never seen clearly before brings an immediate improvement. It's a magical moment, resulting in tears, hugs, and kisses, that opens the eyes of our employees as surely as those of our recipients. Gift of Sight is one of the reasons LensCrafters was rated by *Fortune* as one of the "100 Best Places to Work in America" for five consecutive years.

We created LensCrafters Foundation, a 501(c)(3) public operating charity, in order to conduct fundraising activities with our suppliers, employees, and local foundations. We raise about $1 million in cash (35 percent from employees) and $2 million in goods annually to supplement LensCrafters' commitment of overhead and staff (12 full-time people plus access to the expertise of every single store and department).

In summary, principles that worked for us and may work for others include the following recommendations:

- Focus your community service on your product.
- Involve employees in hands-on giving.
- Push program ownership to the local level.
- Brand the program with a strong, single identity.
- Forge partnerships.
- Set, communicate, and track program goals.

WHEN SHOULD A CORPORATE CAUSE PROMOTION INITIATIVE BE CONSIDERED?

Assuming that a cause has been selected that the organization wants to support, the following circumstances should lead to considering a cause promotion initiative to support the cause, either in addition to other initiatives or in preference to other initiatives:

- When a company has easy access to the target markets, as did British Airways for Change for Good, PETsMART for animal adoption, and *PARADE* magazine for generating interest in bake sales.
- When the cause can be connected and sustained by a company's products, as with The Body Shop's product labeling and Ben & Jerry's new flavor and packaging.
- When the opportunity exists to contribute underutilized in-kind services, such as in-house printing or corporate expertise, as evidenced by Johnson & Johnson's contribution of marketing expertise to the "Campaign for Nursing's Future."
- When employee involvement will support the cause and employees get excited, as they were at Wal-Mart in support of Children's Miracle Network and at LensCrafters in delivering eyeglasses and eye care to those in need.
- When a company wants to limit its involvement and commitment to raising awareness and concern, versus the often more difficult

effort of changing behaviors, handling and fulfilling calls to action, and creating infrastructures to support these efforts.

- When there is a co-branding opportunity, as there was for Aleve with the Arthritis Foundation, where promotional materials will support the cause and the brand with target audiences.

DEVELOPING A CAUSE PROMOTION CAMPAIGN PLAN

Perhaps the most important decision to be made once a social issue has been identified and a cause promotion initiative has been selected is to confirm whether the campaign will include partners and, if so, to identify them. Campaign plans should then be developed together, up-front, as they will include critical decisions on target audiences, key messages, campaign elements, and key media channels.

One of the most effective ways to make these decisions is to develop a document that will provide direction for developing messages, designing campaign elements, and selecting media channels. A useful tool is a creative brief, typically one to two pages in length. It will help ensure that all team members, including external partners, are in agreement on target audiences, communication objectives, and key assumptions, prior to the more costly development and production of communication materials. Typically, a creative brief to support the development of a promotional campaign includes the following six sections:

1. *Target audience.* This section includes a brief description of the target audience, including estimated size, demographics, geographics, psychographics, and behavior variables.

2. *Communication objectives.* This is a statement of what we want our target audience to *know* (facts, information), *believe* (feel), and perhaps *do* (e.g., donate or volunteer for a cause), based on exposure to our communications.

3. *What benefits to promise.* This is the identification of key factors that will motivate target audiences to participate in volunteer efforts or to make donations—in other words,benefits they will experience by taking these steps.

4. *Openings.* Michael Siegel and Lynne Doner describe openings as "the times, places, and situations when the audience will be most

attentive to, and able to act on, the message."[26] This information will be key for determining media channels.

5. *Positioning and requirements.* This section describes the overall desired tone for the campaign (e.g., serious versus lighthearted), as well as requirements such as the use of corporate logos.

6. *Campaign goals.* This is an important section to consider in selecting media channels, as it outlines quantifiable goals for the campaign. These may include process goals (e.g., desired reach and frequency goals) or actual outcome goals (e.g., number of people to sign up for the race).

This document will then lead to development of campaign elements including slogans, headlines, and copy; graphic images; materials; selection of media channels; evaluation plans; budgets; and implementation plans, including responsibilities and target dates for campaign activities.

SUMMARY

A corporate social initiative is categorized as a cause promotion when the core element of the effort is promotional in nature. Primary strategies utilized are persuasive communications. Communication objectives focus on building awareness and concern; persuading people to find out more; persuading people to donate their time, money, or nonmonetary resources to a cause; and/or persuading people to participate in events to benefit a cause. Most commonly, corporations partner with nonprofit organizations and special interest groups, although a few initiate and implement campaigns on their own. In many cases, the corporation is given visibility on promotional materials and in the media in exchange for its support.

Most corporate benefits are marketing related, with advocates asserting that a cause promotion can strengthen brand positioning, create brand preference, increase traffic, and build customer loyalty. Many corporations experience additional benefits, noting increased employee satisfaction and the development of new and strong partners in the community.

Several potential downsides for the corporation are inherent in these promotional campaigns: Visibility for the corporation can get lost; most promotional materials are not sustainable; tracking investments and return on promotional investments is difficult; this endeavor, because of its visibility, may generate too many additional requests for support from other organizations connected to the cause; this approach requires more time and involvement than writing a check; and promotions are often easy to replicate, potentially removing any desired competitive advantages.

Keys to success include recommendations to carefully select an issue (up-front) that can be tied to your products and your company values. It should be a cause that management can commit to long-term, that is a concern for your customers and target markets, motivates your employees, and has the most chance for media exposure. When developing cause promotion plans, take care to connect the campaign to your products, develop partnerships, incorporate and ensure visibility for your brand, and figure out a way to measure and track results.

This initiative should be given serious consideration when a company has easy access to a large potential target audience; when the cause can be connected and sustained by the company's products; when opportunities exist to contribute to the campaign using in-kind services; when employees can get excited about the effort; when it's desirable to limit the company's involvement and commitment to just raising awareness and concern about an issue; and when there is a co-branding opportunity, versus being one of many sponsors.

Steps in developing a plan begin with decisions regarding partnerships. Then, working together, planning teams identify target audiences and develop key messages, campaign elements, media channels, evaluation plans, budgets, and implementation plans.

Cause-Related Marketing: Making Contributions to Causes Based on Product Sales

*People often ask why American Express supports so many charitable or-
ganizations around the world and what purpose such efforts serve for the
company. The answer is easy—and it has been the same for the 150
years that American Express has been in business. We have a vested interest in the well-being of our communities. Moreover, many of our major philanthropic efforts are tied directly to the company's long-term
business objectives. Finally, the company's philanthropic activities have
added enormous luster to our brand over the years.*[1]

—Mary Beth Salerno, President,
American Express Foundation

In cause-related marketing (CRM) campaigns, a corporation commits to making a contribution or donating a percentage of revenues
to a specific cause based on product sales. Most commonly this offer
is for an announced period of time and for a specific product and a

specified charity. This *link to product sales* or transactions most distinguishes this initiative, which contains a mutually beneficial understanding and goal that the program will raise funds for the charity and has the potential to increase sales for the corporation. Contributions may be in actual dollar amounts (e.g., $4.95 donation for every high-speed Internet connection installed) or a percentage of sales (e.g., 50 percent of revenues from sales of specified products will be donated to children's charities).

The distinction from other corporate social initiatives is clear on several fronts. First, this is the only one of the six initiatives described in this book where corporate contribution levels are dependent on some consumer action. It is perhaps most similar to cause promotions, where the corporation is supporting awareness, concern, and public contributions to causes. The distinction is that with CRM, the corporation then makes an additional contribution based on consumer response (e.g., matches miles that passengers donate to a cause). Second, CRM initiatives often require more formal agreements and coordination with the charity; important activities include establishing specific promotional offers, developing co-branding advertisements, and tracking consumer purchases and activities. Finally, this initiative typically involves more promotion, especially paid advertising. This makes sense, as there are anticipated economic benefits for the corporation to promote product sales. As a result, this initiative is most likely to be managed and funded by the corporation's marketing department. In ideal scenarios, a formal marketing plan is developed for the initiative, establishing goals and objectives, identifying target markets, developing the marketing mix for the offer, and establishing evaluation and tracking mechanisms.

Most regard the American Express campaign described in Chapter 1, supporting the Restoration of the Statue of Liberty, as the start of what has became known as cause-related marketing. The marketing world was watching and encouraged by the possibility this effort demonstrated—that a single, well-coordinated philanthropic effort could contribute to the company's bottom line and raise money for a charity as well. Subsequent public opinion research helped explain why, with the 1999 U.S.-based Cone/Roper Report indicating that two-thirds of consumers say they are likely to switch brands or retailers to one associated with a good cause, when price and quality are equal.[2]

TYPICAL CORPORATE CAUSE-RELATED MARKETING INTIATIVES

Typical components of a cause-related marketing initiative are outlined in Table 4.1 and include one or more products that the corporation will promote, a cause that will be supported, and a charity or charities that will benefit from the effort. Although the range of corporations participating in CRM initiatives is broad, it is perhaps most ideal for companies with products that have mass market appeal, large customer bases, and wide distribution channels, especially those in the financial services, consumer goods, airlines, and telecommunications industries. Several types of product links and contribution agreements are common, including the following:

- A *specified dollar amount for each product sold* (e.g., Yoplait's 2003 promotion that promised 10 cents to the Susan G. Komen Breast Cancer Foundation for each pink yogurt lid returned by December 31).

- A *specified dollar amount for every application or account opened* (e.g., Wells Fargo branches in Arizona the summer of 2003 donating $10 to local schools for every consumer checking account opened with direct deposit).

- A *percentage of the sales of a product or transaction* is pledged to the charity (e.g., 73 percent of the purchase price of Avon's Crusade Candle is returned to breast cancer causes).

- A *portion of the sale of an item*, sometimes not visibly disclosed, will be donated to a charity (e.g., Windermere Real Estate's commitment that every time a sales associate sells a home, a portion of the commission goes to their foundation that benefits nonprofit agencies dedicated to the homeless[3]).

- The company *matches consumer contributions* related to product-related items (e.g., Northwest Airlines matches miles donated by passengers for children with medical needs for travel).

- A *percentage of net profits* from sales of a product or products is pledged (e.g., Paul Newman pledging 100 percent of all profits and royalties after taxes from Newman's Own products for educational and charitable purposes[4]).

- The offer may be for only a *specific, designated product* (e.g., $1 donated for every Big Mac sold) or it may be for *several or all products* (e.g., Avon's line of "pink ribbon" products).

- It may be for a *specific time frame* (e.g., for Big Macs sold on World Children's Day) or *open-ended* (e.g., an affinity credit card for Rotarians that makes ongoing contributions to the International Foundation with every purchase).

- The corporation may decide to set a ceiling for their contribution from sales (e.g., Lysol contributing five cents for each product coupon redeemed, up to $225,000).

Although cause-related marketing campaigns support a wide range of causes, those with the most visibility are ones with the biggest followers, most commonly associated with major health issues (e.g., breast cancer, arthritis, heart disease, asthma, AIDS), children's needs (education, hunger, medical needs), basic needs (hunger, homelessness), and the environment (wildlife preservation, nature preserves).

Typically, beneficiaries of funds raised are existing nonprofit organizations or foundations. However, a foundation or nonprofit is sometimes created by the corporation (e.g., the Windermere Foundation) to collect, manage, and distribute funds. Corporations may award funds to a variety of charities or may dedicate proceeds from a campaign to one specific organization. Partnerships may include more than one corporation, as well as a public agency (e.g., schools).

Table 4.1 presents examples of causes supported by nine major corporations featured in this chapter.

POTENTIAL CORPORATE BENEFITS

By design, most corporate benefits from a cause-related marketing campaign are marketing-related. As the following examples demonstrate, successful initiatives can support efforts to attract new customers, reach niche markets, increase product sales, and build positive brand identity. In addition, such initiatives may also be one of the best strategies for raising significant funds for a cause.

Table 4.1 Examples of Cause-Related Marketing Campaigns

Corporation	Cause	Apparent Target Audiences	The Offer	Major Partners
Financial Institutions	Affinity cards for a wide range of nonprofit organizations and member associations	Current and potential donors and members of associations, clubs	Donations made by financial institution to charity based on charge card applications and activities	Nonprofit organizations and member associations
Avon and the Avon Foundation	Breast cancer	Women who buy cosmetics and care about the breast cancer cause	Percentage of sales of "pink ribbon" products donated to the Avon Foundation	Avon sales representatives Breast cancer research and patient services
QVC	Tobacco cessation	Family and friends of women who smoke	$5 donated with every sterling silver *Circle of Friends™* pin sold	American Legacy Foundation
Lysol	Litter prevention and cleanup	Purchasers of household disinfectants and cleaning products	$.05 donation for specific Lysol products associated with coupon redemptions	Keep America Beautiful

(Continued)

Table 4.1 (Continued)

Corporation	Cause	Apparent Target Audiences	The Offer	Major Partners
Target	School equipment and programs	Parents with kids in school grades K-12	One percent of purchases donated to eligible K-12 school of the guest's choice and 0.5 percent of Target Visa purchases made elsewhere	Public schools
AT&T Broadband/ Comcast	Families of sick children	Internet users	Donation of $7 with installation of high-speed Internet service	Ronald McDonald House Charities
Athena™ Water	Women's cancer	People concerned with women's cancers	100 percent of net profits donated to medical research	Research and health care organizations
Northwest Airlines	Travel for sick children	Members of Northwest mileage plans	Member miles that are donated are matched by the airline	Children's charities
American Express	Hunger	Credit card customers and potential customers	Donation made for applications and transactions	Hunger relief charities

Attracting New Customers

Inspired perhaps by the success of the innovative American Express credit card campaign in the early 1980s that generated increased card usage, new member applications, and more than $1 million for the Statue of Liberty restoration fund, financial institutions have been partnering with nonprofit organizations and foundations for more than 20 years to develop and promote affinity card programs. Financial institutions believe they can give consumers a sense of purpose with their plastic and a reason to pick their cause-related option over the many other cards in their wallet. How this works and why this cause-related initiative continues to be popular is described in the following summary:

Example: Financial Institutions and Affinity Cards

Most commonly, nonprofit organizations develop an exclusive arrangement with a financial institution that makes a donation linked to one or more specific consumer actions, including applying for a card, using the card for a purchase (donation amounts sometimes increase with greater purchases), transferring a balance, or receiving a cash advance. Annual percentage rates most commonly range from 15 to 22 percent; many carry annual fees; and some reports suggest the average donation for charges is about .05 percent, about a half a cent for every dollar.[5]

Consumers apparently like affinity cards, as they are often a visual symbol and reminder of something they feel strongly about. By using the card they are able to generate contributions (at no apparent cost to them) to a charity or association they care about. It also gives them a frequent opportunity to share their passion with others, especially at cash registers and with fellow members of an organization (e.g., an alumni card used at a dinner with a fraternity brother). For the nonprofit, of course, this word-of-mouth promotion is invaluable, as is the mass exposure that a bank's marketing power might offer. For the financial institution, benefits can go beyond increased applications, card usage, and word-of-mouth from passionate cardholders, as some charities even agree to share their mailing lists with the bank. Apparently this relationship is mutually rewarding as, according to the Nilson Report, affinity cards accounted for 29 percent of all credit cards in circulation in 2001.[6]

But experts caution that successful relationships (a win-win for the charity and the financial institution) require important criteria. Visa USA, for example, suggests that the nonprofit organization will likely need to have a current member/donor base that could be anticipated to generate a desired 50,000 cardholders. If 10 percent of the base responded, this would mean that the organization would actually need to have 500,000 potential names, or even as many as one million if only 5 percent are expected to respond.[7]

Although many organizations are not willing to share financial numbers, a few have published impressive results:

- Working Assets, a long distance, wireless, credit card, and broadcasting company in San Francisco, has generated $40 million from its affinity credit card since 1985. With every purchase made using the Working Assets credit card, 10 cents is donated to nonprofit groups working for peace, human rights, equality, education, and the environment. Promotional messages encourage potential applicants to "Start changing the world a dime at a time."[8]
- The World Wildlife Federation in Washington, D.C., has earned almost $8 million from its affinity credit card since 1995.[9]
- The American Lung Association's affinity card with Citibank has generated over $1 million to help fight lung disease. For every account activated, Citibank donates $30, as well as a percentage of every purchase made with the card.. Promotional materials note that if 100,000 cardholders spent $5,000 a year on their card, it would amount to more than $3 million a year for the American Lung Association.[10]
- A mailing in 2003 urged Rotarians to apply for the premium Platinum Plus MasterCard credit card to help increase public awareness and visibility of Rotary International and raise funds to benefit the Rotary Foundation. Since the launch of this program in 2000, more than

$1 million has been raised. Their 2003 mailing closed with the message that the next $1 million in affinity card proceeds would be designated for the association's polio eradication program (see Figure 4.1).

Raising Funds for a Cause

The Avon Breast Cancer Crusade is perhaps one of the most well-known and long-standing cause-related marketing campaigns of our time, and a prime example of a win-win for a company and the cause. Pringle and Thompson elaborate on the value of cause-related marketing to the Avon brand, as well as to the breast cancer cause, in their book *Brand Spirit*. "A global brand such as Avon has built its market position by recruiting, training, and motivating a vast and evolving army of representatives. In the process it has created valuable relationships with millions of women. As such Avon has had the authority to embark on an ambitious cause-related marketing campaign focused on a highly personal issue, namely breast cancer. This campaign from a trusted brand has probably done more than any governmental organization to demystify, educate, and help prevent this debilitating and often fatal disease."[11]

Figure 4.1 The Rotary Foundation receives a donation equivalent to one-half of 1 percent of every purchase charged to the card.

Example: Avon Breast Cancer Crusade[12]

Avon's desired position, as well as their mission, is made clear in their slogan, "AVON—*the* company for women." Their association for more than a decade with the cause of women's breast cancer has certainly assisted in securing and affirming this position. Their corporate vision is "to be the company that best understands and satisfies the product, service, and self-fulfillment needs of women globally. Our dedication to supporting women touches not only beauty—but health, fitness, self-empowerment, and financial independence."[13]

The Avon Breast Cancer Crusade was founded in the United Kingdom in 1992 and launched in the United States in 1993 with a mission to fund access to care and help find a cure for breast cancer, and includes a focus on medically underserved women. The cause has resonated well with the company's market as well as with sales representatives. The Avon Foundation awards funds for medical research, screening and diagnosis, clinical care for cancer patients, support services for patients and their families, educational seminars, and early detection programs. In addition, Avon supports programs for breast cancer and other vital women's health issues in more than 50 countries worldwide. Funds raised by all corporate and foundation initiatives in the United States are managed and disbursed by the Avon Foundation.

The Avon Breast Cancer Crusade raises funds through many social initiatives. They support cause promotions, including local fundraising programs, direct online donations, and a national se-

Figure 4.2 Avon's Heart of the Crusade Pin is priced at $3.00, with 83 percent of the purchase price being returned to the breast cancer cause. (Reprinted courtesy of Avon.)

ries of fundraising walks. Their philanthropic initiatives include providing grants to beneficiaries ranging from leading national cancer centers to community-based breast health organizations. Of special interest in this chapter is their cause-related initiative, the year-round sale of special "pink ribbon" products.

Pink ribbon products, marketed by Avon Products, Inc., over the decade have included lipsticks, pens, mugs, candles, stuffed bears, cosmetic cases, umbrellas, and the Heart of the Crusade pin see Figure 4.2). Net proceeds (above cost of goods) donated to the breast cancer cause range from 50 to 83 percent of the purchase price. Most products are priced low, at $7.00 or under; each is gift-boxed and accompanied by an informational brochure, "Guide to Better Breast Health."

Since 1993, 600,000 independent Avon sales representatives in the United States alone have generated over $55 million from sales of pink ribbon products. Total net funds raised worldwide exceed $300 million.

Reaching Niche Markets

A growing number of companies are discovering that cause-related marketing initiatives can be an effective way to reach and connect with specific demographic, geographic, or otherwise defined targeted markets (e.g., tobacco users; friends and families of cancer victims; school teachers; homemakers). The nonprofit foundation featured in the following example forged a partnership with an e-commerce leader reaching tens of millions of homes a day, as a way to reach niche audiences and generate grassroots interest in an important and potentially life-saving campaign.

Example: QVC and the American Legacy Foundation,

In February 2003, QVC and the American Legacy Foundation announced the availability of the *Circle of Friends* Sunburst Pin, a wearable icon representing a new movement in support of women struggling with tobacco addiction (see Figure 4.3). The American Legacy Foundation, created as a result of the 1998

Figure 4.3   Sterling *Circle of Friends*™ Sunburst Pin. QVC price was $16 plus shipping and handling, with $5 from each sale donated to American Legacy Foundation. (Reprinted courtesy of American Legacy Foundation.)

Master Settlement Agreement between the tobacco industry and attorneys general in 46 U.S. states and five U.S. territories, reports that one in five women in America smoke and more than 178,000 die each year from a tobacco-related disease.[14] QVC, Inc., partnered with the foundation's *"Circle of Friends"* initiative, providing a national audience that could learn more about *Circle of Friends* and the importance of supporting smokers who want to quit, as well as the Sunburst Pin product offering. QVC broadcasts live 24 hours a day, 364 days a year, and introduces 250 new products every week to viewers in an estimated 84 million homes across the United States. Jewelry lines account for an average of 29 percent of QVC programming.[15] It seemed a natural fit that QVC's audience would respond well to a beautiful piece of jewelry with a symbolic meaning.

The sterling silver pin was designed by a world-renowned jewelry designer, with the Sunburst logo intended to be a symbol of hope and inspiration for women and families choosing a tobacco-free future. The pin also reflects a movement of people joining together to help loved ones and friends in their attempts to quit smoking. Print advertisements in magazines featured celebrities and highlighted the message that "Quitting isn't easy, but when friends and loved ones are there to help, smokers are 50 percent more likely to succeed."[16]

The pin was offered exclusively through QVC for $16.00 plus shipping and handling. For every pin sold, $5 went to the American Legacy Foundation to help fund programs for women dedicated to living smoke-free lives, including a toll-free helpline. Pins could be purchased online or by calling a toll-free number.

Foundation president and CEO Dr. Cheryl Healton commented at the time the initiative was announced, "We are delighted to welcome QVC into our *Circle of Friends* and invite its national viewing audience of more than 84 million cable households to join in the cause."[17]

Increasing Product Sales

Keep America Beautiful (KAB) is a national nonprofit public education organization with affiliate chapters across the nation, enhancing environments in more than 14,000 communities.[18] Their focus is on litter prevention, beautification, community improvement, and waste reduction. In the following example, brand managers for LYSOL® share their cause-related marketing campaign that both benefited KAB and supported marketing goals for increased awareness and purchase of multiple LYSOL® products.

Example: LYSOL® and Keep America Beautiful

For over 100 years, LYSOL® Brand has strived to set the gold standard in disinfecting and cleaning, with the goal of helping protect families from illness-causing germs. As a category leader, we seek to align ourselves with partner organizations based on their having similar missions and values as ours. The Keep America Beautiful (KAB) Great American Cleanup encourages individuals across the country to take greater responsibility for improving their community environments. For LYSOL® Brand—whose goal is to help maintain clean, vibrant, and productive homes, schools, hospitals, and other institutions—it was a natural fit to extend the family protection message to a broad, community-based activity.

In the spring of 2003, LYSOL® developed a freestanding newspaper insert with a circulation of 40 million to launch our involvement in the program. Approximately 10,000 grocery stores had LYSOL® and the Great American Cleanup shopping cart ads (see Figure 4.4). Then, to support specific cleanups, LYSOL® contacted the leaders of all KAB affiliates in every state, offering them the opportunity to use our products as part of their volunteers' Great American Cleanup activities. We donated nearly 25,000 products with a total retail value of approximately $105,000 across all 50 states, and in many cases had LYSOL® representatives on-site to assist with the cleanups, conducted at day care centers, senior housing, public transportation shelters, park facilities, and schools. Six thousand T-shirts with the LYSOL® logo and Great American Cleanup logo were produced for local cleanup events, along with signage on banners and buckets as well. We leveraged public relations and media exposure at the national and local levels to make consumers aware of our involvement with the cleanup, and had significant signage, paraphernalia, and other items on-site and in grocery stores to demonstrate our support. We also provided information on the LYSOL® web site for the event and a hot link to the Keep America Beautiful site for specific market level cleanup information.

Five products were featured in the newspaper insert, offering a five cent donation to KAB for every coupon redeemed, up to $225,000, and in the summer of 2003, LYSOL® donated $225,000 to KAB.

Our involvement in KAB's Great American Cleanup generated significant recognition for the LYSOL® brand in communities across the country and showed our relevance in serving people's needs in disinfecting and cleaning. This relationship supports our brand leadership platform, builds brand equity, and demonstrates that we are highly involved with causes about which Americans care.

From a product perspective, and based on the structure of our cross-product promotion, we generated sales of multiple products in the LYSOL® franchise to the same customer. This was important to us, as it helped raise consumer awareness of the range of products we offer. One of our goals was to promote and sell multiple products in the LYSOL® franchise to our target consumers. We were pleased with results that demonstrated cross-promotions do work and do lead to trials of additional products.

LYSOL® is proud to once again sponsor the Keep America Beautiful Great American Cleanup for 2004. This year we began to plan programs with affiliate leaders much earlier, and have involved our trade partners. We have arranged with various retailers to do in-store promotions, radio spots, and other activities as a shared commitment to supporting this cause and to building their business.[19]

Building Valuable Partnerships that Support the Effort

As noted earlier in the chapter, corporations have several options for partnerships for cause-related marketing initiatives. They may partner with a nonprofit organization or foundation that is not connected or

Figure 4.4 LYSOL® grocery cart ad promoting donations tied to purchase of specific products. (Reprinted courtesy of LYSOL®.)

Figure 4.5   Target's School Fund-Raising program raised $27 million for 110,000 schools in 2003 alone. (Courtesy of Target Corporation, Minneapolis, MN.)

associated with the corporation, or they may designate their own foundation or nonprofit organization as the recipient of funds raised during the campaign effort. The following example illustrates an additional option, in which a company brings another for-profit corporation into the partnership, extending the visibility, reach, and appeal of the initiative.

Example: Target's School Fundraising

Since it was introduced in 1997, Target's "Take Charge of Education" initiative has contributed more than $100 million to support educational programs all across the country.

One effort within this initiative is a cause-related program they've named "School Fundraising," in which every time guests use their Target® Visa® or Target Guest Card® at a Target store or at target.com, an amount equivalent to 1 percent of their purchases will be donated to the eligible K-12 school of the guest's choice (see Figure 4.5). In addition, a donation will be made of 0.5 percent of Target® Visa® purchases made elsewhere. In 2003, this program raised $27 million for the more than 110,000 schools enrolled in the program.[20] The recipient K-12 schools can use the dollars for anything they need, from books to playground equipment.

Guests are invited to apply for a Target® Visa® and/or Target Guest Card® and then designate a school online or by calling an

800 number. Purchases are tracked and donations are then made to schools twice a year. The program is supported through advertising, including print ads.

As might be expected, individual schools promote the program with their students' parents as well. In one school's e-mail message, the information included program results, showing the amount of donations made from the program to the school to date, and encouraged parents to click on a link to apply for the program or to call the 800 number to designate their school.

Copromotions also support the program. In the fall of 2003, Target partnered with Red Brick Learning, a provider of educational materials, and offered schools an opportunity to double their donations, as the company promised to match every Target School Fundraising dollar that schools apply to the purchase of Red Brick Learning educational materials.

As of September 2003, more than eight million Target guests were enrolled in the program.

Building Positive Brand Identity

By their nature, cause-related marketing campaigns are most successful when the word is spread far and wide, and most corporations involved in these campaigns will devote marketing resources to help assure this. By association, then, the company is co-branded with the cause (e.g., Windermere with Habitat for Humanity, and Target with local public schools). The Comcast brand enjoyed association with Ronald McDonald House Charities and gained publicity for their initiative, described in the following example.

Example: Comcast and Ronald McDonald House Charities

Comcast Cable is reported to be the largest provider of cable services in the United States and is expanding its cable operations to deliver digital services and provide faster Internet service.[21] Cause-related marketing initiatives have been included to support this expansion, with a seeming intention to create a buzz about their services. Their co-branding effort with Ronald

McDonald House Charities, named by *Worth* magazine as one of "America's 100 Best Charities of 2002," apparently did not go unnoticed.

In 1999, a cross-promotion between AT&T Broadband/Comcast and McDonald's in Southern California targeted the Hispanic market with a television spot and direct-mail piece containing the message: "Receive the very best of cable programming for the entire family and team up with AT&T Broadband/Comcast to help benefit Ronald McDonald House Charities of Southern California (RMHC)." (See Figure 4.6.) The offer was to sign up for cable for only $19.99 a month and AT&T Broadband/Comcast would donate the $7 installation fee to RMHC; six weeks following installation, AT&T Broadband/Comcast promised to send the household coupons to redeem for four free McFlurry deserts or soft-serve cones at participating McDonald's locations in Southern California. Liz Castells-Heard, president/CEO of Castells & Asociados, the Los Angeles–based Hispanic marketing and advertising agency that developed the cross-promotion, believes that the partners "did well by doing good," generating "short-term sales with minimal incremental cost." "We get extreme satisfaction by partnering our existing clients to support such worthy causes for the benefit of the community."

Liz estimated that McDonald's received $1 million worth of cable TV and direct-mail exposure; that Ronald McDonald House Charities® received $85,000; and that AT&T Broadband/Comcast got a "cool freebie to entice subscribers, additional media through McDonald's ubiquitous store point-of-purchase displays and co-op radio, and, most importantly, benefited from McDonald's long-established high Hispanic brand equity and community entrenchment." She also commented that the media engagement was very high. "Radio deejays raved about McDonald's yummy desserts and the benefits of cable television for the entire family. The charity check was presented at a high-visibility family event covered by local TV and radio. We made it on the news. We got on talk shows and got sound bites on how we helped Latino kids. The promotion exceeded expectations by 30 percent, and RMHC's proceeds tripled."[22]

Figure 4.6 A partnership benefiting Ronald McDonald
House Charities®. (Promotional materials shown are for 2002 program.)
(Reprinted courtesy of Castells & Asociados.)

In summer 2002, Castells & Asociados again partnered their AT&T Broadband/Comcast and McDonald's clients to support RMHC with a promotion that featured a festive, piñata-themed television spot and direct-mail piece with the message: "Save Big and Help the Community." For every cable subscription, the $4.95 installation fee went directly to RMHC. The new customer then received a coupon for a free Crispy Chicken Extra Value Meal.

The promotion has been considered so successful that several Comcast markets, such as western Washington, emulated the cross-partnership in subsequent years with positive results in the general market.

POTENTIAL CONCERNS

It appears there may be as many concerns with this initiative as there are potential benefits. Some are unique to CRM and others are common challenges associated other social initiatives as well. Those most significant for CRM include the following, having the greatest implications for increased staff time and funds and potential legal and marketing risks.

- Contractual agreements specifying contribution conditions need to be drawn up between the corporation and the charity, taking more time and attention than with other initiatives such as a cause promotion or volunteering in the community.
- Legal restrictions and required disclosures need to be investigated and abided by, again consuming more staff time on and attention to campaign details and coordination with partners.
- The corporation as well as the partners need to establish reliable tracking systems to ensure consumer commitments are fulfilled. Such systems can be very labor intensive (e.g., a campaign where schools receive funds associated with the return of cereal boxtops will involve recording the number of returns and ensuring the appropriate schools will be credited with the appropriate amount of funds).

- Since per item donations are often small (e.g., 0.5 percent of purchases on a credit card), participation levels will need to be high in order for the effort to be worthwhile, for the corporation as well as for the charity. This often requires an investment in paid promotions, including advertising, point-of-purchase signage, and/or direct mail, in order to obtain a reach and frequency threshold with target audiences.

- Consumers can be especially skeptical of campaigns like this, as it will be seen (and rightly so) as more than a philanthropic effort. This will be especially true for campaigns that do not provide easy access to information regarding what portion of the proceeds of the sale will go to the charity or how much money is expected to be raised from the effort. The perception among many consumers is that the amount is probably small and won't make a big difference and that the corporation is using its association with the charity for purely profit motives. If amounts are not disclosed, this skepticism can rise, a tough dilemma if in fact the per sale donation will seem very small and not reflect the total potential amount.

- Though not common, some customers may have concerns about the charity the brand is being associated with and may not want to purchase the product as a result. This may happen, for example, when a charity has a mission or is associated with some value that is inconsistent with those of the consumer or if a recent scandal (e.g., management of funds of the charity or membership discrimination) has received significant publicity.

- Promotional executions and media channels will need to be developed with the cause partner, who will also have guidelines and priorities related to brand identity and graphic standards. The charity partner may, for example, have a target market they want to reach (first or most) that is not as attractive to the corporation or not a priority for marketing resources.

KEYS TO SUCCESS

Keys to success take into consideration the challenges and potential downsides of CRM. Many are illustrated in depth in the three cases presented in this section. Perspectives are offered from managers involved in developing and executing these initiatives, along with their recommendations, which include the following:

- Select a major cause that your company and your target audience has passion about.
- Choose a charity partner that has a broad base of existing and potential relationships, as the amount per transaction generated by the campaign may be small and therefore high volumes will be key to a successful campaign.
- Target a product offer that has the most chemistry with the cause, looking for the intersection between your customer base, your products, and people who care about the cause.
- Research the idea with targeted customers, or consider a pilot in one market to gauge general appeal and refine marketing strategies.
- Give the effort considerable visibility with potential buyers. Small mentions on product labels or small type added to existing ads may go unnoticed.
- Keep the offer simple, to avoid consumer suspicion and significant paperwork. Consider the benefits of disclosing the actual or anticipated amount to be donated to the charity (e.g., the next $1 million raised will be designated to eradicating polio in the world).
- Be willing to recognize errors and make changes.

Northwest Airlines and Its AirCares® Charitable Support Program

Prior to the early 1990s, Northwest's corporate giving strategy consisted primarily of the community relations department simply writing checks to the various causes it supported. Not surprisingly, perhaps, there was little awareness or visibility among the employees or passengers with regard to the company's role in the communities it served. In 1992, charitable activities at the corporate level were organized under a new initiative called the Northwest AirCares® charitable support program, described by Northwest:

Interestingly, this took place at a time when the airline—and the entire airline industry—faced serious financial problems, with the Gulf War, high fuel prices, and overcapacity among the airlines. Despite all this, we were committed to being a responsible corporate citizen and looked for ways to use our resources to support causes around the world.

The program began as an in-flight fundraising project for nonprofit organizations, a cause promotion effort. Northwest has a captive audience of more than 50 million people a year who were then exposed to the program and the mission of its charitable partners. Each quarter, Northwest profiled a different partner charity through its various onboard communications and asked passengers to contribute money or frequent flyer miles to the nonprofit organization. We featured the charity partner over each three-month period through in-flight videos and onboard flight attendant announcements, ads in *USA Today*, and featured articles in the *Northwest WorldTraveler* magazine.

Over the years, we learned that some of the causes that were featured did not resonate as well as others with passengers in terms of their giving. We also found that after dozens of partnerships and causes were featured over the years, it was difficult to find new charity partners that caught as much of the passengers' attention or generated employee enthusiasm. What we noticed was that passengers were most moved by opportunities to help children, especially sick children.

The program then evolved to where since the end of 2002, Northwest's AirCares emphasis has been exclusively on its KidCares® program (see Figure 4.7). The KidCares medical travel program provides travel for a child, accompanied by one parent or guardian, to obtain needed medical treatment, a critical element when a child's health depends on receiving treatment far from home. This travel is made possible by mileage donations from Northwest's generous WorldPerks® travel program members that are then matched by the airline (a cause-related marketing effort).

Internal support for the program is provided by the marketing

Figure 4.7 Northwest Airlines' medical travel program is made possible by customer donations of miles that are then matched by the airline. (Reprinted courtesy of Northwest Airlines.)

department that is responsible for tracking donated miles and managing communications about the program to the millions of members enrolled in WorldPerks through member statements and Northwest's web site. Corporate communications dedicates one page from each edition of the *Northwest WorldTraveler* inflight magazine to communicate about the program. To date, KidCares has provided free travel for more than 600 children and an accompanying adult.

Through the AirCares program, the company has been better able to communicate that it is a caring corporate citizen, concerned with various issues around the world. In fact, recently the company's Air-Cares program received an award from the International Leadership Institute in Minneapolis/St. Paul. The award, the 2004 Twin Cities International Corporate Citizen Award, is "given to corporations in the community who have made outstanding contributions to both the local and global communities and who have demonstrated a strong commitment to international understanding, cooperation and mutual respect."[23] The Institute said that it looks for organizations that don't brag about how much they do but are, instead, just out there doing what needs to be done for people.

We have also been able to leverage our relationship with charity partners. For example, when we run a special fare promotion, we can ask the current partner charity to share this promotion with its membership (staff and supporters).

Employees are taking more pride in the program and becoming involved in supporting the charity partners. As an example, our technical operations department, one of Northwest's largest employee groups, contributes an estimated $25,000 per year to AirCares partners by individual employee donations through fundraising. An extraordinary fundraising effort took place during the last quarter of 2003 when during Northwest's United Way campaign, the Technical Operations employees conducted a garage sale, of sorts, selling extra tools and toolboxes both to Northwest employees and to the general public. Their goal was to raise $50,000 to be given to a designated AirCares charity organization; that goal was exceeded within the first three hours of the sale with the end result of the sale raising $150,000. The money was divided amongst three of Northwest's Air-Cares charity partners. Their efforts helped a lot of people in need and built team spirit for the employees.

This program has provided several lessons learned and the following recommendations for others:

- We learned how important it is to target issues and develop initiatives that relate to the company's core business, what you know best. Northwest is in the business of air transportation and it makes sense (to us and our customers) for the airline to use its resources to help sick children or people in need of travel. Likewise, restaurants and grocery stores may want to tackle the hunger issue and women's retail stores may want to support [victims of] breast cancer or domestic violence and a real estate or mortgage company would do well to consider supporting the homeless or Habitat for Humanity. It's about finding a natural, easy match.
- Don't be shy about trying to have the initiative be a win-win situation for both the corporation and the charity. There's nothing wrong with doing well by doing good.
- Be willing to shift program emphasis if something isn't resonating with your customer base. Follow their passion.

American Express

Following the terrorist attacks of September 11, 2001, American Express recognized the need for, and committed itself to being an active part of, a process of healing, renewal, and revitalization in lower Manhattan. The decision reflected the company's commitment to its home community in New York, and its recognition of the critical role that business could play in revitalizing that community. A corporate executive for American Express shares how a variety of corporate social initiatives were used in this effort, with a special highlight on a familiar cause-related marketing effort.

Nowhere has American Express' community support been more focused or more prevalent than in New York City—the company's corporate home throughout our 154-year history. Most recently, American Express has been at the forefront of efforts to revitalize downtown New York in the aftermath of September 11—from returning 4,000 displaced employees to our corporate headquarters (damaged after the 9/11 attacks) in lower Manhattan, to helping draw millions of visitors to downtown New York through our sponsorship and support of various events and initiatives. American Express has pledged to partner with corporate, community, and government leaders to help make lower Manhattan the place to be for arts, entertainment, shopping, dining, and business.

The company initiated and supported a wide range of corporate social initiatives in downtown New York to fulfill this commitment. Immediately following September 11, we created the American Express World Trade Center Disaster Relief Fund, which contributed $5 million to help the community respond to the disaster and to assist those most affected by the tragedy. For downtown merchants, company staff went door-to-door offering help to get merchant systems up and operating following 9/11 and ran advertising campaigns encouraging patrons and visitors to come back downtown. In the spring of 2002—at a time when many people were still reluctant to come downtown—we became the founding sponsor of the Tribeca Film Festival, drawing thousands of people to lower Manhattan for a series of premiere movie events, a free rock and comedy concert in Battery Park, and a free family day. The Tribeca Film Festival attracted more than 150,000 people to lower Manhattan that spring, more than 300,000 in 2003, and more than 400,000 people in 2004, our third year of support. We also were the title sponsor of the first-ever Downtown NYC River to River Festival in 2002, which featured more than 500 mostly free performances and cultural events in downtown Manhattan. River to River has successfully drawn one million patrons to lower Manhattan in each of the festival's first two years.

Most recently, American Express launched the Campaign to Reopen the Statue of Liberty (see Figure 4.8). Recognizing the importance of the statue as a world symbol of liberty and freedom and its place as one of the most significant attractions in bringing people to lower Manhattan, American Express pledged a minimum of $3 million to the Statue. The funds will help support critical safety improvements to the statue, which has been closed to the public since September 11, 2001. The American Express contribution has two parts. First, the company donated one cent for every purchase made on an American Express Card—up to $2.5 million—from December 1, 2003, through January 31, 2004. The company made a direct contribution from its philanthropic program of $500,000.

These recent initiatives, as well as our history of involvement in social responsibility, have led us to adopt several guiding princi-

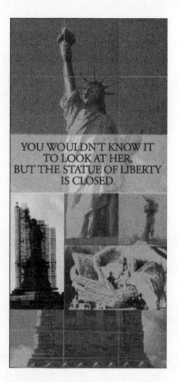

Figure 4.8 Promotional material for American Express's campaign to help reopen Lady Liberty. (Reprinted courtesy of American Express.)

ples to ensure we do the most good for our communities as well as our company:

- We achieve greater success with corporate social responsibility initiatives when our efforts are a natural and logical extension of the business and brand of the company. For American Express, service has always been a hallmark of its brand. We also have been strong supporters of culture and the arts—as have our Cardmembers. The company's efforts in New York align well with this historic commitment to service, culture, and the arts.
- We leverage our resources—in funding, marketing, advertising, planning, and so forth—with those of a wide range of civic, cultural, community, and business groups. The strength of public-private partnerships, the collective commitment of the

community, and the combining of resources make it possible for these initiatives to achieve far more than would have been possible through the efforts of any individual organization.

- We involve many different parts of the company—from staff groups to core business units—to think creatively, act generously, and work collectively on corporate social responsibility initiatives.

- We recognize the importance of long-term commitment. Despite the significant progress in the past two years, much work in rebuilding and revitalizing lower Manhattan remains. That is why we have supported many of these projects beyond just the first year—when emotions and support were high—as an acknowledgment of the considerable work that lies ahead and, with it, the need for sustained support throughout the community.

Athena™ Water and Women's Cancers

Paul Newman began selling food products under the label "Newman's Own" in 1982 with a $40,000 investment, pledging all after-tax profits to charities. Food industry experts predicted that the operation would lose $1 million in the first year. After the 12th month of business, Newman ended up giving close to $1 million to educational and charitable organizations. Since 1982, he has contributed over $150 million to thousands of charities. He attributes this success in part to providing consumers opportunities for "eating good food and doing good at the same time."[24]

The following more recent case may someday further demonstrate the power of a cause to enhance a product, even when it has few if any other points of differentiation. Athena Water's story is shared by Trish May, the company's founder and CEO, a former marketing manager from Microsoft who is a breast cancer survivor:

The $3.5 billion-a-year bottled water market is extremely crowded and includes giants like Coca-Cola's Dasani and Pepsi's Aquafina. And yet, in the summer of 2003, I decided to enter the fray, determined to capture a share of the bottled market in the Northwest and at the same time raise money for women's cancer research.

I wanted to create a product where people could make a difference every single day, one that didn't require you to run a race or attend a fundraising lunch. I considered everything from nuts to fruits to tofu and more, and when I landed on the idea of bottled water, I knew it was right. It was something everyone needs. It's associated with health and is a frequent purchase. The name Athena Water also seemed right as the Greek goddess Athena was known as the goddess of war, wisdom, and healing, and our initiative is about fighting the battle for a cure in an intelligent way.

We first introduced the water in July 2003 as a product of Athena Partners™, a nonprofit organization with a mission to raise funds for women's cancer research and education, which exemplifies a new type of not-for-profit, considered a social enterprise as it sells a product or service to support its cause rather than depend on donations. I funded the investment and pledged to donate 100 percent of net profits from bottled water sales to cancer research and education (see Figure 4.9). Pricing is in line with most other bottled waters with a suggested retail price of $3.29 for a six-pack of 500 milliliter bottles and $1.29 for single one-liter

Figure 4.9 Athena Water's donation of all profits to breast cancer research provides it with a point of difference in a crowded category. (© 2003, Athena Partners.) (Reprinted courtesy of Athena Partners.)

bottles. I estimated at the time that if we could eventually capture 5 percent of the bottled market in the Northwest, we would be able to donate $1 million a year.

By November of 2003, only four months later, Athena had gained a distribution into 75 percent of the grocery accounts in western Washington, a rapid entry especially for a new product from a new company. We were also picked up by food service outlets (Tully's Coffee), and a local health care organization started giving patients a bottle of Athena with every mammogram and when undergoing chemotherapy. Most recently, a popular box lunch caterer signed up and now includes Athena water in 5,000 to 6,000 boxed lunches it delivers each week to area businesses. Early in 2004, we anticipate donating at least $10,000 in profits from 2003, our first year. Funds will be split among cancer research organizations based in the Northwest.

Three factors give me a great sense of optimism about what lies ahead and the potential for this product to make a real difference:

1. The market for bottled water is strong and growing. Even though the market is crowded, it is estimated to be growing at 30 percent a year and is a product that appeals to the target market, women.

2. There is strong appeal for the woman's cancer cause. I believe it is the largest and most successful cause for which funds are raised each year. It resonates deeply with people as it touches everyone directly or indirectly and is a topic about which women bond and which they are comfortable discussing. It is also an area that other vendors want to support or feel a social responsibility to report.

3. Cause-related marketing has proven it can be successful. There are numerous examples of successful cause marketing products such as Yoplait yogurt and the U.S. Postal Service breast cancer stamp. The stamp has raised millions by adding a few cents to a commodity product and demonstrates the power of the cause to enhance a product, even when it basically has no other point of differentiation. The cause, together with the 100 percent of profits donation, gives the water a unique point of differentiation in a crowded, undifferentiated category.

WHEN SHOULD A CAUSE-RELATED MARKETING INITIATIVE BE CONSIDERED?

Although most companies have the potential for developing and implementing a CRM initiative, those most likely to experience success are those with products that enjoy a large market or mass market appeal, have well-established and wide distribution channels, and would benefit from a product differentiation that offers consumers an opportunity to contribute to a favorite charity. It should be considered when increased product sales, visibility, or co-branding with a popular cause would support corporate marketing objectives and goals for a product or products.

It may also be most successful in situations where a company has an existing, ideally long-term association with a cause or charity and then adds this initiative to the lineup, in an integrated fashion. For example, consider a scenario where a life vest manufacturer had been partnering for years with a local children's hospital on a variety of corporate social initiatives related to drowning prevention among children. Efforts included participation in a cause promotion to increase awareness and concern about unintentional drownings among children by sponsoring paid public service announcements on television and promoting a children's health fair where drowning prevention information was distributed. Imagine, too, that they were involved in a social marketing initiative with the hospital that encouraged parents to put life vests on children at beaches, and a philanthropic effort that included donating loaner life vests at community beaches and swimming pools. A cause-related marketing initiative might best be added at this point, where a donation to the children's hospital is promised with every toddler life vest sold. Because at this point the consumer associates the life vest manufacturer with the drowning prevention campaign and the children's hospital, the new effort may be perceived as an authentic, natural extension of the apparent commitment to children and injury prevention.

DEVELOPING A CAUSE-RELATED MARKETING CAMPAIGN PLAN

Steps in developing a CRM effort mirror those of traditional marketing plans, beginning with a situation assessment; setting objectives and goals; selecting target audiences; determining the marketing mix; and developing budget, implementation, and evaluation plans. Although this sequential process is not always practical or common, it is recommended by those looking back on both successful and disappointing efforts.

In the situation assessment phase, many suggest to begin by identifying the company's marketing needs. Does the company want to enter a new market with existing products? Is there a new product launch that this effort might help fuel? Or is the market becoming crowded with parity products, offered at similar prices in similar locations, with the company in need of a new strategy for product differentiation?

With this focus, the assessment then moves to identifying a social issue to support. What issues is the corporation already supporting? Would a CRM effort strengthen the company's association and contribution to this cause? What are the major social concerns of target markets? Of these, which one is most closely aligned with the company's core values and has the strongest potential for connections with products that would support marketing objectives? At this point, potential partners are explored. As this will be a co-branded effort, what charity or foundation would be the right match for the company and product's positioning? How large is their membership or donor base and what is their reputation in the community?

Once a social cause and charity have been selected, a marketing plan is developed to include marketing objectives (e.g., increase in new applications) and quantifiable goals (e.g., desired fundraising levels). Working with the charity, target audiences are identified and a marketing strategy is developed that will include products the campaign will be linked with, purchase incentives, distribution channels, and promotional strategies. At this stage, legal agreements and contracts will also most likely need to be developed, as will promotional budgets and implementation plans. Tracking systems will need to be established, with clearly outlined roles and responsibilities for tracking and reporting.

SUMMARY

Cause-related marketing campaigns are most distinct from other corporate social initiatives by the link of contribution levels to corporate product sales; the need for more formal agreements and systems for measurement and tracking with the charity; and the likelihood that the program will be funded and managed by the marketing department, often the recipient of the most corporate benefits. Contribution agreements with the charity and the consumer vary from ones that announce a specified dollar amount for each product sold to ones that promise a portion of after-tax profits. The offer may be for only one specific product or it might apply to a line of products. It may be good for only a brief promotional time period, or it may be open-ended, as with affinity credit cards.

By design, most corporate benefits from a cause-related marketing campaign are marketing-related and include the potential to attract new customers, reach niche markets, increase product sales, and build positive brand identity. In addition, this initiative may also be one of the best strategies for raising significant funds for a cause. Potential concerns and challenges should also be anticipated and addressed, including increased needs (relative to other social initiatives) for promotional funding, staff time for planning and coordination of the campaign with charity partners, and attention to potential legal and marketing risks in comparison to other types of initiatives.

Experts recommend that managers select a major cause their company and target audience has passion for, preferably one the company is already supporting. The ideal scenario is one where the charity partner has a large potential following, the product has good chemistry with the cause, and the incentive (offer) is straightforward and easy to understand. Development of a formal marketing plan is encouraged, one that includes considerable promotional effort and resources, recognizing that success will most likely depend on high participation levels, especially when contributions per transaction are small.

Corporate Social Marketing: Supporting Behavior Change Campaigns

Creating public-private partnerships, such as Crest Healthy Smiles 2010, can help affect change in the oral health of our country. These collective efforts can help educate both the public and health professionals, as well as provide the health care services and oral care tools needed to help end the current disparity in our nation's oral health.
— Former U.S. Surgeon General Dr. David Satcher[1]

Corporate social marketing is a means whereby a corporation supports the development and/or implementation of a behavior change campaign intended to improve public health, safety, the environment, or community well-being. *Behavior change* is always the focus and the intended outcome. Successful campaigns utilize a strategic marketing planning approach: conducting a situation analysis, selecting target audiences, setting behavior objectives, identifying barriers and benefits to behavior change, and then developing a marketing mix strategy that helps overcome perceived barriers and maximize potential benefits. It relies on the same principles and techniques used in developing and implementing marketing strategies for corporate goods and services.

It is most easily distinguished from other corporate social initiatives by this behavior change focus. Although campaign efforts may include awareness building and educational components or efforts to alter current beliefs and attitudes, the campaign is designed primarily to support and influence a particular public behavior (e.g., keeping a litterbag in the car) or action (e.g., voting). This initiative is probably most similar to cause promotion initiatives where, as described in Chapter 3, the corporation is providing funds, in-kind contributions, or other corporate resources to increase awareness about a cause or to support fundraising or volunteer efforts for a cause. When, however, campaign goals, objectives, messages, and related activities are "selling" a particular desired behavior, we categorize it as a corporate social marketing initiative and recommend specific program planning and implementation principles.

Philip Kotler and Gerald Zaltman launched social marketing as a discipline more than 25 years ago in a pioneering article in the *Journal of Marketing*.[2] It is more recently described by Kotler, Roberto, and Lee as "the use of marketing principles and techniques to influence a target audience to voluntarily accept, reject, modify, or abandon a behavior for the benefit of individuals, groups, or society as a whole."[3] Over the past three decades, interest has spread from applications for improving public health (e.g., HIV/AIDS prevention) to increasing public safety (e.g., wearing seat belts), and more recently to protecting the environment (e.g., water conservation) and engendering community involvement (e.g., organ donation).

Most commonly, social marketing campaigns are developed and implemented by professionals working in federal, state, and local public sector agencies, such as utilities, departments of health, transportation, and ecology, and in nonprofit organizations. Of interest in this chapter is the application for professionals working in for-profit corporations or their foundations.

TYPICAL CORPORATE SOCIAL MARKETING CAMPAIGNS

Corporate social marketing campaigns most commonly focus on promoting behaviors that address specific issues such as the following:

- *Health issues* including tobacco use prevention, secondhand smoke, breast cancer, prostate cancer, physical activity, fetal alcohol syndrome, teen pregnancy, skin cancer, eating disorders, diabetes, heart disease, HIV/AIDS, and oral health.

- *Injury prevention issues* including traffic safety, safe gun storage, drowning prevention, suicide prevention, and emergency preparedness.
- *Environmental issues* including water conservation, electrical conservation, use of pesticides, air pollution, wildlife habitats, and litter prevention.
- *Community involvement issues* such as volunteering, voting, animal rights, organ donation, crime prevention, and blood donation.

Selection of issues is most often influenced by a natural connection to a corporation's core business (e.g., Crest and children's oral heath). A decision to support a behavior change campaign may then be sparked by some growing, perhaps even alarming trend (e.g., increases in child obesity rates). This interest may be initiated by an internal group or staff member, such as a product manager who monitors specific consumer groups and their issues. Or the corporation may be targeted and approached by a public sector or nonprofit organization to partner in an effort (e.g., a medical center approaches a retail store regarding discounts on lock boxes for safe gun storage).

As outlined in Table 5.1, a wide range of industries participate in social marketing efforts. Major campaign elements include forming partnerships, determining a behavior objective, selecting target audiences, and developing and implementing campaign strategies. More detailed steps recommended for developing a social marketing plan are outlined at the end of this chapter.

Although campaigns may be developed and implemented solely by the corporation, it is more common that partnerships will be formed with public sector agencies and/or nonprofits who provide technical expertise regarding the social issue (e.g., heart disease); extend community outreach capabilities (e.g., access to Boys & Girls Clubs); and add credibility, even luster, to the campaign effort and the brand (e.g., American Heart Association partnering with Subway). In typical scenarios, the corporation provides several types of support: time and expertise of marketing personnel; money; access to distribution channels; employee volunteers; and in-kind contributions (e.g., printing of an immunization schedule). Funding may come from several sources within the organization, although

Table 5.1 Examples of Corporate Social Marketing Initiatives

Corporation	Desired Behavior	Target Audiences	Sample Activities	Major Partners
Subway	Practice healthy heart habits	Adults looking for healthy food options	Radio/TV Brochures	American Heart Association
Pampers	Put infants on their back to sleep to help prevent SIDS	Parents and caretakers	"Back to Sleep" logo on newborn diapers	SIDS Foundation Health Canada
Best Buy	Recycle used electronics at our store	Computer and software users	Web site Print Recycling events Radio	Local governmental agencies
Mustang Life Vests	Put a life vest on toddlers at beaches, on docks and on boats	Families with toddlers	Outdoor ads Discount coupons Loaner programs	Children's hospitals Emergency medical services Local government coalitions
Premera Blue Cross	Don't pressure your doctor to prescribe antibiotics	Adults and parents	Posters Newsletter News articles	Statewide Coalition on Judicious Use of Antibiotics

(Continued)

117

Table 5.1 (Continued)

Corporation	Desired Behavior	Target Audiences	Sample Activities	Major Partners
Dole	Eat 5 fruits and vegetables a day	Parents, teachers, children	Web site CD-ROM Cookbook	National Institute of Health Produce for Better Health Foundation
7-Eleven	Dispose of litter properly	People who eat fast food 16- to 24-year-olds People who drive 50-plus miles a day	Point of purchase Special events	Texas Department of Transportation Keep Texas Beautiful
Crest	Ensure good oral health for children	Primarily children in grades K-3	Education Dental care Oral health tools	American Dental Association Boys & Girls Clubs
Safeco Insurance	Take important steps to prevent fire around the outside of your home	Homeowners in high-risk wildfire areas	Printed materials with "10 Tips to Wildfire Defense" Video Speaker events	Fire marshals Local Safeco agents
The Home Depot	Practice these 100 ways to save water	Local residential households	Brochures Workshops Discount coupons Guideline cards	Utilities Water conservation coalitions Media & Communications Firms

marketing is often an enthusiastic contributor, as many of the benefits support marketing objectives and goals.

As suggested in Table 5.1, typical campaigns focus on behaviors that can be expressed as a single act (e.g., get a flu shot) or simple doable acts (e.g., eat five fruits and vegetables a day)—behaviors that the target audience will know if they have done and ones that campaign managers can measure. Market segmentation is common, with a desired focus on target audiences who will benefit most from the behavior change, who are most open to the idea of change, and who can be reached efficiently with available media channels. Typical activities include traditional promotional efforts using a variety of media channels, including broadcast, print, outdoor, promotional items, and special events.

POTENTIAL CORPORATE BENEFITS

As illustrated in the following brief case examples, many of the potential benefits for the corporation are connected to marketing goals and objectives: supporting brand positioning, creating brand preference, building traffic, and increasing sales. Potential benefits beyond marketing include improving profitability and making a real social impact.

Supporting Brand Positioning

Kotler and Armstrong describe a brand's position as "the complex set of perceptions, impressions, and feelings that consumers have for the product compared with competing products."[4] Social marketing is one strategy to achieve a desired brand position.[5] The following case illustrates how a social marketing partnership between a corporation and a publicly funded program provided strong benefits for a brand in the highly competitive fast-food industry and helped to positively influence eating behaviors.

Example: Subway and Heart Health

Subway has a corporate philosophy to offer healthy, convenient fast food and currently features seven sub sandwiches with six grams of fat or less.

On a local level, this core competency made them a natural partner for North Carolina's Heart Disease and Stroke Prevention

Task Force and the North Carolina Cardiovascular Health Program funded by the Centers for Disease Control and Prevention.

Subway sponsored and therefore was associated with messages from these health organizations promoting healthy eating and being physically active. In the year 2000 these cosponsored messages reached over seven million listeners in North Carolina with taglines on Subway's radio and television commercials. Brochures at cashier stands were made available in more than 470 stores throughout the state. Coupons for Subway's healthy "Seven Under Six" meals were featured in newspaper inserts (see Figure 5.1).

Reports indicate that demand for their low-fat offerings increased and that one state legislator asked how he could get a Subway restaurant in his district. The partnership has garnered attention from CDC and the American Heart Association.

On a national scale, in 2003 Subway announced its national sponsorship of the American Heart Association's "America Heart Walk," an annual 5K walk in more than 750 cities across America. Promotional materials including an announcement of the sponsorship on napkins and in a "Nutritional & Dietary Guide" on counters in Subway restaurants, outlining the benefits of exercise, tips for getting started, and how to find time for an exercise routine.

Figure 5.1 Subway's cosponsored messages provide strong support for a desired brand positioning. (Reprinted courtesy of MarketSmart Advertising.)

Creating Brand Preference

Brand preference makes it more likely that a particular product will be selected from a lineup of similar products. Social marketing can create rich associations for the brand by connecting it with a cause. According to Business for Social Responsibility, "A 1997 study by Walker Research found that when price and quality are equal, 75 percent of consumers would switch brands or retailers if a company is associated with a good cause."[6]

In the following example, note the potential for rich associations for the Pampers brand of disposable diapers as a result of supporting a social marketing campaign to influence parents and caregivers to place infants on their backs to sleep, instead of their sides or stomachs.

Example: Pampers and Sudden Infant Death Syndrome (SIDS)[7]

Sudden Infant Death Syndrome (SIDS) is the leading cause of death among infants from birth to 12 months in North America. Importantly, according to the National Institute of Child Health and Human Development (NICHD), the SIDS rate in the United States has declined by more than 50 percent since the NICHD "Back to Sleep" campaign began in 1994. Pampers joined the nationwide Back to Sleep campaign in the United States in 1999 at the encouragement of a forum comprised of leading world child care experts (Pampers Parenting Institute), recognizing Pampers as the leading diaper used in hospitals.[8]

Pampers printed the Back to Sleep logo (featuring a baby sleeping on its back—see Figure 5.2) across the diaper-fastening strips of its diapers for newborns, delivering life-saving information straight to parents and caregivers. In addition to imprinting the Back to Sleep logo on diapers in three different languages (English, French, and Spanish), Pampers included Back to Sleep information in childbirth education packets, booklets distributed through pediatricians' offices, direct mail pieces to households with newborns, and an aggressive media outreach program targeting minority communities. In 1999, it was estimated that the campaign would reach 1.5 million mothers of newborns and that Back to Sleep information in education packets would reach 2.5 million mothers each year.[9]

And in Canada the company supported the creation and distribution of promotional door hangers, distributed educational pamphlets to new mothers through the majority of Canadian hospitals, and promoted SIDS awareness through its own advertising campaigns.[10]

Building Traffic

As noted early in this article, social marketing campaigns influence behaviors, and corporations can leverage these behaviors to increase sales of their products, especially through increased traffic. RadioShack, for example, developed a program that provided a variety of materials and tools for families to help keep children safer from abduction and abuse. One campaign element included offering 800,000 free "Child ID" kits at all RadioShack stores nationwide.[11] Best Buy also demonstrates this traffic-building opportunity.

Figure 5.2   A "just-in-time" message that appeared on Pampers newborn diapers. (Reprinted courtesy of National Institute of Child Health and Human Development.)

2003 Best Buy Recycling Event Locations

June 2003
Denver, CO
St. Louis, MO

July 2003
Minneapolis/St. Paul, MN

August 2003
Boston, MA
Philadelphia, PA

September 2003
Atlanta, GA
San Francisco, CA
San Diego, CA
Washington DC

October 2003
Florida

Figure 5.3   Used electronic equipment is recycled at Best Buy stores, providing opportunities for upgrades and increased sales. (Reprinted courtesy of Best Buy.)

Example: Best Buy and Recycling Electronic Equipment[12]

In summer 2001, Best Buy was among the first electronics retailers to offer consumers recycling opportunities across the country, leveraging the fact that an estimated 50 million computers and televisions are thrown away annually, increasing concerns about landfills and hazardous waste management as well as hazardous materials.

The program encourages consumers to drop off old and unwanted computers, monitors, televisions, VCRs, and other electronic items at select Best Buy stores during specified weekends (see Figure 5.3). A handling fee is charged for CRT-containing items. Best Buy plans to form partnerships with local government agencies, manufacturers, and waste management companies.

This national rollout was launched after a two-day pilot event in autumn 2000 at one of Best Buy's Minnesota stores resulted in a two-day collection of 22 tons of equipment, enough to fill two semitruck trailers.[13] Partners included local government agencies as well. The program was announced at an annual luncheon of the Electronics Product Recovery and Recycling (EPR2) Conference, attended by government agencies, academia, nonprofit organizations, electronics manufacturers, and recycling companies.[14] Best Buy incorporated messages regarding the recycling events in radio and print ads and on their web site.

For Best Buy, this strategy captures opportunities for computer upgrades, builds traffic in their stores with their target audiences, and builds their brand through positive value associations.

Increasing Sales

Perhaps the most attractive of benefit of social marketing initiatives is the potential for increased product sales. This is often possible when there are natural ties with the products and services of corporations that can support desired behaviors (e.g., booster seats, blood pressure monitoring equipment, water conserving appliances, baby safety gates, smoke alarms, mulch mowers, compost bins, exercise equipment, water bottles, and bike helmets). The following case makes this point well.

Example: Mustang Survival Life Vest and Drowning Prevention[15]

Mustang Survival, a life vest manufacturer interested in increased share in the child life vest market, enthusiastically accepted an invitation in the early 1990s to partner with Washington state's Children's Hospital and Regional Medical Center's drowning prevention campaign. After all, the campaign focused on influencing parents to put life vests on their children when on beaches, docks, or boats, in open water, and around swimming pools.

Mustang Survival provided funds for advertisements, featuring the Mustang logo, and for educational materials and displays. It donated life vests for loan programs on public beaches; provided discount coupons for its life vest that were distributed by coalition partners (see Figure 5.4); and created retail displays featuring drowning prevention messages along with its life vests.

Figure 5.4 Coupons distributed by drowning prevention coalition partners assisted Mustang in capturing more of the child life vest market. (Reprinted courtesy of Seattle Children's Hospital and Regional Medical Center.)

After the first year of this campaign, Mustang reported an increase over the prior season of more than 25 percent in this new market; children's life vest ownership and life vest usage increased significantly among parents aware of the campaign.

Improving Profitability Through Reducing Costs

Social marketing campaigns can even contribute to corporate profitability by influencing behaviors that can reduce operating costs or expenses. Prime examples are in the utility sectors (e.g., influencing homeowners to reduce peak energy loads) as well as health care and insurance industries, where health promotion and injury prevention can save costs of delivering health care.

Example: Premera Blue Cross and Judicious Use of Antibiotics[16]

In general, health experts agree that up to 50 percent of all antibiotic treatment may be unnecessary. This issue directly affects public health, overall health care costs, and, to a lesser extent, the profitability of organizations such as Premera Blue Cross, a regional health plan in Washington, Oregon, and

Alaska. In an effort to help reduce the local threat of bacteria growing increasingly resistant to antibiotics, Premera joined a coalition that included the Washington State Medical Association and the Washington State Department of Health to promote the judicious use of antibiotics.

Campaign activities include the following:

- Targeting physicians through printed materials and educational symposiums, and reporting on individual physician prescribing patterns.
- Targeting members through newsletters, posters, and brochures with clear behavior messages: Don't pressure your doctor to prescribe antibiotics; finish the full course; and never save the medication. (See Figure 5.5.)
- Targeting the community through news articles in major newspapers.

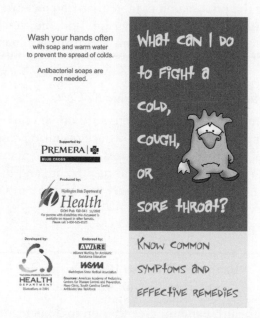

Figure 5.5 Campaign poster to encourage judicious use of antibiotics is also expected to result in savings for Premera Blue Cross. (Reprinted courtesy of Washington State Department of Health and Premera Blue Cross.)

In 2001, Premera estimated that a potential savings on overprescribing for upper respiratory infections alone could reduce health care cost by $8 million per year for this health plan and its members alone (1.1 million members).

Attracting Enthusiastic and Credible Partners

The social marketing initiative, perhaps more than others, is likely to be welcomed and supported by public sector agencies, nonprofit organizations, foundations, and special interest groups often charged with goals and performance measures for influencing public behaviors (e.g., reducing incidence of obesity in children). These organizations and agencies in return offer support in the form of endorsements, expertise, networks, and shared distribution channels, as illustrated in the following example for Dole.

Example: Dole and 5 A Day

The "5 A Day" program was launched by the National Cancer Institute in 1991 with a mission to promote the consumption of at least five servings of vegetables and fruit per day as a way to reduce the risk of chronic diseases.[17]

Unlike initiatives of many government health promotions, the 5 A Day program relies heavily on private industry to achieve its goal of increasing vegetable and fruit consumption. Partners in several industries have stepped forward, including national grocery store chains, produce growers, distributors, and trade organizations.

The Dole Food Company was a welcomed partner and one of the original program sponsors, contributing to the program since its beginning. Programs Dole has developed to support this effort to encourage children and their families to eat five to nine servings of fruits and vegetables a day include the following:[18]

- *5 A Day Adventures* CD-ROM.
- "Jammin' 5 A Day" music.
- "Fun with Fruits & Vegetables" kids' cookbook.
- "How'd You Do Your 5 Today?" Chart.

- "5 A Day Live!" musical performance kit.
- Dole 5 A Day web site (see Figure 5.6).
- "5 A Day Friends" e-mail.
- 5 A Day Student Ambassadors.
- 5 A Day Supermarket Tours.

Dole's contribution to the program is acknowledged by educators, children, parents, and U.S. government health and education agencies for following important principles including maintaining integrity of nutritional messages, creating noncommercial materials and programs, maintaining a strong partnership with the National Cancer Institute, and supporting the national 5 A Day for Better Health campaign.[19]

Between 1991 and 2003, the Dole 5 A Day program provided free nutrition education materials to more than 38,000 schools and 115,000 elementary teachers in the United States.[20]

Figure 5.6 A logo that provides a strong co-branding message. (Courtesy of Dole Food Company, Inc.)

Having a Real Impact on Social Change

Perhaps more than any other social initiative, social marketing has the potential for impacting positive behaviors of large populations, and thus having an impact on social change. Support from organizations like 7-Eleven can make or break efforts to reduce litter.

Example: 7-Eleven and Litter Prevention

"Don't Mess With Texas" is a tough-talking litter prevention campaign sponsored by the Texas Department of Transportation. This social marketing campaign launched in 1986 seeks to persuade Texans to keep their trash in the car and off the roads—and apparently it is working. Between 1995 and 2001, litter thrown on Texas highways decreased by more than 50 percent and cigarette butt litter decreased by 70 percent.[21]

7-Eleven, Inc.'s decision to support the campaign made sense on a couple of fronts. First, research indicates similarities in the demographic profiles between convenience store customers and people who litter. Those littering are more likely than most to eat fast food at least three times a week, be under age 24, and drive more than 50 miles a day. Second, 7-Eleven is said to have coined the phrase "dashboard diner®," as it is known for its portable food and drink offerings and, as a good corporate citizen, wants to encourage proper disposal of its containers. Corporate leaders viewed the partnership as a way for 7-Eleven to have a major impact, because of the large number of state residents coming to their stores each day.[22]

Campaign activities supported by 7-Eleven included in 2001 posting a 6-by-12-inch decal on sales counters, encouraging customers to "Dine on the Dash but Stash Your Trash" (see Figure 5.7). 7-Eleven unveiled what is believed to be the worlds' largest trash bag at a "Don't Mess With Texas" local rally and cleanup event that offered customers a chance to practice tossing trash into a bag while enjoying refreshments. Each store had decals identifying it as a "Don't Mess with Texas" partner posted on the door and at the gas islands. Volunteers from Keep Texas Beautiful conducted spot checks for litter at 7-Eleven stores and ranked their exterior appearance. Feedback was then routed to the appropriate 7-Eleven management personnel.[23]

It was estimated that more than a quarter of a million customers shopped nearly 300 Texas 7-Eleven stores each day and saw the antilittering message, which included a reminder about the state's $500 maximum fine for each littering violation.

POTENTIAL CONCERNS

Several significant potential downsides of social marketing campaigns need to be acknowledged and planned for.

Some issues are not a good match for the corporation. Consumers tend to be skeptical about the motivations that a corporation has for promoting or supporting a social issue. It might even be said they have a nose for hidden agendas and will be quick to judge the sincerity and authenticity of the effort. In Chapter 2, for example, we described a social marketing initiative that McDonald's uses to promote timely childhood immunizations. Compare your reaction to this focus to one where a different fast-food restaurant focused on physical activity for children and handed out brochures on recommended exercise levels for children at various ages to avoid childhood obesity. Could this gesture be interpreted

Figure 5.7   This anti-littering message leveraged 7-Eleven's dashboard diner® phrase with strong reach and frequency. (Reprinted courtesy of 7-Eleven.)

by many as a way to justify fast-food eating habits? Similarly, note the potential difference in acceptance and believability between an initiative where a tobacco company sponsors a campaign to increase the number of receptacles available for cigarette butts and to promote their use, versus a campaign to encourage parents to talk with their children about smoking. Will some people doubt the sincerity of the tobacco company's professed desire to prevent teens from smoking?

For many issues and initiatives, clinical and technical expertise needs to be sought.   Many behaviors appropriate for social marketing campaigns need to be grounded and supported by professional opinions (e.g., campaigns for diabetes prevention and control, reducing cholesterol, natural gardening, and protection from the West Nile Virus). As mentioned earlier, this is the advantage and perhaps necessity of seeking partners in the public or nonprofit sector with expertise in the area of focus.

Behavior change and, therefore, impact does not often happen overnight.   Internal publics especially will need to be warned up-front that the campaign will have milestones and that interim measures that indicate progress will need to be established and monitored. A litter reduction campaign, for example, may focus the first year on creating awareness of fines, the second year on convincing citizens that fines will be enforced, with real behavior change not expected until the third year of the campaign.

Be prepared for criticism from those who view social marketing campaigns as none of your business.   Some citizen groups believe fervently that campaigns about issues that seem to only impact the individual (e.g., smoking) are interfering with personal rights and should not be of concern to governmental agencies or corporations. In some states where primary seat belt laws have been adopted, for example, citizen groups have been known to advocate for reversal of these policies, arguing that if someone wants to "kill themselves" by not wearing a seat belt, that's the individual's choice and right. The best preparation for these situations is to provide facts regarding potential harm to others (e.g., statistics on increased diseases for children living in homes with a parent who smokes) and impact on public tax dollars (e.g., emergency medical costs for injuries that could have been prevented by a seat belt).

Recognize that developing, even supporting a social marketing campaign involves more than writing a check. To work well, these campaigns involve more staff time for planning, implementation, and coordination with partners; more integration into current media and distribution channels; increased attention to monitoring and tracking results; and vigilance in keeping updated on trends and events relative to the social issue and related behaviors.

KEYS TO SUCCESS

The following three cases illustrate important principles for successful corporate social marketing campaigns. Highlights include an emphasis on selecting an issue that leverages the company's core business, employee passions, and current marketing strategies; the importance of developing strong and credible partnerships; and the need for long-term plans and commitments.

Crest's Healthy Smiles 2010 Initiative

Brand managers at Procter & Gamble (P&G) consider their Crest Healthy Smiles 2010 initiative a real success (see Figure 5.8). The following is their story of how this initiative was selected, activities that

Figure 5.8   Logo for Crest's "Healthy Smiles 2010" program, which includes public/private partnerships to improve oral health, particularly among underserved minorities. (Reprinted courtesy of P&G.)

were involved, benefits to the brand as well as the cause, and perspectives on keys to this success.

The Crest Healthy Smiles 2010 (CHS2010) initiative was launched in May 2000 in response to the Surgeon General's report describing oral health as a "silent epidemic" in our country, particularly among underserved minorities. In his report, he called for public-private partnerships to close the disparity gap in oral care by the year 2010. As a leader in oral care and historically committed to improving oral health beyond merely selling our products, this call to action was clear and a challenge we felt confident we could address in a meaningful way. Procter & Gamble's core values include improving consumers' lives. Crest Healthy Smiles 2010 is consistent with what we stand for as a company.

To support CHS2010, Crest provides education, access to dental care, and oral care tools to underserved communities through partnerships with community and nonprofit organizations. Through a partnership with the Boys & Girls Clubs of America, every Club across the country was designated a "Cavity Free Zone," a place where oral health is a priority. A curriculum was developed to be taught in these Clubs, and access to dental care is provided through Crest Smile Shop dental clinics located within Clubs as well as in mobile dental units operated in partnership with leading dental schools. Additionally, Crest supports dental professionals and organizations with product and educational materials so they may bring education to their local communities. Finally, national advertising and public relations efforts were deployed to raise awareness about the oral health crisis and highlight Crest's role and commitment to closing the disparity gap. Funding for activities came from the Oral Care category within P&G.

In terms of benefits for the brand, this initiative has accomplished the following:

- Reinforced Crest's commitment to improving oral health.
- Positioned the brand as a leader in Oral Care.
- Built equity for the brand.
- Created goodwill among the dental community—both individual dentists/hygienists as well as professional organizations such as the American Dental Association and state/local societies.

- Delivered significant PR value, driving multiple consumer impressions on both a national and local level, and included influencers (former Surgeon General Dr. David Satcher, the American Dental Association), celebrities (Hank Aaron, Vanessa Williams), professionals, and consumer advocates.
- Generated incremental sales for the brand through partnerships with key retailers.

For the issue of oral health, to date the Crest Healthy Smiles program has touched over 35 million consumers with education, access to dental care, and/or oral care tools. Crest has raised awareness about the oral care crisis and impacted positive change at the community and national level.

Keys to this success include:

- Gaining senior management support.
- Choosing a cause that aligned perfectly with Crest's vision, mission, equity, and core competencies.
- Staying focused on a specific audience and purpose, one where we knew we could make a difference.
- Clearly defining up-front the scope of the project and funding levels.
- Committing to having a real social impact and developing plans to deliver outcomes.
- Setting clear business objectives, goals, and measures of success.
- Having an infrastructure that supported national as well as grassroots efforts.
- Forming mutually beneficial partnerships, ones with shared visions and missions, ones that would extend our reach at local levels and create goodwill and loyalty for the brand (e.g. Boys & Girls Clubs).
- Engaging employees to be ambassadors for the cause.
- Recognizing our limitations and enrolling experts for guidance (i.e., American Dental Association).

Safeco's FireFree Initiative

Safeco, an insurance and investment company based in Seattle, Washington, has been in business for 80 years "to help people protect what they value and secure their financial future."[24]

"FireFree" is a national public campaign designed by Safeco to increase resident participation in wildfire defense and mitigation behaviors (see Figure 5.9). It encourages homeowners to take 10 steps to create defensible space around their homes. Rose Lincoln, assistant vice president and director of community relations, describes a model for social initiatives that Safeco thinks works.

> Safeco developed FireFree in reaction to two fires in the 1990s in the Bend, Oregon, area. Both fires resulted in significant damage to property, including the outright loss of over 50 homes. When we approached fire officials about providing a grant, they instead suggested the company create an awareness campaign focused on teaching homeowners that by taking just 10 simple steps—a weekend's worth of work—they can create defensible space around their property and lessen the chance of loss in the event of a fire.
>
> In 1996, a $150,000 grant went toward the development of campaign materials that promoted "10 Tips to Wildfire Defense." A video and brochure were created for firefighters to use in educating communities. In 1997 the campaign was launched in Bend with a citywide cleanup. Print, television, and radio ads promoted the event and the 10 tips.
>
> We continue to spend about $50,000 each year to produce and distribute brochures and videos that are available at no charge to fire

Figure 5.9   Logo for Safeco's program promoting "10 Tips to Wildfire Defense." (Reprinted courtesy of Safeco.)

officials and to Safeco agents across the country who live and work in wildfire-prone areas and want to mobilize their communities to defend against wildfire. Safeco's Community Relations department provides the funding. As of September 2003, the company had shared nearly 165,000 brochures and over 750 videos in approximately 500 cities and 36 states across the country.

In Bend, the message continues to be delivered via mass media advertising, a public speakers program, and through educational materials. There is also an annual awareness campaign in the spring that closes with weekend cleanups coordinated by local fire and forestry officials, homeowner associations, and volunteer FireFree neighborhood coordinators. In other cities, fire officials leverage local organizations' talents, including media, to maximize the reach of the program.

Having Safeco's name tied to a program that helps people prevent loss has had both brand equity and brand preference benefits. We believe in the research that concludes that people prefer to buy products from companies that care. We feel that having Safeco's name tied to a program that helps people prevent loss increases our reputation as a caring company and will help us rise to the top when consumers are looking for insurance and investment products.

Although we haven't tracked the outcomes in each area we've sent materials, we continue to get positive feedback as well as requests from new organizations that have seen the materials and are interested in implementing the program in their communities.

In 2003, we sent out a national news release based on a survey conducted in late 2002 in four wildfire-prone areas (Denver, Colorado; Flagstaff, Arizona; Spokane, Washington; and Bend, Oregon). The survey showed that 8 of 10 people in those areas were concerned about wildfire, and that people who are concerned about wildfire and know there are things they can do to lessen their chance of loss will take action.

We know that the more we create awareness of the importance of defensible space, the more people will take action and less loss will occur during fires. Ultimately, FireFree has the potential to reduce claims in the event of a wildfire. People living in wildfire-prone areas, specifically Bend, are now aware of simple steps they can take to reduce potential loss in the event of a fire, and they take those steps.

We strongly recommend several keys to success:

- Focus on an issue that aligns with a core business issue or corporate strength.
- Select an initiative that will leverage a majority of your corporate citizenship work.
- Build partnerships with knowledgeable organizations—those with common goals and interests. Use the partnerships to create programs that will have the best possible impact and most positive outcomes. This will create a far-reaching campaign that has larger impact than if it were kept solely within the corporation's sphere of influence. And the results are far more powerful than just writing a check.
- Ensure that local distributors and participants in the program are given a clear role in campaign efforts and are provided necessary training and resources.

This social marketing initiative has convinced us that people *are* interested in taking personal responsibility when armed with the facts and when they understand the consequences of inaction.

The Home Depot and Water—Use It Wisely

The Home Depot, a home improvement retailer with over 1,300 locations and more than 250,000 associates, has a commitment to give back to the communities where customers live and their associates work. They call it "Doing Good *and* Doing Well."[25] In 2001, they reported investing $25 million to support communities and over six million volunteer hours.[26] The following social marketing initiative in Arizona illustrates the benefits of a strong private/public/not-for-profit and media partnership to encourage behavior changes in the way people use water. Home Depot's story is told by Park Howell, president of Park and Company, the marketing firm that created the Water—Use It Wisely campaign and the "100 Ways in 30 Days to Save Water" promotion.[27]

In the summer of 2003, The Home Depot in Arizona joined with "Water—Use It Wisely," a national water conservation campaign that incorporates education, community outreach, and mass media, to encourage citizens to save water by showing them how. The majority of the 100-plus water-saving tips at the core of the campaign encourage behavioral changes in the way people use water, including specific recommendations such as use a hose nozzle; sweep your driveways and sidewalks instead of hosing them off; and turn your sprinklers back in the fall. The "100 Ways in 30 Days to Save Water" promotion provided a focused, month-long forum where the city and other "Water—Use It Wisely" partners sponsored weekend water conservation workshops in 39 Arizona Home Depot stores. Phoenix, Mesa, Scottsdale, the Arizona Department of Water Resources, and 17 other "Water—Use It Wisely" partners teamed with Home Depot to develop a comprehensive conservation training program for the home improvement retailer's customers. The city and state conservation experts first trained more than 120 Home Depot managers and their assistants, who in turn trained their store employees, to host weekend conservation classes. Each week featured a new topic. Additionally, Salt River Project (SRP), the Phoenix metropolitan area's largest wholesale water provider and an ongoing campaign partner, cosponsored the promotion, providing considerable financial and media support. Additionally, SRP provided numerous in-kind services including printing of the in-store banners, which contributed to the overall awareness and success of the event.

In-store banners, signage, and a 24-page color consumer guide on water conservation were the primary campaign elements (see Figure 5.10). Awareness was created through statewide advertising and public relations efforts, water bill inserts, NFL Cardinal's football game promotion, and grassroots-level communication via the local Home Depot stores, including in-store signage and banners, Home Depot associate shirts, and buttons. Additionally, wateruseitwisely.com provided the Web portal for detailed information on the 100 ways to conserve water.

Media sponsors bolstered the statewide TV advertising effort with a 95 percent household reach in Arizona. In addition to a $100,000 media buy, News Channel 3 provided extensive news coverage on the promotion, featured it on its Saturday garden show, and allowed the use of its TV personality, Dave Owens, "The Garden Guy." Public relations efforts where coordinated by Park & Co., the creators of the "Water—Use It Wisely" campaign, with Home Depot and SRP support. Additional funding for print advertising was supplied by the City of Phoenix. The promotion generated more than

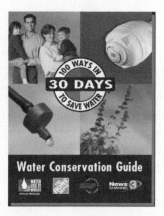

Figure 5.10 This brochure for a public/private partnership featured water-saving devices and clinics available at Home Depot. (Reprinted courtesy of Park & Company and Home Depot.)

4.3 million customer impressions through Arizona Home Depots and millions of impressions through the media. Approximately 40,000 consumer conservation guides were distributed, as well as more than 60,000 "Watering by the Numbers" irrigation guides and countless conservation brochures.

Chicanos Por La Causa (CPLC) was selected as the statewide charity to benefit from the promotion, which included Home Depot retrofitting fixtures and installing low-water-use landscapes in CPLC neighborhoods, offering a very visible example of Home Depot's commitment to its communities and the environment.

From Home Depot's perspective, this effort helped to meet several marketing objectives, including the following:

- Partnering with city and state water conservation officials in a concerted effort to bring conservation training and information to the public.
- Reinforcing Home Depot's and SRP's positions as leaders in environmental initiatives.
- Reinforcing Home Depot's and SRP's character of being good neighbors.

- Generating retail sales of water conservation products, including everything from hose nozzles and water-efficient showerheads and toilets, to low-water-use plants and irrigation systems.

What we believe worked well about this effort is that the cause aligned perfectly with Home Depot's environmental initiatives, and its senior management was instrumental in bringing together all 39 stores for a day of intensive conservation training with the cities and state, a training that led to the ultimate success of the weekend workshops.

A strong recommendation is to get as many people, experts, and organizations involved as possible who are in step with your vision.

WHEN SHOULD A CORPORATE SOCIAL MARKETING INITIATIVE BE CONSIDERED?

Based on the unique characteristic of social marketing campaigns (a focus on behavior change), the following situations should signal an opportunity to consider the social marketing option:

- When the primary objectives of an initiative are to support corporate marketing goals and objectives, versus corporate giving or community involvement agendas (e.g., an electronics store wants to build traffic and advertises that according to the public health department, it's time to check your home fire alarm batteries this weekend, a discount special on them is available in all its locations).

- When the issue the organization wants to support (e.g., healthy children) is one that has the potential for an individual behavior change component (e.g., a fast-food restaurant teams up with the local children's hospital and community health clinics to print an immunization schedule on tray liners).

- When the dollars for support of the initiative are coming primarily from the marketing department and can therefore be managed and integrated into marketing communications (e.g., a produce company putting the national "5 A Day" logo on packaging, advertisements, and coupons).

- When the behavior can be tied to one or more corporate products and then integrated into their features, pricing, distribution channels, and promotions (e.g., a life vest manufacturer attaching water safety tips to labels, creating retail displays on how to choose a life vest that's right for your child, and then distributing discount coupons via a local children's hospital).

DEVELOPING A CORPORATE SOCIAL MARKETING CAMPAIGN PLAN

A planned approach is key to success, the following eight steps and principles are recommended for developing a strategic social marketing plan.[28] It is also highly recommended that partners be identified prior to this formal planning process and be involved in developing each step of the plan.

1. *Conduct a situation analysis*, which begins with a statement of campaign purpose and focus, as well as an analysis of internal strengths and weaknesses and external opportunities and threats. Special efforts should be made at this step to review past and similar campaigns for lessons learned, as well as potential for replication (e.g. the "Click It or Ticket" campaign to enforce seat belt use, adopted by many states across the nation, was initiated by one state, North Carolina).

2. *Select target audiences*, starting with those who have the greatest need, are easiest to reach, are the best match for the organizations involved, and are most ready for action (e.g., newly pregnant women as a focus for a tobacco "Quitline").

3. *Set behavior objectives (the desired behavior) and behavior change goals.* One key to success at this step is to establish behavior objectives that are single, simple, doable acts that become the core of the campaign effort (e.g., put an infant on its back to sleep). Quantifiable goals are established in terms of behavior change in the targeted population, similar to sales goals in the corporate marketing model.

4. *Determine barriers and motivations to behavior change.* Identify perceived costs and benefits to the desired behavior, as they provide

rich material for developing strategies. In addition, it is at this stage that we also identify the competition, namely behaviors the target audience is currently doing or prefers to do (e.g., placing infants on their stomach).

5. *Develop the marketing mix*, including product, price, place, and promotional strategies, ones that uniquely and strategically address the barriers and motivations that target audiences have for adopting the desired behavior. A few keys to success for each of these four Ps include the following:

- *Product:* Include a tangible object or service in the campaign, something that will facilitate the desired behavior (e.g., litterbags handed out by mini-marts in support of a state litter prevention campaign).
- *Price:* Look for nonmonetary forms of recognition that add value to the exchange (e.g., Backyard Wildlife Sanctuary plaques for homeowners agreeing to natural yard care practices, provided by a local nursery).
- *Place:* Look for ways to make performing the desired behavior convenient (e.g., dental care offered in mobile vans sponsored by an insurance company).
- *Promotion:* Develop messages prior to selecting media channels. Focus on messages that are clear, vivid, and concrete (e.g., "Don't Mess With Texas") and media channels that provide constant reminders and are sustainable over time (e.g., state road signs with litter fines and corporate sponsor names).

6. *Develop a plan for evaluation and monitoring.* Evaluation should be based on measuring behavior change goals established in step 3, providing a real outcome measure. In addition, evaluation plans can be developed to measure changes in awareness and attitudes, as well as campaign processes (e.g., reach and frequency of campaigns and dissemination of materials).

7. *Establish budgets and find funding sources.* Opportunities should be explored for corporate partnerships with all sectors: public agencies, nonprofit organizations, foundations, and special interest groups.

8. *Complete an implementation plan.* A three-year plan is ideal, recognizing that behavior change may be slow to come and that time is often needed to educate, change attitudes, and provide infrastructures to support behavior change (e.g., more litter receptacles).

SUMMARY

Corporate social marketing is most clearly distinguished from other corporate social initiatives by its focus on *individual behavior change*, changes that will help improve health, prevent injuries, protect the environment, and increase community involvement. Potential corporate benefits are greatest for supporting marketing goals and objectives including strengthening brand positioning, creating brand preference, building traffic. and increasing sales. Potential and significant additional benefits beyond marketing include improving profitability and making a real social impact.

Several concerns and potential pitfalls with corporate social marketing campaigns are real. Some social issues, although important, are not an authentic fit for the corporation. For many issues and initiatives, clinical and technical expertise needs to be sought. Behavior change, and therefore impact, does not often happen overnight, and key publics and partners need to be forewarned. Be prepared for criticism from those who view social marketing campaigns as "none of your business." And recognize that developing, even supporting a social marketing campaign involves more than just writing a check.

Corporate managers experienced in these campaigns emphasize several keys to success: Pick an issue connected to the organization's core business, employees, and current marketing strategies; focus on an initiative that has the potential for a long-term commitment; gain management support; partner with public sector and nonprofit organizations who can provide expertise, credibility, and extended reach into communities; and develop solid plans (up-front) with established funding, measurable goals, and clear roles and responsibilities. Finally, as with any strategic marketing effort, a sequential planning process is fundamental and will involve audience research and utilization of all key marketing tools.

Corporate Philanthropy: Making a Direct Contribution to a Cause

"Your ads are obnoxious. Sunny is disgusting in them. We swore we would rather sleep on concrete than buy a bed from you because of her ads. But we came because of your role in the community and we stayed because of the service we received at your store."

—Comment card given to CEO Sunny
Kobe Cook, Sleep Country U.S.A.

Corporate philanthropy is a *direct contribution* by a corporation to a charity or cause, most often in the form of cash grants, donations and/or in-kind services. It is perhaps the most traditional of all corporate social initiatives and has historically been a major source of support for community health and human service agencies, education, and the arts, as well as organizations with missions to protect the environment. These corporate donations are often critical to a nonprofit's operating budgets, capital expenditures, and special projects, filling the gap between expenses and revenues from programs and contributions from individual donors. Other terminology most closely associated with this initiative includes community giving, community relations, corporate citizenship, and community affairs.

Some models and definitions include employee volunteerism as a form of corporate philanthropy. We have distinguished community volunteering as a separate initiative in Chapter 7, as it has unique characteristics related to corporate benefits, potential concerns, keys for success, and decision making related to developing and implementing corporate programs. Similarly, we earlier distinguished cause promotions from philanthropy as those communication-oriented initiatives focused on efforts specifically designed to increase awareness and concern about a particular issue.

Most agree that the character of corporate philanthropy has matured over the decades, primarily in response to internal and external pressures to balance concerns for shareholder wealth with expectations to demonstrate responsibility for communities contributing to the corporation's livelihood.[1] Perhaps the most consistent response has been to move to a more strategic approach to selecting social issues to support, with an increased tendency to choose an area of focus and to tie philanthropic activities to the company's business goals and objectives. Second, there appear to be more long-term relationships being developed with nonprofit organizations, ones that look more like a partnership than a casual acquaintance or one-night stand. Third, corporations have expanded their options for giving beyond cash donations to include contributions of other (often less costly) corporate resources such as excess products, use of distribution channels, and technical expertise. Fourth, we see increased interest in involving employees in decision making regarding the prioritization and selection of recipients for philanthropic programs. Fifth, as with other initiatives, the spotlight appears to be fixed on determining ways to track and measure outcomes, even rates of return on contributions. Finally, as a reflection of globalization, giving has now expanded to include international communities where corporations are also doing business.[2]

TYPICAL PROGRAMS

Philanthropic efforts commonly involve selecting a cause that reflects a priority area for the corporation, determining the type of contribution to be made, and identifying a recipient for contributions, most often an existing nonprofit organization, foundation, or public agency such as a school. The range of options for giving are summarized here and, as indicated, are varied, with trends mentioned earlier that are breaking from the tradition of cash donations to creative giving strategies that make use of other (sometimes idle) corporate resources.

- *Providing cash donations* (e.g., making contributions to United Way, providing financial support for a YMCA teen program, or making a donation to provide emergency funding for those who lost their jobs as a result of the attacks of 9/11)

- *Offering grants* (e.g., providing a grant to a nonprofit organization to help with startup costs for offering voice mail for homeless people who are job hunting, or offering grants to nonprofit organizations and schools to support environmental education)

- *Awarding scholarships* (e.g., scholarships that enable minority students to attend college and pursue a career in restaurant management, or scholarships for high school students in a third world country to spend their senior year as an exchange student in the United States)

- *Donating products* (e.g., providing used shoes that can be recycled for athletic tracks, or infant car seats that can be given to families in need when leaving the hospital; or a local diner bringing cheeseburgers and milkshakes to a homeless shelter several nights a week)

- *Donating services* (e.g., printing child immunization schedules for a community health clinic, providing call center support for a hotline to report littering on freeways, or offering free dental care for families in a domestic violence shelter)

- *Providing technical expertise* (e.g., sharing strategies for setting up inventory control systems, or reviewing health education materials for technical content regarding nutritional guidelines)

- *Allowing the use of facilities and distribution channels* (e.g., car dealerships that make room for car seat inspections, or grocery stores that provide space for collection of canned goods for food banks)

- *Offering the use of equipment* (e.g., vans for transporting materials for a science exhibit to schools, or medical equipment offered for use at a health fair)

Recipients of these contributions are most often existing nonprofits and foundations in the community, and may even have an existing relationship with the corporation. They may also be public agencies such as schools or foundations that have been created by the corporation and that then manage and distribute funds. As noted in Table 6.1, there may be additional partners in the effort, even some that also provide funding for the cause.

Guidelines for determining levels of giving vary. Many companies budget their donations based on the prior year's income. Some target a percentage of pretax earnings. Business for Social Responsibility describes giving patterns in its "Issue Brief on Philanthropy," including an estimate that "the average pretax percentage-level of corporate giving ranges from 1.3 percent (according to the American Association of Fundraising Counsel) to 0.7 percent (according to the Conference Board)."[3] In 2002 *Forbes* reported giving levels of the top "Forbes 500" companies, looking at cash donations in 2002 as a percentage of operating income in 2001. It then ranked companies with the top scores, including Target (cash giving at 2.56 percent of operating income), MetLife (2.51 percent), Albertson's (2.42 percent), Best Buy (2.05 percent), Ford Motor (1.76 percent), Cisco Systems (1.6 percent), American Express (1.39 percent), DuPont (1.33 percent), Altria Group (1.29 percent), and J.P. Morgan Chase (1.21 percent).[4]

Table 6.1 highlights examples of philanthropic programs for a variety of firms, for a variety of causes.

POTENTIAL BENEFITS

On the surface, involvement in philanthropic activities appears to contribute most to the image and regard for the corporation among its varied publics, including customers, employees, and community organizations, especially ones that track and report on corporate giving. Many managers point to increased respect and community good will and a stronger desired brand position.

In an article in the *Harvard Business Review* in 2002, Michael Porter and Mark Kramer argue that philanthropic activities can (and should) go beyond generating goodwill. They cite examples of how activities can enhance a company's productivity (e.g., Exxon Mobil making substantial donations to improve roads in developing countries where it operates),

Table 6.1 Examples of Corporate Philanthropy Initiatives

Corporation	Cause	Major Contributions	Recipient(s)	Major Partners
ConAgra Foods	Children's hunger	Funding Delivery trucks Tracking system technology	Food banks nationwide Children	America's Second Harvest Local children's programs and charities
General Electric	Outdoor lighting at national landmarks	Anti-glare fixtures Grants	Yellowstone National Park	Yellowstone Foundation National Parks Service
The New York Times Foundation	Journalism	Cash contributions Institutes for journalists	Universities Students	Universities Experts in the field of journalism
General Motors	Highway safety	Funding and providing vans for car seat inspections and delivery of MADD program materials	National SAFE Kids Campaign® Mothers Against Drunk Drivers (MADD)	Dealerships United Auto Workers NAACP

Company	Focus Area	Program	Recipients	Partner/Example
General Mills	Childhood nutrition and physical activity	Grants for local community organizations	Local nonprofits, community organizations, and schools	American Dietetic Association Foundation
Kenneth Cole	Homelessness, AIDS, handgun control and safety, children in domestic violence shelters	Cash contributions to nonprofit organizations and foundations Cause promotions in advertising	Several nonprofit organizations and foundations with missions supporting these causes	Major nonprofits with missions related to major causes
Microsoft	Technology skills	Grants in cash and software	Underserved communities worldwide	Community-based technology learning centers
Costco Wholesale	Early learning and child care	Funding to support opening of a child care center	Early Learning and Family Childcare Center	Bellevue Community College
REI	Conservation and outdoor recreation	Grants	Nonprofit organizations and community groups	Employees

expand markets (e.g., Apple Computer donating computers to schools, increasing the usage and appeal of their systems), and ensure a strong future workforce (e.g., American Express supporting training for students pursuing careers in travel agencies).[5]

The following examples point to these as well as additional benefits from involvement in corporate philanthropic activities, including strengthening the company's industry (e.g., the *New York Times* educating and inspiring journalists), gaining the satisfaction of having a significant impact on societal problems (e.g., grants from General Mills to support local youth nutrition and fitness programs), and leveraging the availability of excess or idle corporate resources (e.g., General Motors providing vans to support car seat safety inspections).

Building Reputation with Respected Organizations

The U.S. Department of Agriculture estimates that 13 million American children are fighting hunger each year, and America's Second Harvest estimates that one of four people standing in line at a soup kitchen is a child.[6] A partnership between ConAgra Foods, Inc., one of North America's largest packaged-food companies, and America's Second Harvest, the nation's largest domestic hunger relief organization, seems like a natural to address this national challenge.[7] Although the philanthropic nature of this initiative is featured in this example, activities also include various cause promotion efforts and community volunteerism among employees.

Example: ConAgra Foods and Feeding Hungry Children

ConAgra Foods' *"Feeding Children Better"* initiative launched in 1999, represents a multiyear, multimillion-dollar commitment and is reported to be the nation's largest corporate initiative dedicated solely to fighting child hunger in the United States (see Figure 6.1).[8] Efforts are directed in three areas: funding for Kids Cafes, a national program of America's Second Harvest; improving technological and transportation efficiencies of the food bank distribution systems; and raising public awareness of this country's child hunger problem.[9]

Kid Cafes are partnerships with after-school and summer feeding programs that provide children with nutritious meals. ConAgra Foods partners with America's Second Harvest and its national network of more than 200 food banks and food-rescue organizations to help fund Kids Cafes and is the program's national sponsor. Cafes are located in facilities such as YMCAs and Boys & Girls Clubs and in other family resource centers. In October 2003, for example, a news release announced the grand opening of a Kids Cafe at the Lincoln Early Intervention Center in Pocatello, Idaho, that will provide an evening meal once a week for 160 school-age kids.

As a part of this initiative, ConAgra Food also funds Rapid Food Distribution System, a computerized nationwide inventory and trucking system that enables food banks to get food to destinations faster and cheaper. The program is reported to have the potential to reclaim up to 200 million pounds of food available for donation, which might otherwise be discarded.[10]

By the end of 2003, ConAgra Foods had provided funding for more than 160 Kids Cafes, donated 122 trucks for food banks, assisted food banks around the nation with logistics assistance and inventory control system upgrades, and sponsored a national public service advertising campaign to raise awareness of child hunger in the United States.[11]

Figure 6.1 Program logo for ConAgra's initiative to help feed hungry children. (Reprinted courtesy of ConAgra Foods.)

Creating Community Goodwill and National Attention

A GE Consumer Products manager explains that they look for philanthropic projects that are a natural fit for their products and their business, ones where they can lend expertise to the cause and at the same
time support overall corporate citizenship goals. As with most companies, they enjoy projects that will also glean national attention and build
goodwill for the brand, as evidenced in the following initiative.

Example: GE Helps Stars Shine
More Brightly Over Old Faithful

Over the years, GE has been a leader in support of great national
landmarks, including the Washington Monument and the
Statue of Liberty. As national interest in dark skies and concern
with light pollution has continued to grow, GE turned its attention to another national icon, Yellowstone Park, and the historic
Old Faithful geyser area.

In May 2002, the GE Foundation, the philanthropic organization of the General Electric Company, announced a new program in cooperation with the National Park Service and the
Yellowstone Park Foundation to restore the night sky (dark sky)
over Yellowstone in Bozeman, Montana. The program was
timed to celebrate the 100th anniversary of the Old Faithful
Inn and targets the "sky glow" in the Old Faithful village, as
well as other major visitor areas in Yellowstone National Park
(see Figure 6.2).

Based on an audit conducted by the National Parks Service, GE
Lighting, and GE Lighting Systems, GE agreed to donate 50
antiglare fixtures and the foundation made a 2002 grant of
nearly $100,000 to support the overall effort to return the dark
skies over Yellowstone. Over a three-to-five-year period, support
will amount to $200,000 including GE Foundation grants and
product-in-kind donations.

Yellowstone Foundation announced the partnership and the initial grant on their press letterhead. According to a GE
spokesperson, "the media and headline writers liked the irony
that a light bulb manufacturer would take the initiative to lower

light levels." GE also publicized the announcement at a lighting industry trade show press conference.

For GE, this philanthropic initiative provided numerous benefits. A GE manager commented that "being associated with a treasured national park that can use our products to achieve a more aesthetic, environmentally sensitive lighting scheme brings tremendous pride to our employees and gleaned positive press coverage and national attention, promoting goodwill for the brand. Since the press coverage of the program, groups leading similar efforts, such as the International Dark Sky Association, have also contacted us to become even more involved in this cause. And, importantly, this project has proved to be an excellent learning experience for us to develop superior lighting products for diverse lighting applications such as this."[12]

Figure 6.2   GE's products and cash contributions are helping stars shine more brightly over Yellowstone National Park.

Strengthening the Corporation's Industry

Some philanthropic efforts are directed to longer-term benefits, ones that help ensure a stronger future for the company. This may include supporting efforts that train a future workforce, ones that cultivate relationships with high-quality suppliers, and others that build goodwill with the general public, regulatory agencies and policy makers. In the following example, a strong philanthropic effort supports the future of *The New York Times*, as well as that of journalism.

Example: The New York Times
Supporting Journalism and Journalists

The New York Times Company Foundation supports a variety of philanthropic activities, including providing grants to domestic organizations in five fields: journalism, education, culture, environment, and service; matching gifts of employees, directors, and retirees; providing college scholarships; raising funds for the Neediest Cases during the holiday season; and supporting an elementary school in Manhattan named for the publisher who founded the modern *New York Times* in 1896.

In the foundation's 2002 Annual Report, activities reflecting its special emphasis on supporting journalists and the field of journalism were highlighted (see Figure 6.3). In 2000, an initiative was launched to offer week-long courses designed to inspire and educate journalists on emerging new subjects. Participants were supported through web sites that provided a forum for information exchange, which included offering "journalists everywhere access to information about the subject."[13] In 2002, the program continued its expansion, offering five Institutes for journalists: Homeland Security, Theater Criticism, Foreign Language Press, the Age Boom Academy, and Frontiers of Brain Research. In 2002, these Institutes provided specialized training to over 60 writers and producers. Foundation grants also continued to support high school journalism, and the foundation continued to provide a service called Campus Weblines, designed to assist students in creating online school newspapers.

Figure 6.3 The New York Times Company Foundation places a special emphasis on supporting journalism and journalists. (Photo: James Estrin for *The New York Times*.)

Additional philanthropic efforts to support journalism in the past included a contribution in 1997 for $50,000, the first of two installments, to the School of Journalism and Mass Communication at the University of North Carolina at Chapel Hill. The grant was given for purchasing equipment, books, and periodicals. In recognition, the university named a seminar room the New York Times Company Foundation Seminar Room in 1998.[14]

In 2003 the Times Company was ranked number one in the publishing industry in *Fortune's* list of "America's Most Admired Companies," for the third consecutive year. The Times Company was also named in *Business Ethics* magazine's 2003 list of the "100 Best Corporate Citizens."

Building and Securing a Strong Brand Position

The following example, albeit a small company relative to many featured in this book, illustrates the potential for integration of a company's core values with philanthropic choices and desired brand positioning. Perhaps, as some think, this strategy represents a new type of philanthropy, one that is as much a part of the brand as the product itself.

Example: Kenneth Cole and Social Change

The American Foundation for AIDS Research is quoted as stating that "Kenneth Cole has made one of the single most remarkable philanthropic commitments in contemporary America, a commitment that breaks down the barriers between the public interest and corporate sectors and between deeply held personal values of equality and justice and day-to-day business concerns. In doing so, he proves that a social conscience and business acumen are not mutually exclusive and provides a role model for a new kind of corporate philanthropy."[15]

Major causes and organizations that Kenneth Cole Productions, Inc., supports are ones labeled on the company's web site as "Just Causes" and include nonprofit organizations with missions related to AIDS, the homeless, and mentoring for children in domestic violence shelters; the Sundance Institute, which supports screenwriters, directors, and documentary films; handgun control and safety; voting; protecting rivers and watersheds in New York; and providing funds and services to families in the footwear industry.

Historically, the company's advertising campaigns have reflected the founder's social consciousness and have been considered controversial by some, funny by others, and inspiring to many. As a noteworthy potential strategy for others engaged in corporate social initiatives, Cole's philanthropic activities are often integrated in the company's advertisements and, according to a 2003 article in the *Washington Post*, are known for their "snappy one-liners to promote a social agenda, burnish his corporate image, and sell his shoes."[16] Several examples of these one-liners were cited in this article and featured as follows, demonstrating the strategic use of philanthropy to claim and own a brand position:

- "Our shoes aren't the only thing we encourage you to wear" was a tagline that appeared in Cole advertisements in the late 1980s, accompanied by a graphic of a condom.
- "Have a heart, give a sole" was used with a visual where ads showed "tattered work boots of the homeless in lieu of a shiny pair of loafers." (See Figure 6.4.) The ads then promised a discount on a pair of new shoes if a customer donated a pair of their old ones to the homeless.
- "Buy a pair of Kenneth Cole Shoes and you might be responsible for bringing one homeless person in from the cold" read another billboard ad, which, as noted in the *Washington Post* article, was in sharp contrast with others in the industry. "Gucci advertising promises its customers a night of sweaty sex. Hermes ads suggest that a shopper has finally earned the keys to a private club."
- "Red, white and blue. It's the new black" was a line that appeared in January 2002, ringing in the New Year with a little humor, patriotism, and branding combined.[17]
- *Footnotes: What You Stand For Is More Important Than What You Stand In* is the title of a new book authored by Cole and published in the fall of 2003, telling the story of his company.

Figure 6.4   Cole's philanthropic efforts are often integrated
in advertising. (Reprinted courtesy of Kenneth Cole Productions.)

Having an Impact on Societal Issues in Local Communities

Bill Shore asserts in his book *The Cathedral Within* that "the one thing
more tragic than an incurable disease is knowing effective treatment and
withholding it or failing to ensure widespread use. . . . Medical science
does not waste resources by continuing to research a polio vaccine when
we've long had a very good one. The challenge is to take what works and
ensure its wider availability."[18] In the following example, a corporation's
nationwide philanthropic effort seeks to tackle a major societal problem
(youth nutrition and fitness) at local community levels. As described,
the goal of the initiative is to grant funding that will either provide increased access to existing successful programs or will encourage the de-

CommunityAction

• •

GENERAL MILLS

Figure 6.5 Grants for youth nutrition and fitness are a major initiative of the General Mills' community involvement program. (Reprinted courtesy of General Mills.)

velopment of promising programs that might then be replicated in other communities across the country.

Example: General Mills and
Youth Nutrition and Fitness Grants

In 2002, the General Mills Foundation launched an initiative with the American Dietetic Association Foundation and others to encourage communities in the United States to improve the eating and physical activity patterns of young people, ages 2 to 20 (see Figure 6.5). Of real interest was assuring that programs that had been proven through research to be successful were accessible and implemented at local levels. The joint initiative, called General Mills Champions, provides grants for up to $10,000 to 50 community-based groups to help youth maintain a balanced diet and physically active lifestyle. Additional components of the initiative include sponsorship of the Presidential Active Lifestyle Awards (for up to 50,000 youth each year), developing nutrition and fitness mentoring models, and sharing best practices. Annual funding is provided by the General Mills Foundation and ranges from $750,000 to $1 million. In the first year that grants were offered, over 650 applications for the 50-plus grants were received.

Grants are provided to diverse groups and projects. One in Wyoming, for example, targets at-risk girls ages 12 to 19 residing in a state correctional facility. Another in Oklahoma will use Native American cultural activities such as Native dancing as a way to incorporate more physical activity in the classroom. In Missouri, a new "A Healthier You" Girl Scout badge will be introduced. A project in South Carolina will focus on a community garden for underserved youth ages 5 to 14, and in Massachusetts efforts will include audio announcements with nutrition and physical activities messages that will be broadcast over 10 elementary schools' public address systems.

The President of the General Mills Foundation recommends to others considering and developing philanthropic initiatives to "select a focus area that management believes in; make sure it is one you can make a long-term commitment to with a high-integrity nonprofit organization; ensure it is a cause important to your consumers; and find ways for employees to participate."[19]

Providing Opportunities for Noncash/In-Kind Contributions

Corporate philanthropy offers opportunities for corporations to support causes through in-kind donations as well as cash and grant contributions. These may take the form of donations of services or products, or the use of a corporation's existing distribution and communication channels. For some corporations, this provides a more strategic way to contribute to

Figure 6.6 General Motors is a major supporter of the National SAFE KIDS Campaign. (Reprinted courtesy of General Motors.)

causes, as it often provides opportunities to connect the company's products with the cause. In the following example, in-kind contributions, as well as financial support, are closely aligned with the company's core business, products, and consumer markets.

Example: General Motors and Safe Driving

As outlined in their Corporate Responsibility and Sustainability Report for 2001–2002, General Motors supports several social initiatives and programs to encourage safe driving, including ones focusing on child restraint and safety belt use, drunk driving prevention, occupant compartment and trunk anti-entrapment, young drivers, and distracted driving. Some issues are supported with cause promotion initiatives (e.g., support for a campaign to educate the public on the facts associated with restraint); several with corporate social marketing initiatives (e.g., a brochure addressing child safety called "Never Leave Your Child Alone," with millions of copies distributed through dealerships and public health offices); some with socially responsible business practices (e.g., research and development related to technology and standards to minimize driving distractions); and several featuring employee volunteerism (e.g., dealerships participating in car seat safety checks).[20]

In terms of philanthropic activities, the focus of this chapter, several of their major initiatives related to safe driving include partnerships with well-known national organizations and programs, including the National SAFE KIDS Campaign (see Figure 6.6) and MADD (Mothers Against Drunk Driving), United

Auto Workers, and the NAACP.[21] Philanthropic activities to support causes have included financial support as well as those with a core connection to GM products and distribution channels: supporting child safety seat inspection stations; educating dealers on child safety; donating child safety seats to low-income families; and providing fully equipped vans in order to hold a traveling child safety seat check-up event, as well as vans to transport program materials and presenters for MADD programs.

POTENTIAL CONCERNS

Several challenges and concerns associated with philanthropic efforts are similar to those experienced when developing and implementing other social initiatives. Care needs to be given to finding and selecting a nonprofit charity and partner that has a strong reputation, is easy to work with, and has an existing infrastructure that will assure the effective management and utilization of contributions. As with other initiatives, managers may need to address shareholder concerns that the company should not be funding social causes that are or should be within the auspices of governmental agencies. This may be especially true when making large cash contributions.

Many issues, however, are more unique to philanthropic activities. Compared with other initiatives, there is often less visibility for these activities. By their nature, cause promotions, cause-related marketing, and social marketing efforts gain visibility for the company's role through communications inherent in campaign activities. Community volunteerism naturally puts a face on the contributions the company is making, often creating strong personal relationships and goodwill. Socially responsible business practices are often publicized by the corporation, as they represent opportunities to showcase concrete actions the company is taking to contribute to communities and the environment, especially to regulatory and policy making audiences. Some feel strongly that philanthropic activities should not be touted, believing that their actions will speak louder than words and the public will be even more convinced the activity is a public relations stunt if resources are used especially for external communications. Others take note of opinion polls cited in Chapter 1 that indicate the public expects and watches for the company's philanthropic activities and often makes purchase decisions based on awareness and knowledge of a company's giving.

An additional challenge for managers of philanthropic initiatives is to track activities and measure outcomes. Again, communication-related activities in cause promotions can be measured in terms of reach, frequency, and consumer impressions. Cause-related marketing and social marketing campaigns can even take this a step further, with actions and behaviors typically tracked and reported. Employee volunteer hours can be calculated and their impact often weighed (e.g., numbers of pounds of litter collected from a community park). By contrast, philanthropic activities often depend on feedback on outcomes and impact from the nonprofit charity, which may be lacking such measurement systems. Additionally, assigning values to in-kind contributions can be difficult and time consuming, especially for a national or global corporation. Finally, managers in companies without a set of guidelines and targets for giving will struggle for direction and consensus on levels and types of giving.

KEYS TO SUCCESS

Several keys to success for this initiative are similar to those for other initiatives. Choose a cause for contributions that has a connection to your business, your employees, and your overall corporate citizenship focus. Make certain leaders in the company are involved from the beginning, especially in major philanthropic efforts. Select the best grantees, find a way to make a concrete and positive difference, and consider multiyear partnerships with the charity as well as with for-profit corporations that can leverage contributions. Explore opportunities for donations of in-kind services, especially those connected to core products. Finally, don't be shy, but do be appropriate about talking about results and celebrating success.

Executives from Microsoft, Costco Wholesale, and Recreational Equipment Inc. (REI) share their applications of these principles and elaborate on their guidelines for developing and implementing their philanthropic programs in the following three cases.

Microsoft

Of special interest in this next case is the clear integration and coordination of a philanthropic initiative with the corporation's mission and

Figure 6.7   Microsoft's Unlimited Potential initiative is a natural evolution of the company's mission. (Reprinted courtesy of Microsoft.)

branding efforts. Microsoft's Managing Director of Global Corporate Affairs describes a strategic philanthropic initiative and shares what the company did to integrate the effort with the company's mission and brand positioning.

Confirming our belief that amazing things happen when people have the resources they need, Microsoft has seen remarkable results from our community investment efforts.

In today's knowledge-based economy, computer literacy has become a vital workplace skill—a skill that millions of people worldwide still lack. To help narrow this skills gap and aid global workforce development, in September 2003 Microsoft Corporation launched Unlimited Potential (UP), a global initiative focused on providing technology skills for disadvantaged individuals through community-based technology and learning centers (CTLCs) (see Figure 6.7). The program focuses on community technology centers because they exist in nearly every country in the world as a location for people to access information. In the first year since the inception of Unlimited Potential, Microsoft awarded a total of $50 million in cash, software, and technical assistance to more than 150 nonprofit organizations in 45 countries.

Narrowing the "digital divide" requires going beyond providing people with access to technology. The real difference is made when people are equipped with the knowledge and skills to put that technology to use. Computers are amazing tools that can transform lives, businesses, and even entire economies—but only if people know how to use them. Our goal is to make computer literacy a reality for underserved communities worldwide.

UP will provide funding to help CTLCs hire and train technology instructors, and will also make basic computing curriculum available to these centers. In later phases of the initiative, Microsoft will partner with others to establish a global support network delivering technology curriculum, research, tools, and services to CTLCs worldwide. The company will also sponsor a global and regional awards program, to recognize effective and scalable information technology solutions that deliver social benefits. The awards are designed to encourage innovation and provide the funding necessary to help the best information technology solutions scale for broader use.

UP grants are made through Microsoft's U.S. and international subsidiaries, working closely with local organizations to identify community-based centers where technology skills training is a primary focus. Grant recipients span regions around the world, including Africa, Asia, the Caribbean, Central America, Europe, Latin America, the Mediterranean, the Middle East, Mexico, and the United States.[22]

The connection of this community investment initiative to mission is more than coincidental. It is intentional. Microsoft's mission is "To enable people and businesses throughout the world to realize their full potential." The Unlimited Potential initiative is in complete alignment with this corporate purpose and provides a mechanism for us to deliver on it.

Our current corporate advertising campaign reflects Microsoft's desires to "unleash the potential in every person, family, and business. We want to help you do the things you do every day—express your ideas, manage your finances, build your business—faster, easier, and better. At Microsoft, we see the world not as it is, but as it might someday become." The campaign slogan is "Your Potential. Our Passion." This consistency is possible because we have made a corporate-wide decision to align the work of our product teams; our communication and outreach efforts; and our community investments around our company's mission.

To support this integrated approach, several efforts were key:

- *Referencing the corporation's mission statement at the onset:* The Unlimited Potential initiative is a natural evolution of our company's mission, and of its 20-year history of community outreach. As we developed Unlimited Potential, we made sure that the program continued to align with our efforts to help people and communities realize their full potential.

- *Working with the marketing department and the advertising and communication agencies responsible for external corporate communications:* Microsoft's brand group provided significant counsel as we developed the Unlimited Potential name and visual identity, thus ensuring consistency with the corporate brand.

- *Highlighting UP stories in external communications vehicles:* We've seen incredible things happen as a result of our philanthropic outreach. When technology and technology skills are made available to individuals and communities who previously lacked digital access, it transforms lives and creates amazing opportunities. Sharing these stories is a great way to demonstrate what our company is all about and the impact we hope to have through the power of technology. UP projects have been integrated into executive speeches, business presentations, the corporate advertising campaign, our annual report, our external web site, and other communications vehicles.

- *Focusing on internal communications as well as external communications:* A company's brand isn't just communicated through advertising and public relations. Brand is also transmitted—perhaps most powerfully—through our people. We work hard to ensure our employees not only understand our community investment efforts but also have a chance to get involved. When they share their experiences and their own personal transformations, it's one of the most effective brand tools we have.

Costco Wholesale

Opened in 1976, Costco Wholesale is the world's first warehouse membership club, and in early 2000 had more than 32 million members, 335 warehouses, and nearly 80,000 employees worldwide.[23] Costco's strong corporate culture includes a belief in the importance of giving back to those who have contributed to its success and an interest in creating positive social change. The following example of a philanthropic effort is

shared by a Costco executive who offers recommendations to others engaged in similar community philanthropic efforts.

Costco's community support concentrates on children and education. We believe education is a great equalizer and have worked over
the years to improve the educational opportunities for children,
ranging from elementary school age children through our Back to
School Backpack program, to college age students through our
scholarship program for underrepresented minority students. Recently, we expanded our efforts to include the education of children
from birth to age five.

We learned from recent brain research that education of children begins at birth and that the critical years in a child's development (zero to five) are the same years during which over 70 percent
of children are placed in some type of child care away from home.
Many child care centers and family child care providers are not able
to fully promote the healthy development of children during these
crucial years, and these years become, at times, years of missed opportunities to educate our children when they need it most. In addition, there is a severe lack of affordable quality child care.

We also believe that the lack of quality and affordable child care
needs to be addressed and corrected by the entire community, and
we determined that a collaborative approach was needed among
business, government, parents, teachers, academic institutions, and
the community. No one group can do it alone. We also realized that
this collaborative effort would be important in order to reduce costs,
make child care more affordable, and increase quality.

Costco partnered with Bellevue Community College (BCC)
over four years to develop this collaborative effort, and together they
built the Early Learning Family and Childcare Center on BCC's
campus (see Figure 6.8). This effort included the design, development, and construction of the facility, fundraising through grants
and donations from the private and public sectors, and the implementation of a high-quality program for children ages three months
to six years.

Costco contributed $1.5 million to the project. We also con-
tributed in-kind services and coordinated additional in-kind services
from our general contractor, architect, legal counsel, and vendors.
BCC provided funding and coordinated the fundraising campaign

Figure 6.8　The Early Learning and Family Childcare Center supported by Costco.

through its 501(c)(3) foundation, grant writing, and other means. As a result of our participation, Costco employees have access to 50 percent of the available child care slots, at the same tuition rates.

However, our primary reasons for participating in this project are to provide a model of affordable quality child care that hopefully will be replicated, to increase awareness of the importance of early learning within the business community, and to increase parental involvement in early learning.

Many communities across Washington state and the nation have inquired about the project. We've given tours and have spoken with various communities to share what we have learned. This project has been featured in various articles, and Costco's CEO and others have spoken to business groups around Washington, promoting the importance of early learning and the collaborative model. Costco has received recognition from the Bellevue Chamber of

Commerce as a recipient of the 2002 Eastside Business Award for Corporate Citizenship and the Leadership Award from the Foundation for Early Learning. Finally, BCC has spoken about the project around the country and both the architect and general contractor have received recognition for their involvement in this community service endeavor. While we appreciate the recognition we have received, what matters most to us is that we hope this will inspire other businesses to champion early learning in their communities.

When choosing among causes to support, focuses for efforts, and decisions regarding partnerships, we strongly recommend the following principles:

- *Don't try to be all things to all causes.* Focus on one or two areas.
- *Find a way to make a concrete difference.* We believe that campaigns that do the most good for the community in which the company does business will eventually do the most good for the company.
- *Collaboration is key.* As a result of collaboration, the actual cost of the building was below market value and the construction cost was fully funded, leaving the building debt-free. This substantially reduced operating expenses, allowing more affordable tuition levels and higher wages for caregivers.
- *Recognize that collaboration takes patience, perseverance, and executive support from the collaborators.* Costco and BCC committed senior level people to work on the project, and all collaborating partners did the same. These people had the authority to make decisions on the spot, and the expertise to solve problems creatively and react immediately.

REI

Recreational Equipment Inc. (REI) is a renowned supplier of specialty outdoor gear, currently operating more than 70 stores in 24 states. Retail stores include a variety of facilities for testing equipment, including bike test trails, climbing pinnacles, and camp stove demonstration tables. REI stores also provide opportunities to learn about the outdoors and muscled-powered sports through frequent in-store clinics and REI-sponsored events, and through association with local outdoor organizations. For seven consecutive years, REI has been recognized by *Fortune* magazine's

"Best Companies Special Report" as one of the "100 Best Companies to Work for in America." The following summary of REI's Grants Program, provided by REI's corporate giving manager, reflects their cultural focus on the great outdoors as well as on their employees, who are recognized throughout the outdoor industry for their product knowledge and expertise. (See Figure 6.9.)

> REI's Grants Program is unique as it calls on our employees to nominate potential grant recipients. Although a budget and plan has final approval by the board of directors and REI's leadership team, employees are solicited to nominate nonprofit organizations with which they volunteer who share our values and funding priorities. Organizations that have been nominated by an employee are sent grant applications and, when funding decisions are made, retail employees actually award the grants to the organization they nominated.
>
> Grants are funded by our public affairs department at about $1.8 million per year and focus in two areas. Conservation projects are intended to protect lands and waterways, make these resources accessible to more people who enjoy the outdoors, and better utilize and preserve our natural resources for recreation (e.g., a grant to promote dialogue between user groups and policy makers). Outdoor recreational project grants support increased access to outdoor activities

Figure 6.9   REI's giving program reflects its focus on the outdoors and relies on employee nominations for grant recipients. (Reprinted courtesy of REI.)

(e.g., one that provides sleeping bags and tents for students while attending an outdoor adventure education program), encourage involvement in muscle-powered recreation, and promote safe participation in outdoor muscle-powered recreation and proper care for outdoor resources.

Program success is evaluated on a variety of metrics, including measuring the number of hours of volunteer service, number of miles of trail work completed, number of children participating in an outdoor program, number of people benefiting from donated gear, or number of participants in a program. We believe successful projects then support our own long-term business goals by preparing our future's environmental stewards, promoting outdoor activities, and preserving places for recreation.

Surveys have indicated that our grants program has been a source of pride and loyalty for our employees. We believe it has strengthened our brand with customers, nurtured an internal culture of stewardship, and created partnerships with external organizations that have added value to the campaigns.

We believe in these keys to a successful philanthropic program:

- *Actively engage employees at all levels of the company, particularly those at retail stores.* By directing our corporate dollars to projects in which our employees are personally involved, we reinforce our commitment to stewardship and volunteerism as well as support meaningful projects at the grassroots level that are relevant, strategic, and unique. Although other models for grant making may be simpler and cleaner, we believe involving our employees in the program makes it more relevant, strong, and impactful.
- *Secure the support of leadership.* REI has a long history of giving back to the community and the value held within the company. Having the support of our senior leadership team and the board of directors insures that our program and commitment to stewardship remain bold, consistent, and alive.
- *Communicate results.* We repeatedly communicate the results of our giving efforts. This is done online, through our employee newsletter, in our stores, in our annual dividend packet, in catalogues and mailers, and through speaking engagements of REI leaders.

- *Celebrate success.* Recognize individuals and employee groups for their volunteerism. Participate in nonprofit partners' events and activities supporting environmental stewardship. Send personalized notes, e-mails, and articles about the difference we are making in the community through the donation of time, money, and products.

WHEN TO CONSIDER CORPORATE PHILANTHROPY

In reality, philanthropic activities are the norm for most corporations and are always a consideration when the corporation has citizenship or philanthropic goals. They should also be considered when community organizations and agencies would benefit from excess or idle corporate resources. Emphasis is placed in this chapter on developing philanthropic initiatives that are strategic, having the most impact on the social cause as well as providing the maximum benefits for the corporation.

DEVELOPING PHILANTHROPIC ENDEAVORS

Major decisions related to philanthropic activities will include selecting a cause to support, choosing a nonprofit charity or other recipient for contributions, determining levels and types of contributions, and developing communication and evaluation plans. Guidelines for each include the following:

- Selecting a cause to support should ideally begin by referring to already established philanthropic priorities, ones that have been chosen by the company as areas of focus based on a variety of factors including business goals, employee passions, and customer concerns. This will help ensure management support for the effort, as well as the possibility that contributions will be connected to causes currently being supported by other types of social initiatives. The chances for making a real impact in a particular cause area are then increased. Having these areas of focus will also help guide managers at remote or local levels, increasing the likelihood that corporate giving will be integrated throughout its various markets.

- When choosing a nonprofit partner, managers might first look at existing partnerships and build on ones where there is a good working relationship, a history of good fiscal management, and a track record of collaboration. Other criteria that might be used to select a partner include looking for one where there is the possibility of making a meaningful contribution by providing nonmonetary resources such as corporate products, use of distribution channels, and technical expertise.

- Determining levels of contributions ideally should also begin with a reference to established corporate guidelines for giving, ones that may specify a percentage of pretax profits, a percentage that varies at different profitability levels, or a fixed dollar amount, or may even be based on some other index such as the number of corporate employees.

- Developing a communication plan is an often-overlooked step for philanthropic initiatives. For some it is a deliberate move. Managers are encouraged, however, to develop an internal communication plan that informs employees regarding giving programs and levels of contributions. Plans for celebration should also be considered, especially when concrete results can be reported and shared. In terms of external communications, most would agree that at a minimum, giving programs should be described in corporate reports and on web sites, as many consumers, investors, and suppliers may in fact be looking for them and be surprised (or concerned) when they are not found.

- Though it is often difficult to do so, managers are encouraged to establish tracking and measurement tools that will account for total cash contributions, estimate the value of any in-kind services, and, ideally, provide information on outcomes and impacts for the social cause. There is some evidence that progress is being made to support evaluation strategies. For example, in the Spring 2003 issue of *New Century Philanthropy*, a publication of the Committee to Encourage Corporate Philanthropy, Charles Moore, executive director of the committee, said that initiatives are in the works to establish "industry-led guidelines to account and report cash and value-in-kind contributions across the entire corporation, and enable comparable internal and external benchmarking."[24]

SUMMARY

The current range of options for philanthropic giving is broad, breaking from traditions in the past that focused on cash donations to more creative giving strategies including donating products and services, providing technical expertise, and allowing the use of facilities, distribution channels, and (idle) equipment.

Major strengths for this initiative are building corporate reputation and goodwill; attracting and retaining a motivated workforce; having an impact on societal issues, especially in local communities; and leveraging current corporate social initiatives. Of late, experts are challenging corporations to look also at the potential for philanthropic initiatives that will actually increase productivity, expand markets, and ensure a strong future workforce. The greatest concerns expressed by many were the challenges associated with evaluating and choosing a strong cause partner, dealing with shareholder concerns for issues that have been selected, achieving (tactful) visibility for the corporation for its efforts, and tracking and measuring impact and outcomes, even just determining (quantifying) levels of giving.

Strongest recommendations to address these downsides include choosing social issues that have a connection to the corporation's mission, involving other departments in selecting causes and giving levels. When developing programs, engage employees, secure leadership support, and develop a communications plan, even if it is just an internally focused one.

Community Volunteering: Employees Donating Their Time and Talents

At Timberland, we're about more than the rugged boots we've made for 30 years. We believe that companies have the power and the responsibility to effect positive and lasting change in the world. When you layer in community organizations and individuals who share this passion, the vision for what we can achieve together is limitless.[1]

—Jeffrey Swartz, president and CEO,
The Timberland Company

Community volunteering is an initiative in which the corporation supports and encourages employees, retail partners, and/or franchise members to *volunteer their time* to support local community organizations and causes. Volunteer efforts may include employees volunteering their expertise, talents, ideas, and/or physical labor. Corporate support may involve providing paid time off from work, matching services to help employees find opportunities of interest, recognition for service, and organizing teams to support specific causes the corporation has targeted.

Distinguishing community volunteering from other initiatives is not difficult, as it alone involves employees of a corporation personally volunteering at local organizations (e.g., Boys & Girls Clubs) and for local cause efforts (e.g., picking up litter on roadways). Volunteering in the community is not a new corporate initiative. What is new and noteworthy, however, is an apparent increase in the integration of employee volunteer efforts into existing corporate social initiatives and even connecting the volunteer efforts to business goals. Once more, a strategic approach appears to be the norm, where employees are often encouraged to volunteer for causes that are currently supported by other corporate social initiatives, frequently connected to core business values and goals. IBM, for example, has had a long-standing commitment to education through an initiative called "Reinventing Education" and supports employees in becoming mentors to school youth; and FannieMae employees are encouraged to support the foundation's "Help the Homeless" program.

Volunteering in the community, and corporate support to do this, is viewed by many (including executives sharing their stories in this chapter) as one of the most genuine and satisfying of all forms of corporate social involvement. In his book *Revolution of the Heart*, Bill Shore shares perspectives and insights that may be contributing to this revival and encourages corporations, as well as individuals, to "contribute through their unique skills and creative abilities." He says that by doing this, "they are giving the one thing that is most genuinely theirs and that no one can take away."[2] It means "teaching nutrition and food budgeting to young mothers if you're a chef, tutoring math if you are an accountant, coaching if you are an athlete, examining children if you are a doctor, building homes if you are a carpenter or a builder."[3] He writes about "the yearning people have to be connected both to something special inside themselves and, at the same time, to something larger than themselves and their own self-interest."[4]

TYPICAL PROGRAMS

Corporate support for employee volunteering ranges from programs that simply encourage their employees to give back to their communities to those representing a significant financial investment and display of recognition and reward. Examples representing types of support include the following:

- Promoting the ethic through corporate communications that encourage employees to volunteer in their community and that may provide information on resources to access in order to explore volunteer opportunities.

- Suggesting specific causes and charities that the employee might want to consider and providing detailed information on how to get involved, often with causes and charities supported by other current social initiatives.

- Organizing volunteer teams for a specific cause or event, such as a United Way "Day of Caring" event, where, for example, employees paint the interior of a child care facility for homeless children.

- Helping employees find opportunities through on-site coordinators, web site listings, or, in come cases, through sophisticated software programs that match specific employee interests and criteria with current community needs.

- Providing paid time off during the year to do volunteer work, with typical benefits ranging from offering two to five days of annual paid leave to do volunteer work on company time, to more vigorous programs that provide opportunities for an employee to spend a year on behalf of the company working in a developing country.

- Awarding cash grants to charities where employees spend time volunteering; grant amounts are then often based on numbers of hours reported by employees.

- Recognizing exemplary employee volunteers through gestures such as mentions in internal newsletters, awards of service pins or plaques, and special presentations at department or annual company meetings.

Types of projects that employees volunteer for range from those that contribute to a local community to ones that improve health and safety for individuals, to those that protect the environment.

Community projects, perhaps the most common, include efforts such as building homes, collecting food for food banks, answering phones for public radio pledge campaigns, organizing teams for walk-a-thons, cleaning parks, reading to kids, mentoring youth at risk, volunteering in the classroom, visiting children in hospitals, spending time with seniors in nursing homes, teaching computer skills, befriending people in a homeless shelter, handing out meals at a soup kitchen, building playhouses for orphans, and staffing an adopt-a-pet booth.

Health and safety-related projects where employees volunteer their time include such activities as screening kids for dental problems, leading youth physical activity programs, conducting a car seat safety check, handing out educational brochures on HIV/AIDS, driving seniors to get an annual flu shot, and training children on how to use crosswalks.

Environmental volunteering might involve litter pickup, tree planting in areas destroyed by fires, seed propagation for highway beautification, salmon habitat protection, plant identification, weed control, removing alien plants, wetland rehabilitation, cleaning polluted waterways, and clearing storm drains of debris.

Table 7.1 highlights examples of programs for companies featured in this chapter.

POTENTIAL BENEFITS

According to executives contributing to cases and examples in this book, many of the benefits for this initiative reflect its unique capacity to build strong and genuine relationships with local communities and to attract and maintain satisfied and motivated employees. This may also be one of the best initiatives for augmenting and leveraging current involvement and investments in social initiatives. As with several of the other initiatives, additional potential benefits have been experienced as well, including contributions to business goals, enhancing corporate image, and providing opportunities to showcase products and services.

Building Genuine Relationships in the Community

Recipients of volunteer efforts recognize the spirit of commitment that a company has when volunteers show up personally to help their organization's cause. The relationship and community building opportunities for these sincere contributions are perhaps strongest for this corporate social initiative. It seems that anyone can write out a check or provide space for cause promotional materials in retail stores. But it takes real commitment and caring to give your employees time away from the production lines or for people who have a full-time job to give some of their free time to support a cause.

Table 7.1 Examples of Corporate Community Volunteer Activities

Corporation	Example of a Cause Supported	Examples of Activities	Examples of Support
Ford Motor Company	Affordable housing	Participating in building homes for Habitat for Humanity Detroit	Organizing efforts and employee recognition
Hewlett-Packard	Global access to technology	Working in underserved communities including rural India	Placing employees in these locations for a period of time
FedEx	United Way, National Safe Kids Campaign, and American Red Cross	Participating in United Way "Day of Caring"	Time off from work to participate in "Day of Caring"
Fannie Mae	Making home ownership more possible	Participating in the foundation's "Help the Homeless" program	One-on-one match program Paid leave
Shell	Environmental protection	Weed and litter removal in coastal regions; studying waterbirds	Organizing activities and funding employees to participate in specific programs
AT&T Wireless	Red Cross and other charities selected by employees	Teams volunteer for a specific community group	Awarding grants to charities where employees volunteer
Timberland	Local community organizations	Participation in high impact community service events	Up to 40 hours of paid community service time per calendar year
IBM	Mentoring school-age youth	One-on-one mentoring of students by IBM volunteer employees	Providing software that supports secure online mentoring
Levi Strauss & Co.	HIV/AIDS	Volunteering in food delivery programs, outreach, and education	Engaging employees throughout the company

Example: Ford Motor Company

Henry Ford was said to have had a strong sense of community and demonstrated this commitment early on through such efforts as helping to build subdivisions in Detroit to provide affordable housing for thousands of workers, and establishing Detroit's first large general hospital. Today there are thriving examples that this culture for community goodwill is still alive, offering salaried employees 16 hours of paid community service a year.[5]

Ford Motor Company has been a partner and supporter for Habitat for Humanity, especially in Detroit, for many years. Over 1,000 Ford employees, for example, volunteered their time between the year 2000 and 2002 to help build Habitat homes in Detroit, providing families in need with a safe, affordable place to live. Appreciation for Ford's volunteer efforts was clear in a statement from the executive director for Habitat for Humanity Detroit: "Ford has been one of the reasons that Habitat for Humanity Detroit has been successful in building homes and revitalizing neighborhoods. It's a great opportunity for Ford employees to spend time with each other outside of work while working for a good cause and giving back to the Detroit community."[6] The company also has a philanthropic initiative with Habitat for Humanity Detroit, with a commitment of $125,000 for the organization made in 2000.[7]

And for the 10th consecutive year, Ford participated in an initiative that uses greeting cards to support abandoned and neglected children (see Figure 7.1). This unique program involved company employees collecting old and used greeting cards that are then sent to children at St. Judes Ranch for Children in Nevada, who then use them to make new cards that are sold to support the nonprofit. The children at the ranch earn money as well for every new card they make. In February 2003, 350,000 cards (two tons) were sent to St. Judes kids. A Ford company executive commended the effort: "Our six dozen Ford Motor Company volunteers should be proud. This was another successful year and their effort not only helps Mother Nature with tons of material diverted from the waste stream but also helps deserving young people from St. Judes as well."[8]

Figure 7.1 Ford volunteers collected used and old greeting cards for children at St. Jude's Ranch, who resold them to earn money. (Reprinted courtesy of Ford and St. Jude's Ranch.)

Contributing to Business Goals

Many companies like Hewlett-Packard believe corporate social initiatives can be both a good business investment as well as a social one. They believe that by assisting communities in realizing the potential that technology can have on economic development, for example, they can also build new markets for the company. In the following example, Hewlett-Packard's chairman and CEO, Carly Fiorina, presents perspectives that counter many of those presented in Milton Friedman's seminal work 33 years ago entitled *The Social Responsibility of Business Is to Increase Its Profits*. He argued that business leaders had "no responsibilities other than to maximize profits for the shareholders." To this Ms. Fiorina commented in a recent keynote address, described in the next example, "The idea that companies have no responsibility to the communities in which they operate, that in other words, we operate in a vacuum, or the idea that our actions have no consequences on the world around us is short-sighted at best, and it is certainly not sustainable for very long."[9]

Example: Hewlett-Packard

Hewlett-Packard (HP) has a vision of a future where everyone in the world has access to the social, educational, and economic opportunities offered in this digital age. In 2002 alone, HP invested more than $62 million in resources worldwide to forward this vision. Part of this investment came in the form of employee volunteer efforts in underserved communities.[10]

Carly Fiorina, chairman and CEO of HP, articulated her views on corporate responsibility in a keynote address delivered at the Business for Social Responsibility Annual Conference in November of 2003. She said that they have found, when they get involved in communities and "back it with real resources—not just money and time, but more importantly, HP people and products—we become a catalyst for change because governments and NGOs and community leaders and even other companies are then more willing to make a commitment themselves."[11]

She cited an inspiring example of where an investment of people on the ground, working on community development projects, is also expected to bring benefits to the company. A program called "i-community" places employees for up to three years to work side-by-side with citizens in underserved communities, helping them achieve their goals by contributing management expertise and training on use of technology (see Figure 7.2). In one rural, impoverished community in India, when employees observed that electricity was unreliable (to say the least), a new product idea was conceived: a solar-powered printer and a solar-powered digital camera. The idea then became a business for the community—a solar-powered digital photography studio. In India every citizen is required to have a national ID card with their photograph on it, and people in rural communities needed to travel into a city to have their photograph taken. The photography studio became a new venture for several women entrepreneurs who traveled from village to village creating identity cards. "What happened in that process?" asked Carly. "We've developed a new product; we've helped create new businesses that are sustainable; and we've also created partners and customers for life. Yes, it's a small start, but imagine the potential of something like digital photography in a market like India."[12]

The company's appreciation and recognition for employees was apparent in one of her final comments. "I guess the last thing I would say is that the people of HP represent all that is good and true about this company—including the power of our aspiration and the power of our contribution. And when

Figure 7.2 HP's model for its "i-community" approach underscores a belief that business investment in association with employee volunteerism can lead to a positive social impact through the development of new technology and creation of new markets. (Courtesy, Emerging Market Solutions, Hewlett-Packard Development Company, L.P.)

you have 140,000 employees, they also, by their own personal example, can have a big impact, and I know they do."[13]

Increasing Employee Satisfaction and Motivation

As research highlighted in Chapter 1 indicated, a company's reputation
for community involvement, including support for employees to volunteer for causes, can influence their morale, as well as their choices about
where they work. After 9/11, for example, a Cone/Roper's study indicated
that 76 percent of respondents said a company's commitment to causes
was important when deciding where to work.[14] And in their 2002 Citizenship Study with a national cross section of 1,040 adults, 80 percent of
respondents say they would be likely to refuse to work at a company if
they were to find out about negative corporate citizenship practices.[15]

Example: FedEx

Every year, thousands of FedEx employees volunteer their talent,
resources and time (about 200,000 hours' worth) to support
charitable organizations with which FedEx has an established
strategic relationship, including United Way, March of Dimes,
National SAFE KIDS Campaign, and American Red Cross.

Of special interest in this example is the impact that this involvement has on employee volunteers (see Figure 7.3). FedEx
features their inspiring personal stories on their web site, with a
few highlighted below:[16]

- A manager in Buffalo was moved to see the difference his
  company made on their United Way "Day of Caring" event
  in an impoverished community in his area. "When word
  got back to officials of the City of Buffalo about FedEx
  Trade Networks descending on the area with an army of
  volunteers to clean it up, they sent street-cleaning trucks
  and a dump truck to help. Generally, the city neglects this
  impoverished area; the trucks were there as a result of
  FedEx involvement. We truly made a huge impact on that
  area of the neighborhood that day. It was great to see."
- A senior service agent for FedEx Express who participated
  as a "Loaned Executive" in the United Way campaign is

passionate about her experience and promotes volunteerism to other employees as well. "It's about getting them in touch with something they didn't know existed. It changes you, there is no way around that; no way to ever say I'll walk away being the same person I was walking in here. There's just not."

- An operations manager in Spokane, Washington, volunteers to support the local "SAFE KIDS Walk This Way" program. She has encouraged more than 25 fellow employees to do the same. "In some small way, if we can help with the traffic issues it's worth it. If we can save one child, it's worth it."

In recognition of their 2002 campaign, United Way of America honored FedEx with the Spirit of America Award, its highest tribute for corporate community involvement, recognizing the company's corporate giving, in-kind service, and volunteerism.[17]

Figure 7.3 FedEx employees support a "SAFE KIDS Walk This Way" program, an initiative of the National Safe Kids Campaign. (© 1995–2004 FedEx. All Rights Reserved.) (Reprinted courtesy of FedEx.)

Figure 7.4   Logo for Fannie Mae Foundation's "We Are Volunteer Employees" program. (Reprinted by permission of the Fannie Mae Foundation.)

Supporting Other Corporate Initiatives

Supporting employees to volunteer for causes that are a strategic focus for the organization can leverage the contributions already being made through other initiatives such as cause promotions and philanthropy. In the following example, a corporation has had a long-standing philanthropic focus for contributing to affordable housing and home ownership. It makes real the concept and synergy created when yet one more initiative is integrated into the current strategic mix.

Example: Fannie Mae

In 1990, the Fannie Mae Foundation established a formal program to support volunteer efforts of employees of both Fannie Mae and the Fannie Mae Foundation. The program, called WAVE (We Are Volunteer Employees), was developed to assist employees in finding meaningful volunteer opportunities, provide support for participation in volunteer activities, and recognize employees for their accomplishments (see Figure 7.4). In 2002, more than 1,400 employee volunteers contributed more than 41,000 hours of service in the communities where they work and live.[18]

Support includes a one-on-one match program that helps employees find volunteer opportunities in the community that appeal most to them. A paid release time program offers employees 10 hours of paid leave per month to participate in these activities. Teamwork is built through community projects that involve employees working together, and a formalized recognition programs thanks employees for their efforts through gifts and awards.[19]

Many volunteer efforts support the foundation's commitment to improving affordable housing and home ownership opportunities, especially for low-income and minority families. One program, called "Help the Homeless," started out as a relatively modest, employee-driven walk in a local park to raise money for nonprofit organizations working with local homeless citizens. "The year was 1988. Fannie Mae employees, walking to and from their office in an affluent Washington, D.C., neighborhood, encountered a distressing sight. Increasing numbers of homeless men and women walked the streets. They asked for money; they looked for shelter. Often, homeless children trailed behind a parent. This new reality hit hard—especially for people who devoted their professional lives to expanding home ownership. Concern soon became action. With the blessing of then–Fannie Mae Chairman David O. Maxwell, Fannie Mae employees organized a charity walk to raise money for the overwhelmed nonprofit organizations working with local homeless citizens."[20]

In their first year, walkers raised $90,000 for organizations serving the homeless. To capitalize on the momentum, Fannie Mae employees then contacted local businesses to enlist corporate support for future walks. For 16 consecutive years, the Fannie Mae Foundation has engaged people in the Washington metropolitan area in this grassroots initiative. By 2003, the event had grown to involve more than 100,000 children and adult participants and generated $6.5 million. The total raised by the Fannie Mae Foundation's "Help the Homeless" program now stands at more than $40 million.[21]

In 1995, the WAVE program was recognized by the Points of Light Foundation with an Award for Excellence in Corporate Community Service.[22]

Figure 7.5   Logo for a joint effort between Conservation Volunteers Australia and Shell Australia to protect Australia's coastal regions. (Reprinted courtesy of Shell Coastal Volunteers.)

Enhancing Corporate Image

Many companies are discovering that strong reputations for corporate social responsibility can be enhanced, even won, through the generous actions of employees whose volunteer efforts bring them face-to-face with cause partners, citizens, and neighbors in need. Among all the corporate social initiatives, perhaps this one has the most ability to generate feelings of goodwill among employees and members of the community at the same time.

Example: Shell Australia

Perhaps not surprisingly, volunteer projects that contribute to the environment appear to be increasingly popular for companies having a direct impact on the natural environment, ones such as Shell Australia. Although "Shell Volunteers," a program that began in Australia in 1990, encourages employees to provide their time, energy, and skills to areas that interest them most (e.g., taking young children on outings, planting native trees and grasses, collecting gifts), a coordinator of the program notes that involvement in environmental projects has increased. And this focus is good for the company as well, as she commented: "Shell's involvement in volunteering, while largely generated by the employees, is in line with the company's commitment to sustainable development."[23]

A particular program called "Shell Coastal Volunteers" is a joint effort between Conservation Volunteers Australia and Shell Australia to help confront serious threats to Australia's coastal regions including pollution, marine biodiversity, and habitat degradation (see Figure 7.5). Volunteers work with community groups, government agencies, local governments, and other land managers to provide a range of practical conservation activities including weed and litter removal. In the past three years, there were more than 13,000 volunteer days, 80 kilometers of beach cleaned, more than 490,000 square miles of area revegetated, and 220 kilograms of seed collected. The plan, as reported in 2003, will include undertaking 100 urban and regional projects per year and contributing more than $2 million worth of assistance.[24]

Shell also has a partnership with Earthwatch Australia and funds a number of its employees to participate in environmental research projects, such as studying waterbirds.

Volunteer efforts provide a powerful visible symbol of commitment, as reflected in a statement that Shell Australia's chairman and CEO wrote in *Business/Higher Education Round Table News* in November 2000: "Nothing is likely to galvanize community protest and action against a company more than if it appears to hold 'double-standards.' . . . You cannot say that you take corporate social responsibility seriously and then not engage effectively with the communities in which you operate."[25]

Providing Opportunities to Showcase Products and Services

Philanthropic initiatives that include donations of products and services can be enhanced through volunteer efforts that provide additional opportunities to associate products with corporate community goodwill. This was noted in the example in Chapter 3 where Lysol volunteers showed up at Great American Cleanup events with supplies of their products, increasing in some cases awareness of the range of product in their lineup. In the following example, we see similar opportunities for AT&T Wireless through their community volunteer efforts.

Example: AT&T Wireless

No doubt the vision statement for AT&T Wireless has been guiding their business as well corporate social responsibility efforts: "We envision a world where wireless seamlessly and simply connects us to the people, information, and things we care about most, enabling us to be simultaneously connected and free."[26]

In a press release in 2002, the American Red Cross announced an expanded relationship with AT&T Wireless, a longtime supporter of the organization's disaster relief efforts. Enhanced activities included technical assistance, corporate volunteerism, and outreach to over 1,000 Red Cross chapters around the nation. Included in this expansion was a donation of phones to chapters across the country and a commitment of AT&T Wireless employee volunteer service to local community groups, among them the Red Cross. A senior vice president for the American Red Cross described the benefit of the contribution: "The AT&T Wireless relationship enables Red Cross workers to communicate with each other during times of disaster, ensuring that families can be reconnected with each other, for example. We appreciate the services that AT&T Wireless provides to our communities and we are proud that they are committed to training their own employees in lifesaving CPR and first aid skills."[27]

The company launched a new program, "VolunteerConnection," in November, 2003, to encourage employee volunteerism by awarding grants to nonprofit organizations where employees invest their volunteer time (see logo in Figure 7.6). VolunteerConnection operates in conjunction with VolunteerMatch, an ongoing program that links employees to nonprofit groups in need of support and tracks employee volunteer hours. VolunteerMatch maintains a nationwide database that enables employees to log on to their company's intranet, enter their zipcode and volunteer interests, and a search produces a listing of available opportunities in their community. Employees can then link to the opportunity they are interested in pursuing.

POTENTIAL CONCERNS

Perhaps unique benefits, as just described, bring unique concerns as well. Concerns with types and amounts of corporate support for employee vol-

Figure 7.6 Logo for 2003 AT&T Wireless community volunteer programs. (Reprinted courtesy of AT&T Wireless.)

unteering are real and expressed frequently with challenges and questions such as the following:

- *This can get expensive.* If, for example, a company with 300,000 employees offers 24 hours of paid time off per year for volunteering, and 50 percent of employees participate, the company is donating 3.6 million hours of potential productivity. It may be a complex exercise to evaluate this against options for giving grants and direct cash contributions, and it may look riskier than just encouraging volunteer efforts on the employees' own time.

- *With so many employees, efforts may get spread over so many issues that we don't really make a social impact.* This may be of special concern, for example, in corporations that encourage employees to volunteer in the community but do not offer organized programs or matching services that tend to create more clusters of volunteers for specific causes.

- *Similarly, when efforts among employees are dispersed throughout the market, even the globe, how do we realize business benefits for the company as well?* If opportunities for economic as well as social gain from philanthropic initiatives are real, how do we coordinate widespread and diverse efforts so that they are visible and connected with the company and our brand?

- *Being able to track efforts and outcomes for this initiative can be the most difficult of all.* This, once more, can be especially true for global companies with volunteers in diverse markets, and especially a concern when tracking and reporting systems are not centralized and automated.

- *It is particularly tough with this initiative to find the balance between publicizing our efforts and flaunting them.* Perhaps there is something unique about the personal nature of volunteer efforts that makes communications regarding contributions more uncomfortable than for other kinds of initiatives. This then dampens enthusiasm, perhaps even investments, when a company wants this effort to help build the brand or enhance corporate reputation as well.

KEYS TO SUCCESS

Themes for keys to successful corporate volunteer initiatives are familiar. Overall, executives and managers sharing their recommendations tend to stress developing volunteer programs that match real social, economic, and environmental issues with the passion of employees and business needs of the company. They highlight advantages of also connecting volunteer efforts with the company's broader corporate citizenship strategy and to other current corporate social initiatives, such as cause promotions and philanthropic efforts. They stress the need to get management support up-front for long-term commitments and to choose strong community partners. They seem to agree that employees should be supported and recognized for their efforts and that tracking and quantifying impact is ideal. And they disagree somewhat on if, how, and when these efforts should be made known and publicized. The common ground seems to be that the best visibility is when the messengers are recipients of volunteer efforts sharing the difference that was made, or are the employees themselves telling personal stories of inspiration and satisfaction with their experiences.

In the following cases illustrating select application of these themes, executives from Timberland, IBM, and Levi Strauss & Co. share specific examples of corporate support for community volunteering and offer their perspectives on keys to success and principles to guide decision making.

Timberland

For every year since the list began, Timberland has been named one of *Fortune* magazine's "Best Companies to Work For." This award is one of many the company has received, in part, due to the unique employee benefits offered through a bold program to support employee and citizen volunteering. A corporate contributions executive at Timberland shares the program's background, as well as the company's challenges and recommended guidelines for developing a winning program.

The "Path of Service™" program began with a simple request in 1989. A small program called City Year needed 50 pairs of boots for participants in its "urban Peace Corps." Timberland donated the boots, and a relationship was born. Instead of a thank you note, City Year gave Timberland a service day for employees to serve alongside corps members in the community. The day was so meaningful, and the implications were so clear. We realized a similar experience could have an enormous effect on all Timberland employees. The Path of Service employee volunteer program was born, a program that gives full-time employees 40 hours of paid community service time per year; part-time employees get 16 hours per year.

Path of Service (POS) is the cornerstone of Timberland's community investment as our employees have contributed over 200,000 total hours of service around the world. That commitment has proudly benefited over 200 community organizations in 13 countries, 26 states, and 73 cities. Departments and cross-functional teams utilize their service hours to build team and morale, improve communication skills, and discover unique and hidden assets of colleagues. Individuals utilize their hours to develop a skill, find motivation, and spend valuable time in the community (see Figure 7.7). Nearly 95 percent of our employees use their POS benefit, and an overwhelming majority cite it as one of their top two Timberland benefits.

Most recently, we have launched an initiative called the "Community Builders Tour," which is a mobile service caravan visiting select markets. In the pilot phase of this program we are partnering with select retailers to engage consumers, employees, and civic leaders in high-impact community service events tailored to the host community's needs. Rather than just telling consumers what we do, we seek to engage them in our brand experience.

We believe this program is a means to strengthen our relationships with our shareholders, customers, employees, and communities, and provides an opportunity for our employees to make their difference in the communities in which they live and work. In annual surveys, our

Figure 7.7   Timberland offers full-time employees 40 hours of paid community service time each year. (Photo courtesy of John Gillooly/PEI.)

employees rate POS and other community initiatives as key components of job satisfaction, and our key retailers are eager to join us on our expanded Community Builders Tour.

For the most part, Timberland has not chosen to highlight its community initiatives in the marketplace—both because it seems self-congratulatory and because we believe consumers become skeptical of brands that use their corporate citizenship for market advantage. External communications are limited primarily to editorial opportunities, our CEO speaking frequently on the topic, and a specialized web site distinct from our commerce site. Recently in our retail stores we have added Community Kiosks for the posting and promotion of community service events.

The program, of course, does not go without costs and challenges:

- Path of Service costs the company in terms of lost time on the job. And to make this even more challenging to evaluate, we have not been able to truly value this cost as we have lacked a sophisticated tracking system, but we are currently developing one. That said, we believe the high correlation to job satisfaction (seen in retention rates and annual survey results) more than offsets the costs.
- As we are an increasingly global brand, we are challenged to find the appropriate means for effectively translating the ethos of service into a myriad of cultures, customs, and social, and governmental frameworks.
- While other companies have pet causes, we have come to realize that our commitment is to the ethos of service itself. This means that we support a wide variety of causes in the name of helping people to discover the joy and power of giving of themselves through volunteerism. Sometimes this is messier and harder to communicate and coordinate than a focused approach.

Several principles guide the management of our programs, and may be helpful to others as well:

- Choose what feels most authentic to the business or brand. Anything that is forced or undertaken merely as a marketing initiative will fail with stakeholders.

- See corporate citizenship investments as a means of building equity rather than short-term gain.
- Make corporate citizenship a part of the core business strategy, and make sure it is widely communicated and adopted.
- Consider the needs and aspirations of all stakeholders.
- Giving money away is regarded less favorably than investing time. Combining the two strategically has worked best.
- Choose community partners who are willing to work in partnership, those that have mutual goals.
- Be cautious about flaunting corporate citizenship in the marketplace. It can backlash if perceived to be disingenuous.
- Be prepared to stand by these articulated principles during difficult times. That will be when stakeholders will be measuring integrity.[28]

IBM

In the following case, Stanley S. Litow, vice president for corporate community relations and president of the IBM International Foundation, shares the On Demand Community, an innovative employee volunteer program that IBM believes has effectively leveraged its existing corporate social initiatives, as well as invigorated its workforce. IBM has developed a reputation for state-of-the-art community programs that capitalize on IBM know-how and expertise. Their award-winning programs feature world-class technology solutions to address social problems and are characterized by buy-in and support of community leaders; broad promotion of programs to its employee population; adjustment of technology solutions as necessary to make them more immediately responsive; linkage of programs to other corporate activities; and monitoring and evaluation plans that have helped IBM determine program effectiveness and improvements that needed to be made.

IBM's commitment to corporate citizenship extends back to when Thomas J. Watson Sr. founded the corporation in 1914. His vision for the corporation explicitly staked IBM's reputation not only on technical leadership, but on community leadership as well. He knew that the future of IBM was inextricably linked to the communities in which it did business. No company could be successful if it was part of an unsuccessful community.

Just as IBM has led a remarkable technological revolution, we also have been at the forefront of corporate citizenship. IBM's commitment to social responsibility has stood the test of time; in our nearly 90 years of operations and community involvement, our work has changed and evolved with the changing business environment.

Today, IBM is one of the largest corporate contributors of cash, equipment, and people to nonprofit organizations and educational institutions across the U.S. and around the world. In more than 160 countries, we help people use information technology to improve the quality of life for themselves and others.

In November 2003, IBM launched the On Demand Community (see Figure 7.8). Through this unprecedented program, IBM is contributing technology and expertise to help develop and sustain strong communities where employees live and work. This is accomplished by building on the success of IBM's award-winning community relations programs, such as Reinventing Education, KidSmart, MentorPlace, and TryScience. The new volunteer offerings built around these programs plus other brand-new solutions are aimed specifically at meeting the changing needs of communities worldwide. They provide both IBM technology and talent to schools, not-for-profit organizations, and economic development groups, focusing on communities threatened by the "digital divide"—the discrepancy between those who have the skills and tools to use information technology and those who don't.

On Demand Community is a coordinated effort allowing IBM volunteers to provide Web-based solutions and assistance to schools and service agencies. A vast array of information and resources has been combined in a way that will help make employees better volunteers, able to offer valuable assistance to school and organizations.

For the first time, employees everywhere are able to go online on the IBM Intranet for the full resources of the company in order to

Figure 7.8 IBM's On Demand Community supports IBM volunteers to provide Web-based solutions and assistance to schools and service agencies. (Reprinted courtesy of IBM.)

serve their communities. This approach to community service plays to IBM's strengths in innovation, expertise, reliability, and trust.

On Demand Community has expanded to include over 15,000 registered volunteers in 55 countries. The ongoing addition of new volunteer solutions will expand the ways we can make a difference.

We've learned some important lessons from this initiative. We learned that the IBM volunteering spirit and support for K-12 runs very deep and strong. We also found that more IBMers than we anticipated, especially outside the United States, were looking for just such an initiative. And importantly, we solidified strong views that have helped establish guidelines for our future efforts. In general terms, these are:

- *Make sure there is a connection between the effort and the core of the company.* In our case we endeavored to connect our employees to programs they were already broadly aware of, had significant interest in, and were able to partner with.
- *Make sure you don't compromise the content of what you do.* Keep your eye on the most valued customer, which must be the community in which you are engaged. Provide your employees with the tools and resources they need to be successful, and be prepared to deliver measurable returns calculated in a definable impact on education or on society.
- *Include promotional strategies.* To reach employees and the community you are serving, you must publicize your programs both internally and externally and capitalize on efforts to recognize and share employee contributions and effective practices whenever possible.
- *Develop and implement measurement systems.* Independent process and outcome evaluations must be in place to determine what is working and what is not, and the type of resource investments that will help you to be successful.
- *Conduct due diligence, learn from history but always innovate.* It is critical to learn from past efforts by companies and foundations. Use available research literature to help design program elements. Don't just modify and adapt as you go along, but in everything you do, think bigger and better. Make sure that promising ideas are nurtured and foster a culture of innovation so that programs and people reach higher.[29]

Levi Strauss & Co.

In the following case, the director of community affairs for Levi Strauss & Co. describes the rationale behind their company's commitment for two decades to one of the major social problems of our time. This depth of experience has built a strong set of principles he shares with others involved in engaging employee volunteer support.

Twenty years ago, a group of Levi Strauss & Co. (LS&Co.) employees sought support to distribute leaflets about a mysterious new disease that was devastating the gay community in San Francisco. The employees, however, were not sure if company policy allowed them to circulate such information and were also concerned that distributing these leaflets might lead to misperceptions about their own health. Senior executives of LS&Co. not only endorsed the idea to distribute materials, but joined staff members and handed them out in front of the company's headquarters to show their support for this effort to educate their fellow employees.

Twenty years ago, given the fear and stigma surrounding HIV/AIDS, supporting prevention efforts was not seen as an opportunity to burnish the company's image or as a clever way to increase sales of pants. Even today, questions are routinely asked as to why LS&Co. is so involved in the issue. Providing resources to community organizations was initiated in response to the immediate and growing threat that AIDS posed to the San Francisco community—including many Levi Strauss & Co. employees who worked at the company's headquarters. Doing the right thing is a strong part of the company's 150-year history. Levi Strauss & Co. did not ignore this crisis.

Several efforts of Levi Strauss & Co. and the Levi Strauss Foundation support HIV/AIDS prevention, including the following:

- Providing financial contributions to community-based organizations in the United States and around the world where the company has offices and/or production facilities.
- Offering employees release time to volunteer at local HIV/AIDS service organizations.
- Supporting employee-led Community Involvement Teams, where employee volunteers direct donations to local AIDS nonprofit organizations.

In cash contributions alone, Levi Strauss & Co. and the Levi Strauss Foundation have contributed over $26 million to fight the spread of HIV/AIDS since the early 1980s. In addition, LS&Co. employees have given thousands of hours through AIDS Walks, food delivery programs, and outreach and education projects (see Figure 7.9). These activities have contributed to a heightened awareness about the cause of the disease and ways to prevent it, and the stigma associated with the disease is diminishing, albeit slowly.

Although LS&Co. has enjoyed a good reputation for its progressive social responsibility practices, selling more clothing is not the motivation behind working in the community. Corporate social responsibility is consistent with the company's values, which are empathy, originality, integrity, and courage.

Prospective employees report being drawn to the company, in part, by its commitment to important social issues, such as HIV/AIDS. Although the public knows of its efforts through the

Figure 7.9   Levi Strauss & Co. staff members participating in the 2003 San Francisco AIDSWALK. (Reprinted courtesy of Levi Strauss & Co.)

Levi Strauss Foundation's published "Charitable Giving Guide-lines" and Levi Strauss & Co.'s web site, we let organizations that receive our support speak to the value of the company's contributions.

We consider several factors important to the selection and implementation of corporate social initiatives, especially when considering employee participation and volunteer efforts.

When selecting a social issue to support . . .

- Choose issues and organizations that are relevant to the lives of the company's employees.
- Support causes and projects that improve the social and economic environment in the locations where the company has its physical facilities.
- Don't be afraid to tackle complex social issues that may, at first, frighten people.
- Ensure that the projects, issues, and organizations supported reflect the values of the company and have the support of senior leadership involvement, including the CEO and chairman of the board.

When developing a program plan . . .

- Engage employees throughout the company in the effort—employees at the top, middle, and bottom.
- Develop partnership between Community Affairs and brand managers.
- Collaborate with community organizations that are behind the most innovative responses to the social issue.

For successful implementation . . .

- Stay committed to the issue for an extended period of time instead of jumping around between different causes. Positive change takes time, requiring a long-term investment. Be patient. Many of the benefits of supporting worthy social causes are not immediately evident.
- Provide flexible support for community partners, letting the organizations use the money for their most urgent needs.
- Let the organizations receiving support from the company tell the story of the company's involvement.

- Use all of the company's resources, including cash contributions, employee volunteering, and executive service on nonprofit boards, to support a cause or an organization.
- Use the most creative people on your team to develop truly inspirational campaigns.[30]

WHEN TO CONSIDER EMPLOYEE VOLUNTEERING

The reality is that most large corporations and many smaller ones encourage their employees to volunteer in the community. The dilemma facing most executives centers more around decisions regarding levels and types of support to provide and whether to promote specific volunteer opportunities or to let employees feel free to follow their interests. Increased and more formalized support for employees and promotion of focused causes are best considered under the following circumstances:

- *When current social initiatives would benefit from a volunteer component* (e.g., home supply retail store promoting natural gardening offers employees an opportunity to help build a native plant garden in a local community park).

- *When a group of employees express an interest in a specific cause* that has strong connections with business and corporate citizenship goals (e.g., employees of an outdoor recreational equipment company want to volunteer to help prevent forest fires by removing hazardous brush in threatened mountains).

- *When a community need emerges*, especially an unexpected one that is a good match for the resources and skills of a workforce (e.g., the example presented earlier where American Express helped small businesses in lower Manhattan).

- *When technological advances make it easier to match* employees to volunteer opportunities.

- *When a strong community organization approaches a business* for support, represents an issue of interest to employees, and has a natural connection to strategic corporate citizenship and business goals.

- *When a volunteer effort might open new markets or provide opportunities* for new product development and research (e.g., as presented in the example of Hewlett-Packard's involvement in underserved communities).

DEVELOPING COMMUNITY VOLUNTEERING PROGRAMS

Assuming a company has an interest in developing a formal volunteer program and has decided to go beyond informal communications that simply encourage the workforce to be involved in the community, the following six steps can then be taken.

1. Develop guidelines for employee involvement.

Decisions will be made regarding whether employees will be encouraged to volunteer for causes that (only) interest them, or whether one or more specific charities or cause efforts will be promoted. Most commonly, the decision is to adopt a combination of these options. If it is determined that specific causes will be promoted, the selection of causes is best made by referencing the company's mission statement, overall corporate citizenship focus, current social initiatives, employee interests, existing community partners, and pressing needs in the community.

2. Determine types and levels of employee support.

Program options include providing monetary incentives, such as paid time off and offering cash grants to charities based on the number of volunteer hours spent by individual employees or teams of employees. Nonmonetary support may include organizing teams of employees to participate in specific events, and offering software programs that match employee interests with a database of local volunteer opportunities.

3. Develop an internal communications plan.

Spreading the word to employees at all levels and locations can be critical to fulfillment of a successful companywide volunteer program. Traditional communication planning elements are appropriate, including developing a program name and graphic identity along with key messages that communicate the company's commitment, the need for community support, and the desire for employee participation as is evident in the "VoluntEARS" program at Disney (see Figure 7.10).

4. Develop a recognition plan.

Recognition programs may include components such as mentions of volunteer efforts in internal employee communications like intranet and newsletters, and recognition at departmental and company meetings. Some companies also brand this component of the program (e.g., Fannie Mae Foundation's Catch the WAVE® (We Are Volunteer Employees)).[31]

Figure 7.10   Disney VoluntEARS created a special "Sports Goofy" mural for a charity that builds playgrounds for children with disabilities. (© Disney Enterprises, Inc.) (Reprinted courtesy of Disney Enterprises, Inc.)

5. Develop an external communications plan.

As a first step, communication objectives should be determined, addressing the question of what these communications are intended to support. Is the purpose simply to disclose the corporation's community involvement, leading to targeted communications in annual reports, for example? Or are the communications also intended to strengthen a corporation's reputation in the community, which carries implications for broader media efforts? Perhaps the purpose is to support employee recruitment or to provide an additional venue for employee recognition. Once these objectives are clear and agreed upon, action plans follow.

6. Develop a plan for tracking and assessment.

Finally, a plan and system for tracking employee hours and recipients of volunteer efforts must be established. Additionally, measures should be agreed upon for assessing communication objectives established in the communications plan.

SUMMARY

Volunteering in the community, and corporate support to do this, is viewed by many as one of the most genuine and satisfying of all forms of corporate social involvement. Community volunteering as an initiative is clearly distinct from others, and yet we see trends towards integrating these efforts as an additional component of existing corporate social initiatives.

Support for volunteering ranges from programs that just encourage employees to give back to their communities to ones that have formalized written guidelines and make a significant financial investment over a long period of time.

Volunteer programs are said to have contributed to building strong and enduring relationships with local communities, attracting and retaining satisfied and motivated employees, augmenting and leveraging current involvement and investments in social initiatives, contributing to business goals, enhancing corporate image, and providing opportunities to showcase products and services.

Concerns with developing and managing these programs are real, including concerns with costs, having a meaningful social impact, realizing business benefits (appropriately), and tracking and measuring outcomes.

Many keys to success are familiar: Match real social, economic, and environmental issues with the passion of employees and business needs of the company; connect volunteer efforts with the company's broader corporate citizenship strategy and other current corporate social initiatives; gain management support up-front for long-term commitments; choose strong community partners; support and recognize employees for their efforts; and establish systems for tracking and measurement. Though there is debate regarding the extent and nature of external communications, it seems that the best visibility is when messengers are either the recipients of volunteer efforts or employees sharing personal, inspirational stories.

Increased efforts for employee volunteer programs should be considered when current social initiatives would benefit from a volunteer component; a group of employees express an interest in a specific cause; a community need emerges; technological advances make it easier to match employees to volunteer opportunities; a strong community organization approaches a business for support; or when a volunteer effort might open new markets or support new product development. Enhanced programs will benefit from strategic plans that call for developing guidelines, determining types and levels of employee support; and developing plans for internal communications, a recognition plan, external communications, and tracking and assessment.

Socially Responsible Business Practices: Discretionary Business Practices and Investments to Support Causes

Motorola envisions a future in which our factories are accident-free, create zero waste, emit only benign emissions, use energy in highly efficient ways, and use our discarded products as feed for new products. . . . We are on the threshold of a new era in which all of us—corporations, individuals, government, and other organizations—can join together to cooperate on the healing of our earth. We can no longer afford to view ourselves as separate. We are all interconnected and part of the whole and what we do matters and affects the whole. When we harm the environment, we harm ourselves. Our challenge for the new millennium is to learn how to live in harmony with our earth.[1]

—Motorola's Environmental
Vision Statement

Socially responsible business practices are where the corporation adapts and conducts discretionary business practices and investments that support social causes to improve community well-being and protect the environment. Key distinctions include a focus on activities that are *discretionary*, not those that are mandated by laws or regulatory agencies or are simply expected, as with meeting moral or ethical standards. *Community* is interpreted broadly to include employees of the corporation, suppliers, distributors, nonprofit and public sector partners, as well as members of the general public. And *well-being* can refer to health and safety, as well as psychological and emotional needs.

Over the last decade there has been an apparent shift from adopting more responsible business practices as a result of regulatory citations, consumer complaints, and special interest group pressures, to proactive research exploring corporate solutions to social problems and incorporating new business practices that will support these issues (e.g., Kraft deciding in 2003 to revise several business practices to help address the continued rise in obesity in our nation).

Why this shift?

- There is increasing evidence being documented and shared demonstrating that socially responsible business practices can actually increase profits (e.g., Chiquita quantifying a $5 million annual savings by using fewer agrichemicals) and has the potential for increasing revenues (e.g., what McDonald's is most likely hoping as a result of a new adult "Happy Meal" that includes a salad, an exercise booklet, and a pedometer).

- In our global marketplace, consumers have more options and can make choices based on criteria beyond product, price, and distribution channels. Research presented in Chapter 1 emphasized that consumers are also basing their purchase decisions on reputation for fair and sustainable business practices and perceptions of commitment to the community's welfare.

- Investors and other stakeholders may also be the driving force, with increased public scrutiny and use of more sophisticated pressure tactics, including use of the technology and power of the Internet (e.g., an e-mail broadcast sent from an antitobacco group, letting consumers know that a major retailer had not accepted their requests to carry pocket cigarette butt containers).

- An interest in increased worker productivity and retention has turned corporate heads toward ways to improve employee satisfaction and well-being (e.g., Coca-Cola bottlers in South Africa launching an HIV/AIDS prevention program in the workplace).

- Technology and increased third-party reporting has given increased visibility and coverage of corporate activities, especially when things go wrong, as with current corporate scandals that have made the public more suspicious of business, creating the need for businesses to put a positive shine on their activities. This is even more critical today, with instant access to 24-hour news channels such as CNN, online news articles, and e-mail alerts (e.g., recent publicity that a major communications firm had violated the "do-not-call list" regulation, and announcement of potential associated fines).

- The bar for full disclosure appears to have been raised, moving potential customers from a "consumer beware" attitude to an expectation that they will be fully informed regarding practices, including product content, sources of raw materials, and manufacturing processes (e.g., Kraft's initiative to label smaller snack and beverage packages with the nutrition content of the entire package).[2]

TYPICAL SOCIALLY RESPONSIBLE BUSINESS PRACTICES

As might be expected, most initiatives related to socially responsible practices relate to altering internal procedures and policies, such as those related to product offerings, facility design, manufacturing, assembly, and employee support. An initiative can also be reflected in external reporting of consumer and investor information and demonstrated by making provisions for customer access and privacy, and can be taken into consideration when making decisions regarding hiring practices and facility and plant locations. Common activities include the following:

- *Designing facilities* to meet or exceed environmental and safety recommendations and guidelines, such as for increased energy conservation.

- *Developing process improvements*, which may include practices such as eliminating the use of hazardous waste materials, reducing the amount of chemicals used in growing crops, or eliminating the use of certain types of oils for deep-fat frying.

- *Discontinuing product offerings* that are considered harmful but not illegal (e.g., McDonald's discontinuing their supersize portions of french fries).

- *Selecting suppliers* based on their willingness to adopt or maintain sustainable environmental practices, and supporting and rewarding their efforts.

- *Choosing manufacturing and packaging materials* that are the most environmentally friendly, taking into consideration goals for waste reduction, use of renewable resources, and elimination of toxic emissions.

- *Providing full disclosure* of product materials and their origins and potential hazards, even going the extra mile with helpful information (e.g., including on product packaging the amount of physical exercise needed to burn the calories and fat contained in the candy bar, or the number of pounds of pollutants that will be generated from a gas mower).

- *Developing programs to support employee well-being*, such as workplace exercise facilities, on-site day care, and Employee Assistance Programs for those with drug-related additions.

- *Measuring, tracking, and reporting* of accountable goals and actions, including the bad news, as well as the good.

- *Establishing guidelines for marketing to children* to ensure responsible communications and appropriate distribution channels (e.g., not selling products online to children ages 18 and under).

- *Providing increased access for disabled populations* using technology such as assisted listening devices, voice recognition mechanisms, and alternate print formats.

- *Protecting privacy of consumer information*, an area of increasing concern with the sophisticated data collection, recognition, and tracking of individuals and their movements, especially via the Internet (e.g., an online retailer allowing the customer to purchase products without providing demographic profile information).

- *Making decisions regarding plant, outsourcing, and retail locations*, recognizing the economic impact of these decisions on communities.

As represented in Table 8.1, although a wide range of industries participate in incorporating responsible business practices, the field appears to be dominated by those in the manufacturing, technology, and agricultural industry categories, where more decisions are made regarding supply chains, raw material, operational procedures, and employee safety. Those involved in proposing and developing socially responsible business practices most often include operation, facility, corporate social responsibility, and other senior managers, and to some extent marketing and strategic planners. Communications regarding the adoption of socially responsible business practices are most often aimed at regulatory agencies, investors, customers, and special interest groups. Although most often the corporation develops and implements practices on its own, it may also do this in partnership with public agencies, nonprofit organizations, suppliers, and distributors.

POTENTIAL CORPORATE BENEFITS

As will be illustrated in the following examples, a wide range of benefits have been experienced by corporations that adopt and implement socially responsible business practices, and there appears to be an increasing ability to link these efforts to positive financial results.[3]

Financial benefits have been associated with decreased operating costs, monetary incentives from regulatory agencies, and increased employee productivity and retention. Marketing benefits are numerous as well, with the potential for increasing community goodwill, creating brand preference, building brand positioning, improving product quality, and increasing corporate respect. And, as with other social initiatives, these activities also provide opportunities to build relationships with external partners such as regulatory agencies, suppliers, and nonprofit organizations.

Decreases Operating Costs

In this example, adoption of discretionary business practices saved the company money, contributed to environmental sustainability, and increased energy consciousness among employees.

Table 8.1 Examples of Socially Responsible Business Practices

Corporation	Cause	Target Audiences	Sample Activities	Major Partners/Others
Cisco	Energy conservation	Facility planners and managers	Energy saving devices Plant design	Local utility EPA
Coca-Cola	HIV/AIDS	Employees with HIV and AIDS	Education policies	UNAIDS Governments Pharmaceutical suppliers
Nike	Use sustainable raw materials	Environment-oriented customers and potential customers	Policy development Changes in product content	Employee action teams
Motorola	Waste reduction	Operations managers Facility managers	Recycling Process redesign	EPA
Intel	Workplace safety	Employees in the manufacturing environment	Change in processes Communications Promotions	Suppliers
White Wave	Fuel efficiency	Consumers interested in wind power	Replacing electrical power with wind energy in manufacturing plants	EPA
Starbucks	Protecting tropical rainforests and supplier relations	Suppliers/farmers Employees	Developing guidelines Training New coffee product	Conservation International
Kraft Foods	Obesity	Customers Employees	Labeling Packaging size Education	External council of advisors
Chiquita	Responsible reporting	Employees Special interest groups	Certification standards Guiding values	Rainforest Alliance

Example: Cisco and Energy Conservation

Cisco's philosophy for new construction is to "plan it right," which means thinking about energy efficiency during the design phase. And for Cisco, this also means bringing together employees who specialize in the design side with those who have day-to-day working familiarity with facilities, leveraging each other's expertise.

Cisco used innovative energy conservation technology to design and build its San Jose headquarters campus to meet and often exceed California's energy conservation standards and to help maintain its valued site certifications. This facility was built to exceed California State's Title 24 energy standards by 15 to 20 percent. By exceeding these standards, Cisco not only lowers costs and lessens environmental impact but also takes advantage of incentives offered by its local energy supplier, Pacific Gas & Electric (PG&E). "At two of our headquarters sites, which include 4.9 million square feet of space in 25 buildings, we conserve an average of 49.5 million kilowatt-hours per year. We expect to save about $4.5 million per year in operating costs. On top of that, those energy savings qualified us for $5.7 million in PG&E rebates when construction was completed," says Sheikh Nayeem, energy manager.

The environmental benefits of Cisco's energy conservation at its San Jose headquarters are also measurable and impressive. "The 49.5 million kilowatt-hours per year that Site 4 and 5's 25 buildings save could power 5,500 homes. Those facilities are also producing almost 50 million fewer pounds of carbon dioxide per year and 14,300 fewer pounds of nitrogen oxide. That's the equivalent of removing 1,000 cars from the road," says Nayeem.[4]

Increases Community Goodwill for the Corporation

Imagine the goodwill generated across Africa from the strong commitment that Coca-Cola has made to abate the tragic epidemic that has cost more than 20 million lives across the countries of sub-Saharan Africa. In 2003 an estimated 23.1 million adults age 15–19 and 1.9 million children under the age of 15 were living with HIV/AIDS and close to 9,000 new infections occurred each day.[5]

Example: Coca-Cola and HIV/AIDS in Africa

The Coca-Cola Company believes that the business community can play an important role in battling AIDS by putting into place important initiatives and programs. Since the launch of its HIV/AIDS program in November 2000, one key strategic thrust has been to introduce model workplace programs for their 1,200 African employees.[6]

The HIV/AIDS Workplace Program includes the formation of a local AIDS Committee; free condoms for all associates; AIDS awareness and prevention material; peer counselor identification and training; employee basic HIV/AIDS training; free testing and counseling on a confidential basis, and medical coverage; confidential AIDS testing; and access to antiretroviral drugs and prophylactic treatment.

Along with this program, Coca-Cola developed an HIV/AIDS corporate policy that commits to non-discrimination on the basis of HIV/AIDS status; a right to privacy for employees; encouragement of voluntary disclosure by an HIV positive associate; voluntary testing; reasonable accommodation; encouragement of prevention practices; identification of community resources; and fostering partnerships with government and NGOs for the implementation of its HIV/AIDS programs.

In 2002, it was announced that the Coca-Cola Africa Foundation (see Figure 8.1) was expanding this commitment by working with Coca-Cola's 40 bottlers, which employ 60,000 people across Africa, to put in place similar comprehensive workplace prevention programs. The estimated costs of this initiative to the Coca-Cola Africa Foundation will be between $4 million and $5 million per year.[7]

Creates Brand Preference with Target Markets

As demonstrated in the following example, products can be utilized to showcase a company's responsible business practices, providing a reason beyond price and distribution channels to chose one brand over another,

Figure 8.1 Coca-Cola bottlers in Africa have received support from the company's foundation for comprehensive workplace HIV/AIDS prevention programs. (Reprinted courtesy of Coca-Cola Foundation.)

especially when target markets care about the focus of the particular initiative and the marketplace is relatively undifferentiated.

Example: Nike and Environmental Product Innovation

Until the late 1980s, Nike reported, its environmental commitment was to simply be in compliance with regulations and to support local nonprofit organizations. A small task force of employees then entered the picture and established an environmental steering committee.

In 1993 this group became a formal department called the Nike Environmental Action Team (N.E.A.T.). Efforts focused on compliance, recycling, and education, and included the formation of innovative new programs such as Nike's Reuse-A-Shoe program in 1994. Over the next five years the group's work further strengthened the company's commitment to finding even more ways to help reduce its environmental impact. The group's momentum evolved into the adoption of Nike's Corporate Environmental Policy in 1998. The policy was announced both inside and outside the company, and was endorsed by Nike's CEO and president, who committed Nike to the companywide pursuit of sustainable business practices. This policy served as a tool to communicate the scope of its environmental commitment inside Nike and to those who have a stake in Nike's long-term prosperity.

Nike continues to strive to incorporate environmental responsibility throughout its operations and product life cycle. Environmental responsibility is now an added dimension of Nike's product design innovation platform, and the company has set long-term goals for the environment. This commitment is reflected in decisions regarding products and responds to increasing consumer demand for sustainable options as well as the company's commitment to environmental sustainability. An insignia (see Figure 8.2) was introduced with the intent to engage consumers in conversations about environmental sustainability. This insignia appears on select Nike product and service innovations that focus on creating environmental practices for the business. Examples range from apparel to Nike's Reuse-A-Shoe and Air To Earth programs. Appearing on hangtags, in-store materials, and press releases for select items and programs, the insignia directs people to www.nikebiz.com where they can learn more. Since September 2002, a line of apparel containing cotton that's 100 percent certified organic has carried the logo.

Builds Influential Partnerships

As mentioned in Chapter 1, Business for Social Responsibility asserts that companies engaging in responsible business practices may experience less scrutiny from national as well as local government agencies. "In many cases, such companies are subject to fewer inspections and less paperwork, and may be given preference or 'fast-track' treatment when applying for operating permits, zoning variances, or other forms of governmental permission. The U.S. Federal Sentencing Guidelines allow penalties and fines against corporations to be reduced or even eliminated if a company can show it has taken 'good corporate citizenship'

Figure 8.2 This insignia has been used at times on products and services focused on responsible environmental business practices. (Reprinted courtesy of Nike.)

actions and has effective ethics program in place."[8] Note the strong relationship that Motorola has apparently established with an influential regulatory agency in the following example.

**Example: Motorola and the
U.S. Environmental Protection Agency**

Motorola's environmental vision calls for the company to fully support sustainable use of the earth's resources, with responsible business practices concentrated in three major areas: protecting the land, protecting the air, conserving water.[9]

Programs designed to *protect the land* include a program called WasteWise, a voluntary U.S. EPA program where organizations eliminate costly municipal solid waste, benefiting their bottom line and the environment (see Figure 8.3). Since joining the WasteWise program in 1994, Motorola's U.S. manufacturing sites are reported to have recycled almost 125,000 tons of waste. In the year 2000, Motorola was one of three companies to be chosen by the EPA as "WasteWise Partner of the Year for Very Large Business," recognizing these accomplishments in waste reduction.[10]

Motorola has also developed packaging reuse systems, such as the Compack™ system, developed to eliminate the need for separate product packaging by using a standardized tray to receive incoming components from suppliers and then reusing the tray to ship the finished pagers to customers. This system eliminates over 140 tons of packaging waste each year and saves Motorola approximately $4.3 million annually. The Compack system was featured as the "Innovation of the Month" in a U.S. EPA WasteWise bulletin.[11]

To contribute to *protecting the air*, in 1992 Motorola was the second electronics firm in the world to eliminate the use of chlorofluorocarbons (CFCs) from its manufacturing processes. The EPA recognized Motorola with the 1991 Stratospheric Ozone Program Award for its innovative methods for electronic compound cleaning that eliminated the use of CFCs.[12]

Preserving Resources,
Preventing Waste

Figure 8.3   Motorola participates on a voluntary basis in the U.S. Environmental Protection Agency's waste reduction program. (Reprinted courtesy of EPA.)

Enhances Employee Well-Being and Satisfaction

As we have seen, most corporate social initiatives can contribute to enhanced employee retention and satisfaction efforts, as they engender perceptions of pride in being associated with a company with a strong reputation for community building and goodwill. Socially responsible business practices can take this even further, offering the additional benefit of actually contributing to improved employee health and safety, as illustrated in the following example.

Example: Intel and Environmental Health and Safety

Safety at Intel is more than just a corporate initiative; it's an integral part of the company's culture. It wasn't always that way. Ten years ago, Intel's safety performance and programs were fairly average for the semiconductor industry. Today, Intel's safety programs and performance have achieved world-class levels. One of their long-range goals for environmental health and safety is to prevent all injuries in the workplace.[13]

This dramatic change has entailed transforming how people think and act toward safety. Such a change in culture requires motivating employees at all levels to be safety-oriented, and it has demanded the commitment of Intel's entire management team.

In 2001, two company managers in Oregon took a novel approach to safety. They put their hairdos on the line. If the organization could complete 500 days without an injury, they promised to shave their heads. The goal was reached, and both managers had their heads buzzed boot-camp-style bald in front of a cheering crowd. The head of Intel's Worldwide Safety sees two great themes emerging from the organization's excellent safety record: "They have not only achieved and sustained safety excellence, but their management is visibly and personally involved in setting challenges, and this makes all the difference."[14]

Intel's Design for Environment, Health, and Safety program is a prevention program focusing on early identification of safety problems that can result from new tool or process methods. It is believed that "this early intervention and up-front partnering with suppliers is a key reason why Intel is one of the safest places in our industry to work."[15]

Contributes to Desired Brand Positioning

In the following example, we can imagine that this company's voluntary decision to alter a business practice is likely to further position this brand as one with a long history of commitment to sustainable environmental practices and corporate responsibility.

Example: Silk and Wind Power

In February 2003, White Wave, the country's largest soy foods manufacturer and producer of the well known Silk Soymilk, announced it would be replacing the electrical power used in all of its operations with clean, sustainable, renewable wind energy (see Figure 8.4). According to the EPA, "White Wave is the largest U.S. company to purchase 100 percent new wind power for all of its operations, providing an outstanding example of environmental leadership." According to the EPA, White Wave's purchase of wind power will save approximately 32 million pounds of carbon dioxide emissions each year—equivalent to taking 3,200 cars off the road.

"White Wave has always been committed to socially responsible and environmentally sustainable business practices," says Steve Demos, company founder and president. "We have previously demonstrated this through our 25-year devotion to the processing of non–genetically modified, organically raised soybeans. Today our announcement to purchase wind energy is another legitimate step in creating a business model that is both profitable and environmentally sound. We believe this initiative is a partial fulfillment of our corporate responsibility to return to the marketplace a portion of the profits we derive to meaningful and environmentally sustainable business practices. We are delighted to do so without economic impact to the consumer."

White Wave is also encouraging its consumers to purchase wind energy (a cause promotion initiative in our model). Consumers can visit their web site to learn more about wind energy and sign up to purchase wind energy credits for home use.[16]

POTENTIAL CONCERNS

Perhaps more than with any other social initiative, corporate motives for new and more responsible business practices will be questioned, actions

Figure 8.4 White Wave, a soy foods manufacturer, purchased 100 percent new wind power for all of its operations. (Reprinted courtesy of White Wave.)

will be judged, and results will be scrutinized. Audiences will ask, "Is this for doing good or for doing well?" And it will be asked by many, even most, of the company's constituent groups: customers, the general public, employees, investors, regulatory agencies, and the media. Common perceptions include the following challenges:

- *People will be skeptical of the corporation's motives.* They will likely want to believe the news (e..g., decreased use of harmful chemicals in a manufacturing plant) but will wonder whether the news is some type of public relations stunt (e.g., it only applies to one chemical and one type of plant). They'd like to believe this is a real, substantial change in the way the company will be doing business going forward, but they will wonder if the campaign is just to cover up something that the company doesn't want the public to know or whether it is to distract attention from some impending bad publicity.

- *They will look for actions that back up words and fulfill promises.* When a company, for example, announces a major program with a renewed emphasis on sustainable building practices, some will want to know if the company will only make changes in new plants, or if they will retrofit and upgrade existing ones as well. When it is written in an annual report that a renewed commitment has been made to recycling in the workplace, what actual changes in infrastructure will be made? Will separate bins for colored paper, glass, and plastic bottles be provided and conveniently located throughout the workplace, even in conference rooms? Are corporate supplies of paper made from recycled and recyclable materials? Are internal meeting agendas printed on two sides and do staff members get reminders to print out only those e-mails that they need to file?

- *They will want to know if this is a long-term commitment or a short-term campaign.* There will be a big difference in perception between a company that stresses that "this year we want everyone to try to join a carpool or vanpool or take the bus to work" and one that adopts a program that offers free bus passes, covered bike racks, ride matching, flex cars for personal use, monthly incentives, increased parking charges for single-occupant vehicles, and visible publication of the names of all employees who have joined the effort (or not), including senior managers.

- *They will have questions about whether and how the new practices will make a real difference.* It won't be enough to just say this will improve the environment, increase employee safety, or protect consumers. Constituents will want concrete, measurable facts that demonstrate impact (e.g., number of tons of garbage that are now being recycled and not going into landfills, number of employees no longer coming to work in single-occupant vehicles, and the associated reductions in fuel use and air pollution).

- *They will want to know what you used to do.* When a new practice is announced (e.g., more disclosure of product contents), the next most likely question for many will be "What else haven't you been telling me?" Or, when a harmful practice is abandoned (e.g., dumping of pollutants into streams), they will want to know what harm was done all those years before you banned this harmful practice.

- *They will be waiting to hear the results of your efforts.* Once reforms are implemented, audiences will be watching for reports on how you did relative to published goals (e.g., in annual reports) and, if you didn't achieve the desired results, what further measures will be taken. It will be important to report the bad news as well as the good, externally as well as internally.

KEYS TO SUCCESS

Many keys to success described in the cases to follow address ways to deal with challenges and concerns facing the implementation and reporting of new business initiatives. In summary, corporate managers encourage others to decrease skepticism and criticism by being preemptive; by choosing an issue that meets a business as well as a social need; by making a long-term commitment; by building employee enthusiasm; by developing and implementing infrastructures to support the promise; and by providing open, honest, and direct communications.

Starbucks and Conservation International

Starbucks believes in the value of making long-term investments that will produce social, environmental, and economic benefits for the communities in which it operates. The following case features an initiative that reflects this commitment, one that rewards environmental conservation and increases economic opportunities for the people who produce Starbucks' coffees.

This story, told by Starbucks vice president for business practices, makes a strong case that corporate social initiatives should be proactive, rather than reactive, demonstrating a true commitment, not a defensive response.[17]

In October 1998, Starbucks and Conservation International (CI), a nonprofit conservation organization, began a partnership to support farmers of shade-grown coffee while also protecting tropical forests. Through CI's Conservation Coffee program, Starbucks encourages the production of coffee using cultivation methods that protect biodiversity and provide improved economic opportunities for coffee farmers.

Our first project site was at the El Triunfo Biosphere Reserve in Chiapas, Mexico, a region considered to be one of the world's most environmentally sensitive. Conservation International and Starbucks supported farmers who grow coffee under the protection of shade, creating and maintaining a forested buffer zone around the reserve. In 1999, Starbucks made an initial purchase of 76,000 pounds of Shade Grown Mexico coffee and began offering it in our U.S. retail locations.

In 2000, the partnership was expanded to include (1) increasing efforts to promote conservation and improve livelihoods in a wide range of global biodiversity hotspots; (2) supporting the introduction of a year-round product line that reflects Starbucks' commitment to sustainable coffee production; (3) developing coffee-sourcing guidelines that promote conservation and improve the livelihood of farmers; and (4) engaging other leaders from the coffee world in a collaborative effort to set industrywide guidelines for environmental and social quality.

In fiscal 2001 we invested more than $325,000 in the program. and in fiscal 2002 we signed a three-year commitment to provide a minimum of $600,000 to the effort.

Because most of Starbucks' marketing efforts are at the store level, promotional activities primarily focused on supporting purchases of shade-grown coffee with point-of-sale material including informational pamphlets, posters, visibility on packaging, and relying on well-educated partners (employees) (see Figure 8.5). When we introduced the coffee, we also invited local and wire reporters to our headquarters for a coffee tasting and a joint presentation by CI and Starbucks, resulting in millions of media impressions in print and on TV and radio.

In terms of results for the farmers, CI reported that in fiscal 2002 farmers supplying Shade Grown Mexico received an 87 per-

Figure 8.5   Starbucks believes that support for farmers supplying shade grown coffee beans will help provide long-term sustainable suppliers. (Reprinted courtesy of Starbucks.)

cent premium over local prices for their coffee; exports of coffee from this Chiapas Conservation Coffee program increased 100 percent over fiscal 2001; more than 1,000 farmers participated in the program, up from 691 the year before; and the milling yield for coffee (green coffee beans resulting from processing raw coffee) increased from 64 percent to 76 percent. And for the environment, more than 7,400 acres of coffee fields in Chiapas are currently managed using best practices for conservation coffee. Now, Starbucks and CI are developing similar conservation projects in Colombia and Peru.

For Starbucks, this initiative has helped us develop a strong model for how we select and work with an NGO. It has provided the company with a long-term, sustainable supply of excellent coffee, and a product for consumers interested in an environmental attribute; and it is a source of pride for our employees and partners, seen as a serious commitment due to the long-term investment of significant resources. It has strengthened our reputation as a socially responsible company. In 2002, we were selected as a recipient of the 2002 World Summit Business Sustainable Development Partnerships award with CI by the International Chamber of Commerce and the United Nations Environment Program.[18]

Our experience reinforces the following recommendations for a successful program:

- Select an issue that meets a company need, as well a social one. We had a need for a long-term quality supply of coffee, one consistent with our commitment to conduct business in ways that provide environmental, social, and economic benefits to the community.
- Focus on an initiative that can be connected to your business. This adds relevance and credibility to the effort. We were asked to answer tough questions about the value this will have to the company, the customers, and the producers.
- Choosing something that will be easy to talk about in the company will make it easier for you to generate enthusiasm and support.
- Before beginning a partnership with an NGO, prepare a written agreement specifying clear timelines and deliverables. Then have it signed at the highest level, by both CEOs.

Kraft Foods Global Obesity Initiative

The rise in obesity is among the most important public health challenges facing the world today. The people at Kraft Foods believe they have a responsibility along with many others to be part of the solution, and they want to be. They make it clear that the following initiative described by a Kraft executive is not a cause promotion, but rather an initiative directed at their own policies, practices, and behaviors as a corporation. And they say they expect to make a good return on their investment.

In July 2003, we announced that we were initiating a new series of steps to further strengthen the alignment of our products and marketing practices with societal needs. Senior management and functional leaders from corporate affairs, law, marketing, and R&D were the initial drivers but the effort has been embraced by the entire Kraft organization. Their efforts are being supported by a global team of 10 experts from outside the company who will serve on our Worldwide Health and Wellness Advisory Council, formed to help structure policies, standards, measures, and timetables for implementation.

The commitments Kraft is making are global in scope and will focus in four key areas: product nutrition, marketing practices, consumer information, and public advocacy. A few of the planned steps include providing a broad range of portion-size choices, labeling smaller snack and beverage packages with the nutrition content of the entire package, improving the nutrition profile of our products (see Figure 8.6), eliminating all in-school marketing, and advocating for public policies to engage schools and communities in helping improve fitness and nutrition.

Costs associated with the initiative will include costs for research and development, capital investments to change manufacturing and packaging processes, and costs of raw materials, which may go up or down depending on the changes we make.

Awareness of this initiative was created using news releases, the provision of information on our corporate web site, meetings with government leaders, and presentations to key stakeholder groups. We conducted well over 100 media interviews, resulting in widespread media coverage around the world.

At this early stage in the initiative, the primary benefit has been to Kraft's corporate reputation. Feedback from key con-

Figure 8.6 Kraft Foods' Global Obesity Initiative includes improving the nutritional profile of products. (Reprinted courtesy of Kraft Foods.)

stituencies, including policy influentials, the nutrition and health community, activists, and media, has been significant and positive. A U.S. public opinion survey found that the initiative was received favorably by a strong majority of those who had awareness of it and that a strong majority believed Kraft was doing its part to address the obesity problem in a responsible way. We believe there is a significant growth opportunity that this initiative will ultimately help us capture. As more people become convinced of the importance of a healthy lifestyle, they are going to want products and portion sizes that help them meet their goals. We want to be that company.

From a corporate responsibility perspective, our decision to proceed with this initiative was driven by six principles:

1. We believe that companies that are seriously out of touch with societal expectations will find themselves under mounting economic, social, and political pressure. Companies that are well aligned will enjoy growing support in these same three spheres.

2. In deciding which societal concerns a company should address, focus first on the most relevant, close-to-home issues—the ones that are hard-wired to your business, where expectations are the most immediate and the cost of inaction is greatest.

3. Don't wait until an issue reaches a crisis before addressing it. The longer you wait, the bigger the challenge will be.

4. Actions are more important than words. Make sure there's substance supporting the rhetoric.

5. In communicating the steps you are taking, be accessible to those who want to know more.

6. Recognize that change of this magnitude in most large organizations takes time, patience, and consistent effort from a broad array of disciplines to reach the critical tipping point.

Chiquita's Better Banana Initiative

In the following case, the socially responsible business practice of responsible reporting is highlighted.

An article in the December 2, 2002, edition of the *Financial Times* described Chiquita's attempt to break with the past, as demonstrated through its obtaining stringent independent environmental certifications, developing labor agreements with international and regional unions, and signing a groundbreaking accord with Southern Hemisphere unions. The chief operating officer for the company was quoted as saying, "It's hard to change the image of a century-old corporation. But it's not something we belabor. It happened in the past." The headline for the article read, "The Banana Giant That Found Its Gentle Side: Corporate Social Responsibility."[19] Then, in the July/August 2003 issue of green@work magazine, a cover story featured Chiquita and Ben & Jerry's as co-winners of an award for sustainability reporting, with a lead story titled "Banana Split." (See Figure 8.7)

"They couldn't be more different. Ben & Jerry's is the quintessential do-gooder corporation founded by two school chums in a renovated gas station in Vermont that has captured the environmental mantle in the food industry," the story read. "Chiquita Brands, a huge multinational corporation, has had a long and sometimes unsavory history that includes accusations of unfair labor practices and bankruptcy. Aside from

Figure 8.7 Chiquita and Ben & Jerry's were featured as co-winners for sustainability reporting in green@work magazine's July/August 2003 issue. (Photo courtesy of *green@work* magazine, photographer Jim Robinette.)

producing two of the world's favorite foods—ice cream and bananas, which just happen to work well together—they are seemingly poles apart in every way. How is it then that these two ended up as co-winners of an award for sustainability reporting?"[20]

In the following highlight, Chiquita provides more background about the changes that led to this positive visibility for the corporation's effort, and shares what the company considers its five keys to success.

In the late 1990s, Chiquita was the target of significant criticism regarding environmental and labor practices from news media and nongovernmental organizations, even though we had already begun the process of achieving certification for meeting rigorous standards established by the Rainforest Alliance. This led the management team to answer several tough questions:

- We believe we operate ethically, but how do we know?
- Do we have a set of guiding principles to align employees throughout the company?
- How do we know we are living up to them?

We then initiated a comprehensive and very inclusive process to develop Chiquita's guiding values—what we call our Core Values—one of which is the statement that "We communicate in an open, honest, and straightforward manner." These efforts have garnered considerable attention and some important awards. In addition to the co-award with Ben & Jerry's, we were ranked first in the world among food companies by SustainAbility and the United Nations Environment Programmme for our 2000 Corporate Responsibility Report. While we didn't start reporting to win awards, these awards validate that what stakeholders really respect most is openness and honesty in reporting, and it is an indication that we are being recognized for exactly what we are trying to do.

Rather than trumpet our corporate responsibility successes, we have purposely taken a more low-key approach, in particular, letting our actions speak louder than our words, and letting independent observers point out our successes. We believe this approach has been successful and is perceived to be more credible than a high-profile marketing or public relations effort.

It has taken more than $20 million and eight years to fully comply with the Rainforest Alliance certifications standards on

100 percent of our farms in the five countries of Central America where we operate.

We can quantify financial benefits (e.g., in 2002, we saved more than $5 million compared to 1997 by using fewer agrichemicals, and a pallet recycling program saved us $3 million a year) but rescuing our reputation has been priceless. Employee pride has clearly improved. The value of the Chiquita brand has risen. Activist campaigns directed against us in the late 1990s have essentially gone away. The tone of our media coverage has turned around.

We have summarized keys to our success as the "Five Cs":

1. First is *conviction*. Corporate responsibility is about real improvement in business performance, not public relations.
2. Second is *commitment*. At Chiquita, we've made a fundamental commitment to values and assigned ownership and accountability to our operating managers. When we commit, we deliver.
3. Third is *communication*. We have committed to open, honest, and direct communication with all of our stakeholders.
4. Fourth is *consistency*. This is indeed a process of continuous improvement. We have tied corporate responsibility goals to our everyday management and reward systems. Corporate responsibility is an essential part of Chiquita's culture and central to our strategy.
5. And finally, corporate responsibility is about *credibility*. We know that our ability to improve—and your ability to trust our performance—depends on the credibility of our effort. That's why we've committed to achieve verifiable third-party standards, measure our performance honestly, and report our progress transparently—even when we don't always meet certain goals.

WHEN SHOULD A CORPORATION CONSIDER A MAJOR SOCIALLY RESPONSIBLE BUSINESS PRACTICE INITIATIVE?

Some consider the word *responsibility*, whether at the personal or corporate level, to mean "ability to respond," as opposed to a focus on blame. Looking at it from this perspective, a corporation should regularly review and consider new or modified business practices that will improve the quality of life and, at the same time, provide some net benefit to the corporation, ideally financial, operational, relationship-building, or marketing in nature. Circumstances that might provide this optimal situation could include the following (most references are to examples cited earlier in this chapter):

- When a company has been offered a *financial incentive* to alter a business practice for the benefit of the environment, most typically from an external public or regulatory agency (e.g., Cisco's incentive from the local energy supplier to meet or exceed guidelines for energy conservation).

- When the adoption of a new practice would *reduce operating costs*, as well as contribute to a social issue (e.g., Chiquita saving millions each year after reducing its use of select chemicals).

- When a current business practice can be identified (in part) as *contributing to an important social problem*, and modifications and improvements would help address the issue (e.g., McDonald's deciding to phase out supersize options).

- When there is an opportunity to *improve employee health, safety, or well-being* by altering a business practice or investing in infrastructures and educational communications (e.g., Coca Cola's HIV/AIDS workplace program).

- When engagement in this practice can *add an important point of differentiation* to target markets in a crowded, undifferentiated marketplace (e.g., Nike offering a line of products made with environmentally friendly materials).

- When there are *opportunities for alliances that will strengthen the brand's positioning* (e.g., Motorola's participation in EPA's waste reduction program).

- When the adoption of the practice could actually *improve product quality or performance*, providing increased value and points of difference (e.g., compact fluorescent light bulbs that use less energy and last longer).

- When investments or changes in practices will *strengthen relationships with suppliers or distributors* (e.g., Starbucks providing training and economic opportunities to ensure a long-term sustainable supply of excellent coffee).

DEVELOPING THE INITIATIVE

Based on experiences of professionals, including ones contributing to cases in this chapter, major decisions involved in adapting and implementing socially responsible business practices will focus on the process of carefully selecting the social issue that the initiative will support; developing integrated, strategic plans for implementation; and setting and tracking measurable goals.

As indicated in many of the case examples, most recommend that *business needs should be identified first.* There might be an emerging or current objective for reduced operating costs, improved supplier relations, or reduced regulatory oversight, or there may be important marketing challenges such as repositioning of the brand or standing out in an undifferentiated, crowded marketplace. Next, major social problems are identified that the company could contribute to through altered business practices and investments. As with other social initiatives, a cause should be selected that is substantial, consistent with company mission and values, and one that key publics care about. The actual initiative (business practice to be adopted or altered) is then selected based on an assessment of potential for meeting business objectives and contributing to the social cause.

Experienced experts have also stressed the need for an *integrated, planned approach for implementation,* one involving and backed by executive management. New or revised business practices should be supported through employee communications and any related needs for education and training. In many cases, there will need to be important changes to infrastructure to facilitate the adoption of new practices and to ensure more substance than rhetoric.

And finally, encourage accountability by *setting goals and establishing mechanisms for measuring, tracking, and reporting results.* Many recommend developing communication plans that include publishing goals, reporting on progress, and, in the event that goals are not met, identifying and then publishing corrective action plans to ensure continued commitment and progress toward the goal.

SUMMARY

To implement socially responsible business practice initiatives, a corporation adopts and conducts discretionary business practices and investments that support social causes to improve community well-being and protect the environment. Key distinctions from other initiatives include a focus on activities that are discretionary; *community* is interpreted broadly; and *community well-being* can refer to health and safety, as well as psychological and emotional needs.

Over the last decade there has been an apparent shift from adopting more responsible business practices as a result of regulatory citations, consumer complaints, and special interest group pressures, to proactive research exploring corporate solutions to social problems and incorporating new business practices that will support these issues. Several factors may be contributing to this shift: evidence that socially responsible business practices can actually increase profits; a global marketplace with increased competition and consumer options; interest in increased worker productivity and retention; and increased visibility and coverage of corporate socially responsible (or irresponsible) activities.

Most initiatives relate to altering internal procedures and policies, external reporting of consumer and investor information, making provisions for customer access and privacy, and making decisions regarding suppliers and facility and plant locations.

Resultant financial benefits have been associated with decreased operating costs, monetary incentives from regulatory agencies, and increased employee productivity and retention. Marketing benefits are numerous as well, with the potential for increasing community goodwill, creating brand preference, building brand positioning, improving product quality, and increasing corporate respect. These activities also provide opportunities to build relationships with external partners such as regulatory agencies, suppliers, and nonprofit organizations.

Experts warn that corporate motives for new and more responsible business practices will be questioned, actions will be judged, and results will be scrutinized. Corporate managers encourage others to decrease skepticism and criticism by being preemptive; choosing an issue that meets a business as well as a social need; making a long-term commitment; building employee enthusiasm; developing and implementing infrastructures to support the promise; and providing open, honest, and direct communications.

Major decisions involved in adapting and implementing socially responsible business practices will focus on the process of carefully selecting the social issue that the initiative will support; developing integrated, strategic plans for implementation; and setting measurable goals and establishing plans for tracking and reporting results.

CHAPTER
9

Twenty-five Best Practices for Doing the Most Good for the Company and the Cause

It is true that economic and social objectives have long been seen as distinct and often competing. But this is a false dichotomy; it represents an increasingly obsolete perspective in a world of open, knowledge-based competition. Companies do not function in isolation from the society around them. In fact, their ability to compete depends heavily on the circumstances of the locations where they operate.
—Michael E. Porter and Mark R. Kramer[1]

This book has been written to support managers to choose, develop, implement and evaluate corporate social initiatives such that they will do the most good for the company and the cause. Its purpose is to help guide decision making in the area of corporate social responsibility, resulting in efforts that do the most social, environmental, and economic good. It is, in the end, intended to help maximize the return on discretionary corporate investments in improving the quality of life, with the hope that future participation in these efforts is increasingly satisfying. We discussed early on that it is no longer just *acceptable* that the corporation does well by doing good. It is *expected*.

235

Then what can we conclude is *good*?

For the cause that is supported by corporate social initiatives, *good* is the increased realization of several potential benefits. The six corporate initiatives featured in this book have been seen to provide multiple benefits for a cause and for the charities supporting these causes. As many recipients of corporate contributions to their causes have indicated, these initiatives can:

- *Enhance public awareness and concern for the cause* through support of promotional communication efforts (e.g., Ben & Jerry's campaign to increase concern about global warning).

- *Support fundraising* by encouraging customers and others in the community to contribute to causes (e.g., British Airways' campaign that collects pocket change from passengers for children's charities).

- *Increase community participation in cause-related activities* by providing promotional support and use of distribution channels (e.g., PETsMART periodically providing space in their stores for adopting animals).

- *Support efforts to influence individual behavior change and industry business practices* that improve public health (e.g., Coca-Cola Africa Foundation's HIV/AIDS workplace initiative) and safety (e.g., FedEx's SAFE KIDS Walk This Way program) and protect the environment (e.g., Best Buy's effort to support recycling of used computers).

- *Provide increased funds and other resources* that help charities and cause efforts make ends meet and/or expand efforts (e.g., General Mills providing grants for projects that improve youth nutrition and physical activity levels).

- *Increase the number of volunteers* donating their expertise, ideas, and physical labor to a cause by promoting volunteerism in the community and supporting employee volunteer efforts (e.g., Shell employees helping with coastal cleanups).

At the same time, we have seen through examples and perspectives provided by corporate executives how these efforts to give back to the community also give back to the company. They can help:

- *Build a strong corporate reputation*, as key constituents observe actions that support promises of good corporate citizenship and responsibility (e.g., Kraft's initiative to to help address obesity).

- *Contribute to overall business goals* by opening up new markets, for example, or providing opportunities to build long-term relationships with distributors and suppliers (e.g., Starbucks' initiative to support farmers who provide shade-grown coffee).

- *Attract and retain a motivated workforce* by being known for involvement in the community, and for providing employees an opportunity to become involved in something they care about and to receive corporate support and recognition for doing so (e.g., the personal stories shared about volunteering by FedEx Company employees that "changed their lives").

- *Reduce operating costs* by adopting new socially responsible business practices, such as procedures that increase efficiency and reduce costs for materials (e.g., Cisco saving several million dollars each year through energy saving construction and implementation of energy saving guidelines).

- *Reduce regulatory oversight* by working closely with regulatory agencies to meet or exceed guidelines, thereby increasing confidence and building strong relationships for the future (e.g., Motorola's recognition for participation in the EPA's waste reduction program).

- *Support marketing objectives* by building traffic, enhancing brand positioning, creating product differentiation, reaching niche markets, attracting new customers, and increasing sales, especially when products and services are an integral part of program efforts (e.g., Home Depot's initiative to support water conservation, including connections of products to specific conservation practices).

- *Build strong community relationships* with organizations and agencies that can provide technical expertise, extend campaign reach by providing access to members and donors also supporting the cause; and offer credible endorsement for the corporation's effort and commitment (e.g., Aleve's partnership with the Arthritis Foundation, including sponsorship for the nationwide Arthritis Walk).

- *Leverage current corporate social initiative efforts and investments* by including additional ones that further connect the company to the cause, thus increasing chances for both an impact on the social problem and a greater return on current investments (e.g., Dell adding a volunteer component to its recycling initiative by involving employee volunteers in recycling events).

BEST PRACTICES FOR CHOOSING A
SOCIAL PROBLEM TO ALLEVIATE

Social needs seem endless and the options to provide support overwhelming. At a global as well as local level, we should have no problem finding a cause that needs corporate support, from those that help ensure basic needs are met in the community to those that improve health, prevent injuries, increase public involvement, and protect the environment. The problem is in choosing well among the options. The following six practices help guide strategic decision-making.

1. Choose Only a Few Social Issues to Support.

Many executives interviewed for this book stressed the importance of picking only a few major social issues as a focal point for corporate citizenship and giving. Washington Mutual shared that their strategic focus on improving K-12 education had been in place for more than 75 years, since their beginning in 1927. It is clear that Avon is on a crusade for women's health and REI has a passion for environmental protection. The benefits of this practice seem obvious now and are reminiscent of benefits a corporation realizes when it selects target markets and develops entire marketing strategies to win them over. It increases chances that the company can actually have an impact on a particular social initiative, as resources are focused and multiple initiatives aimed at one cause. It makes it easier to "say no" to others, as the company can point to their priority areas for giving. It increases chances that the company will be able to develop long-term, often coveted relationships with strong desirable partners, as they, too, will be looking for a partner willing to provide significant resources and make a long-term commitment. Finally, targeting resources in a few areas increases chances that the corporation will be connected to the cause and will therefore leverage potential brand positioning and other desired marketing benefits.

2. Choose Issues That Are of Concern in the Communities Where You Do Business.

Improving communities where facilities are located, where future workforces will be recruited, and where customers live can support both social and economic goals. As noted earlier, The Home Depot demonstrated this practice when it focused on the issue of water conservation in a community threatened by drought; and Levi Strauss was one of the first to step forward in the San Francisco Bay area to support HIV/AIDS prevention. American Express, with over 4,000 employees displaced as a result of the September 11 attacks, was a natural to help revitalize downtown Manhattan. And Kraft committed to helping reduce obesity in their marketplace—our nation. Focusing on issues of concern in these communities and for those living in them increases chances that efforts will be noticed and valued among key publics. It adds credibility and believability to standard statements in annual reports and sales catalogues proclaiming, "We believe in giving back to the communities where we do business." It may also help solve real problems facing a business, such as ensuring a future trained workforce, quality suppliers, and even a robust economy.

3. Choose Causes That Have Synergy with Mission, Values, Products, and Services.

Just as we develop and offer products and services that are consistent with our company's mission and then promote and deliver them in a way that reflects our company's values, we should also choose areas of focus for social initiatives that have the same synergy. Often the choice will be obvious, as it must have been for Crest when its leaders learned more about the "silent epidemic" of oral disease in America, especially among low-income children. Similarly, it must have been an obvious choice for life vest manufacturer Mustang Survival when it was approached by a regional children's hospital to support a campaign to help reduce the number of drownings among children. For AT&T, a partnership with the American Red Cross that included donations of phones to support the organization's disaster relief efforts seems easy, as does General Motors' dealership support of car seat safety checks. When corporations contribute to causes that make sense, we find consumers are less suspicious, investors are less likely to judge the effort as peripheral, and employees are more likely to have the needed expertise and passion to volunteer.

4. Choose Causes That Have Potential to Support Business Goals: Marketing, Supplier Relations, Increased Productivity, Cost Reductions.

Subject experts such as Michael Porter of Harvard Business School and Mark Kramer, managing director of the Foundation Strategy Group, say this simultaneous support for business goals is true strategic philanthropy. "It is only where corporate expenditures produce simultaneous social and economic gains that corporate philanthropy and shareholder interests converge. . . . It is here that philanthropy is truly strategic."[2] Starbucks was clear that support for shade-grown coffee was important for the environment, but it also ensures a long-term supply of quality coffee. Safeco realized marketing benefits and potential cost reductions through its partnerships with fire departments in communities where home owners (customers and target markets for many of its insurance products) were provided with informational materials on helping prevent or mitigate fire damage. And Chiquita saved millions of dollars a year by using fewer agrichemicals and from its pallet recycling program. In each of these examples, the corporation chose to support a social issue that had potential for contributing to business goals, as well as a connection to the company's mission, values, communities, and products and services.

5. Choose Issues That Are of Concern to Key Constituent Groups: Employees, Target Markets, Customers, Investors, and Corporate Leaders.

Support for social initiatives will be leveraged when the cause is also one near and dear to our key publics, both internal and external. LensCrafter's successful collection of used eyeglasses is a reflection of the involvement and enthusiasm that customer-contact staff have for giving the "Gift of Sight." Parents concerned with SIDS were most likely grateful for the just-in-time reminder from Pampers to place an infant on its "Back to Sleep." Potential customers for Silk Soymilk may be motivated to choose this product from the lineup on the shelf when they hear of the parent company's commitment to using 100 percent wind power for all of its operations. Investors were perhaps encouraged if they read reports from Motorola that their new packaging reuse systems were expected to save several million dollars each year. And corporate leaders are probably pleased, perhaps even relieved, when they receive reports on employee volunteer efforts such as Shell's coastal cleanup effort in Australia. The successes of most social initiatives reviewed in this book have clearly relied on the connection and resonance the efforts have with one or more of these key constituent groups. Such connection should therefore be factored into decisions on what causes to support.

6. Choose Causes That Can Be Supported over a Long Term.

Achieving maximum benefits for the company (and the cause) often depends on long-term commitments, frequently considered three or more years. As with most communication efforts, it takes numerous exposures to messages and events before an effort is noticed and before targeted audiences for fundraising efforts and especially behavior change campaigns will act. It also most often takes a long period of time to make a dent in a social problem, whether supporting medical research for cancer cures or reducing levels of toxic emissions from manufacturing plants. Long-term commitments can also be more economical, as early years in program efforts are often consumed with steep learning curves and coordination with cause partners, and efforts get more efficient in subsequent years. And finally, those companies who stick with the cause over the years are more likely to be able to own it, as does The Body Shop after staying the course with campaigns "Against Animal Testing" in the cosmetic industry. Even if a competitor decided to move in on this point of differentiation, many consumers are likely to know that The Body Shop was there first.

Those who practice this principle ask themselves and their partners whether this effort will be one that will be a social concern over the next several years; whether it will have continued connection to the company's mission, values, products, and services; and whether key publics will continue to care. Given these criteria, it seems it would make sense for Lysol to make a long-term commitment to Keep America Beautiful; for Target to continue to help local public schools, for Aleve to continue sponsoring walks for the Arthritis Foundation; for ConAgra to help feed millions of hungry children in our country; and for Microsoft to "unleash the potential in every person, family, and business" by providing people with access to technology and the education to put it to use.

BEST PRACTICES FOR SELECTING A SOCIAL INITIATIVE TO SUPPORT THE CAUSE

Once a social issue has been chosen (ideally as an area of focus for the company), all six initiatives should then be evaluated for potential to contribute to the cause, as well as to the company. Table 9.1 summarizes major strengths associated with each initiative, both for the company and for the cause. As the following guidelines suggest, managers will

Table 9.1 Major Potential Benefits from Corporate Social Initiatives

	Cause Promotions	Cause-Related Marketing	Social Marketing	Corporate Philanthropy	Community Volunteering	Socially Responsible Business Practices
For the Cause						
Increased awareness and concern for the cause	Major strength	Major strength	Major strength			
Support for fundraising	Major strength	Major strength				
Increased participation in cause	Major strength		Major strength		Major strength	Major strength
Changes in public behavior			Major strength			
Increased funds and other resources	Major strength	Major strength		Major strength	Major strength	

For the Company

Build strong corporate reputation	Major strength	Major strength	Major strength	Major strength	Major strength
Contribute to general business goals		Major strength			Major strength
Attract and retain motivated workforce	Major strength	Major strength	Major strength	Major strength	Major strength
Reduce operating costs					Major strength
Reduce regulatory oversight					Major strength
Support marketing objectives	Major strength	Major strength	Major strength		
Build strong community relationships	Major strength	Major strength	Major strength	Major strength	Major strength
Leverage current corporate social initiatives	Major strength	Major strength	Major strength	Major strength	Major strength

evaluate initiatives relative to their potential for contributing to specific business and cause-related objectives and goals. These best practices also incorporate additional considerations based on perspectives of managers interviewed for this book, as well as academic and other experts on corporate social responsibility.

1. Select Initiatives That Best Meet Business Objectives and Goals.

As illustrated with numerous examples throughout this book, corporate involvement in social initiatives can support a variety of business objectives and goals. At this phase in the planning process, managers should identify priority needs that might be met through supporting cause efforts, considering financial, marketing, corporate reputation, operational, and employee-related goals. Premera Blue Cross's interest in reducing costs associated with upper respiratory infections, for example, was one factor that guided their decision to partner with others to support a cause promotion initiative that would increase public awareness and concern with the overuse of antibiotics, and a social marketing initiative to encourage physicians to practice more conservative measures when prescribing antibiotics.

2. Select Initiatives That Meet Priority Needs for the Cause.

Initiatives that have the potential to meet business objectives and goals are then evaluated against priority needs that have been identified for a cause, zeroing in on those with the most perceived potential to meet both needs. In the case described in Chapter 5 where Safeco (a personal and business insurance company) decided to support a social marketing initiative, Safeco's first offer to the fire department in Oregon was actually to donate money to help purchase firefighting equipment—a philanthropic initiative. Further discussions with the fire marshal in Oregon, however, shifted the initiative to supporting a social marketing campaign that would persuade home owners to establish defensible space around their house. The reasons were expressed well by the fire marshal, who claimed, "A new piece of equipment might save one more home. But to really save homes, individuals have to take personal responsibility for their property before the fire."[3] This social marketing initiative has the potential to do the most good for Safeco, supporting marketing goals and potential cost reductions, as well as for the prevention of wildfires in this region and in others around the country.

3. Select Multiple Initiatives for a Single Cause, Adding Ones Missing for Current Cause Efforts.

Just as skilled marketers practice a fundamental principle of integrated marketing communications, those involved in selecting social initiatives can benefit from a similar practice. In the case of an integrated marketing approach, a company's communications and media channels are co-ordinated so that messages regarding the company and its products are "consistent, clear, and compelling."[4] Similarly, when a company engages in a variety of initiatives to support a chosen social issue, it increases the likelihood that the company will be clearly associated with the cause, and at the same time will be able to provide more support for the cause than it might through just one initiative. Ben & Jerry's global warming campaign exemplifies this practice. As noted in Chapter 3, one component of this effort was a cause promotion to increase awareness of the threats of global warming. The effort was integrated into other initiatives as well. It included a cause-related marketing effort, where a percentage of sales of the One Sweet Whirled ice cream flavor have gone to organizations that are working to fight global warming; a social marketing component, where consumers were encouraged to send letters to congress and to make personal pledges to reduce their carbon dioxide emissions; a philanthropic initiative, where grants have been provided for efforts aimed at addressing global warming; a community volunteer component, in which employees are encouraged to "park your car for a day" and find alternative transportation to work; and socially responsible business practices. One example of the latter was announced in August 2002: The company would offset one year's carbon dioxide emissions from its Vermont ice cream production facilities by supporting the construction of a new wind turbine in South Dakota.[5]

4. Select Initiatives Representing the Most Potential for Strong Community Partners.

Companies should also evaluate potential initiatives relative to their ability to create relationships with partners in the nonprofit as well as public sector, ones that will add resources as well as credibility to the initiative. As we saw, Crest's interest in improving oral health, especially among children in underserved minority communities, resulted in a cause promotion and social marketing partnership with the Boys & Girls Clubs of America that was applauded by the U.S. Surgeon General. And

Johnson & Johnson's campaign to enhance the image of the nursing profession built relationships with key publics for the company, including health care organizations and nursing associations around the world.

5. Select Initiatives Where You Have a History of Experience.

Each of the six initiatives has its own unique set of keys to success, as well as challenges. One consideration when choosing among potential new initiatives is the company's track record and experience in developing and managing prior initiatives, providing an opportunity to capitalize on lessons learned and to be up and running with greater efficiencies. American Express's most recent campaign to revitalize lower Manhattan no doubt benefited from the company's experience in cause-related marketing efforts over the past two decades. And the experience that Fannie Mae has had over the past 15 years with sponsoring an annual employee volunteer effort in the Washington Metropolitan area to "Help the Homeless" has enabled it to grow the program from raising $90,000 the first year to $6.2 million in its 15th year.[6]

6. Select Initiatives That Will Leverage Current Abundant Resources.

Consider which initiative(s) will leverage current resources, especially those that are both highly valued by the cause and underutilized by the company or that can be provided at low cost. Resources to support cause promotions, for example, may simply require additional messages on existing communications (e.g., *PARADE* magazine's feature story to raise awareness and funds for child hunger relief). Cause-related marketing efforts can often piggyback on current paid product advertising (e.g., LYSOL®'s campaign that included product coupons promising donations from revenues would go to Keep America Beautiful). Social marketing efforts can benefit from existing distribution channels and product labeling (e.g., food growers' support for the 5-A-Day program that includes efforts such as stickers on fruit and the 5-A-Day logo on vegetable packages). Philanthropic initiatives can include donation of existing resources (e.g., Microsoft providing technology skills training for disadvantaged individuals through community-based technology and learning centers, including grants of software). Community volunteering efforts can be tied to existing research and development activities (e.g., Hewlett-Packard working side-by-side with citizens in underserved communities, an effort that generated new product ideas and helped build new markets for the company). And socially responsible business practices can be incorporated when designing new facilities and revamping current operational procedures (e.g., Cisco's new facility design to support energy conservation).

BEST PRACTICES FOR DEVELOPING SOCIAL INITIATIVE PROGRAMS

Many of the best practices compiled here for developing corporate social initiative programs have been formulated in response to the concerns and challenges identified by those sharing their experiences in this book, as well as academic and subject experts. We heard of concerns associated with appropriate visibility for the corporation's efforts, coordination with cause partners, staff time for involvement and administration, potential need for external expertise, expenses for promotions, anticipated public skepticism, and tracking resource expenditures. Major concerns associated with each initiative are summarized in Table 9.2, and the following descriptions of best practices are intended to minimize the potential risks and costs associated with development processes and implementation of each initiative.

1. Form Internal, Cross-Functional Teams to Develop Plans.

Program plans often have the most impact and are most efficiently administered when developed by teams with representatives from various departments within the company, teams that may include those from marketing, finance, operations, facilities management, human resources, and executive administration. This is especially important at the beginning of campaign planning, when program objectives and goals are established, as such teamwork can be critical to building internal support for activities as well as setting realistic expectations for program outcomes. Cisco shared its philosophy, relative to designing and building environmentally sensitive facilities, that "planning it right" included combining people who specialized in facility design with people who

Table 9.2 Major Potential Concerns in Undertaking Initiatives

	Cause Promotions	Cause-Related Marketing	Social Marketing	Corporate Philanthropy	Community Volunteering	Socially Responsible Business Practices
Visibility for corporate efforts can easily be lost.	Major potential concern			Major potential concern	Major potential concern	Major potential concern
Coordination with cause partners can be time consuming.	Major potential concern	Major potential concern	Major potential concern			
Staff time and involvement can be significant.	Major potential concern	Major potential concern	Major potential concern		Major potential concern	
Efforts may require external expertise.			Major potential concern			Major potential concern
Promotional expenses can be significant.	Major potential concern	Major potential concern	Major potential concern			
Consumers may be skeptical of corporate motivations and commitment.	Major potential concern	Major potential concern				Major potential concern
Tracking resource expenditures and value can be difficult and expensive.				Major potential concern	Major potential concern	

have day-to-day working familiarity with the buildings. Effective planning required collaboration between groups with different expertise, including those from facility design, operations, and engineering.

2. Include Community Partners in Plan Development.

Similarly, involving community partners early in the planning process will maximize program effectiveness and efficiency. Partners should be included in establishing program goals and objectives, laying the foundation for strategic solutions, and aligning expectations regarding outcomes. They should be included in developing strategic communication plans, especially decisions regarding target audiences, key messages, and key media channels, a process that will help avoid costly and time-consuming reworks of promotional materials. Partner involvement in crafting implementation plans will help avoid misunderstandings and confusions regarding roles and responsibilities. The water conservation campaign that Home Depot participated in, for example, required strategic coordination with all community partners, including more than 25 local water providers, a local news channel, and a communications firm.

3. Establish Clear Objectives and Measurable Goals (Outcomes) for the Company.

The often difficult and elusive task of program evaluation can be eased considerably by taking time in the program planning process to establish clear objectives and measurable goals for the initiative, ones that will then be used to evaluate program success. Corporate objectives may include those related to business needs (e.g., reduce energy costs in new facilities), marketing needs (e.g., increase share of toddler's life vest sales), employee-related needs (e.g., attract talented, motivated employees) or needs related to corporate reputation and goodwill (e.g., reduce levels of toxic emissions). Goals, in this typology, are ideally measurable, specific, realistic, and time-oriented.

4. Establish Clear Objectives and Measurable Goals (Outcomes) for the Cause.

This same practice holds true for the cause as well. In Athena's story, for example, we learned that the company's CEO had established clear objectives to raise money for women's cancer research and specific measurable goals to capture at least 5 percent of the bottled market in the Northwest, which would mean a possible donation of $1 million a year for research and education.

5. Develop a Communications Plan.

As we learned, opinions regarding corporate recognition for social initiatives vary significantly. Some recommend "don't be shy" and others have a company policy to "let others do the talking." Regardless of philosophic perspectives on corporate recognition, developing a communications plan for the initiative is a best practice. Often it will necessitate separate strategies for several key audiences: target markets for the initiative; external publics, such as investors, regulatory agencies, and suppliers; and employees and other internal stakeholders. Communication plans should identify traditional strategic components including communication objectives, key messages, and key media channels for each of the targeted audiences. Communication objectives should signal desired audience outcomes (e.g., increases in awareness, concern, participation, and/or individual behavior change). Including a call to action as a key message has been show to assist tracking and evaluation efforts, and utilization of existing media channels and distribution outlets can help reduce promotional costs.

6. Identify and Plan for Additional Strategic Elements.

Most initiatives will also include additional strategic elements beyond communications that are incorporated into the planning process. Cause promotions often rely on employee involvement, benefiting from a coordinated effort, such as the one that was key to the Wal-Mart initiative to raise money for Children's Miracle Network. Cause-related marketing initiatives involve decisions regarding product ties, timelines, and more complex agreements with cause partners, as must have been the case with Comcast's cause-related marketing effort to raise money for Ronald McDonald House Charities and to coordinate this effort with coupons for McDonald's products. Social marketing initiatives often involve support for public engagement, as illustrated by Dell's printer recycling initiative that included providing prepaid shipping labels and arranging for free pick up of outdated printers. Philanthropic planning efforts will involve deliberation over specific forms of giving, and then development of programs for implementation, as we can imagine must have taken place for General Mills in selecting and administering grants for improved nutrition and physical activity. Community volunteering will also entail selecting types of employee support and then, in many cases, developing systems such as the volunteer match programs offered for AT&T Wireless employees. And socially responsible business practices can require plans for significant changes as they may involve new work processes, negotiations with suppliers, and decisions on facility design and locations.

7. Get Senior Management Buy-In.

Most managers seeking support for corporate social initiatives recognize and report that executives express a desire to give back and to care for the communities that support their business. The challenge is in getting approval for what will be supported and for how much. Earlier in this chapter, a best practice of involving senior management in choosing causes for focus and agreeing on types of initiative to support the cause was emphasized. The same principle holds true for the development of implementation plans, as this is when important decisions regarding budgets will be made, staff resources will be committed, and current business practices may be altered. Planners most likely recognize they need to be prepared for tough questions and straight answers.

Agreement is especially important prior to finalizing program objectives and goals, budgets, and resource allocation. Some executives are reluctant to make a pledge, at the beginning of the fiscal year, of a certain amount of money for corporate social initiatives that can be tied to earnings. Curt Weeden offers this perspective: "CEOs need to accept the premise that the level of social investing is largely a by-product of a company's historic profitability. In a nutshell, here's how it works. Corporations invest a percentage of an average of the pretax earnings of their previous three years. There is an emergency brake that can be pulled if needed—the CEO retains the power to stop social investing in its tracks if the current year's profits are in jeopardy."[7]

BEST PRACTICES FOR EVALUATING EFFORTS

The importance of evaluating efforts and calculating returns on corporate social investments is easily understood. Most recognize it is the right thing to do in order to improve future programs as well as to fulfill commitments for responsible reporting to stakeholders. We know we should practice the same rigorous disciplines that govern our business investments. The challenge is in doing it. Of all best practices related to corporate social initiatives, evaluation strategies remains the least fully developed. The following six best practices suggest at least a structure for identifying data collection needs and a framework for organizing information into meaningful categories, those that are *output-oriented* and those that are *outcome-oriented*.

1. Determine Purpose of Evaluation.

As with most research-related projects, we begin with the end in mind, answering the question "What will the information be used for?" Options range from wanting to improve future efforts, to needing to report back to our partners and stakeholders, to being able to calculate a specific return on our investment, to knowing when we have reached an optimal giving level where further investments have a decreasing rate of return for the corporation as well as for the cause. The answer for many, we suspect, is that we want answers for all of these. But the question should be asked, as resources needed to gather this information have varying monetary implications.

2. Measure and Report Resource Outputs.

The focus at this point is on resources that the corporation contributes to the initiative and the total monetary value of those resources. Basic categories will include cash contributions as well as (ideally) the monetary value of in-kind donations of products and services, staff hours, and retail space. It is important to stress that information gathered from this effort is not intended to measure the impact of these investments. It is to establish a total monetary value for the investment, which will then be used as a base to evaluate the efficiencies and actual costs associated with outcomes produced as a result of these output levels.

Methodologies for collecting this information will include internal record keeping (e.g., number of staff hours), financial reports (e.g., cash contributions), and information provided by cause partners and public relations and advertising firms.

In recent years, progress has been made in developing measurement practices and standards that will assist corporations in calculating and reporting the totality of their giving programs. In 2002, for example, the Committee to Encourage Corporate Philanthropy entered into a strategic partnership with the American Productivity and Quality Center, the Center for Corporate Citizenship at Boston College, and the Corporate Citizenship Company, to build a framework of definitions, processes, and systems that would more effectively measure corporate giving. Included in this effort is the development of a tool kit that will provide users with global standards, measurement frameworks, management tools, and collaborative networks. The intent is to support companies to "effectively and completely capture and communicate their contributions to society according to a common framework."[8]

3. Measure and Report Outcomes for the Company, Based on Initiative Objectives and Goals.

Focus now turns to measuring outcomes associated with corporate outputs, with an emphasis on measurement of accomplishments relative to corporate objectives and goals established in the early planning stages.

Outcomes associated with *general business goals and objectives* would include tracking and reporting on desired accomplishments most often related to enhanced corporate image, strengthened stakeholder perceptions, reductions in operating costs, increases in employee satisfaction, reduction in expenditures related to employee recruitment and turnover, reduction in regulatory oversight, and receipt of any additional incentives or grants for meeting environmental or community impact guidelines.

Outcomes associated with *marketing goals and objectives* would include tracking and reporting on levels of awareness of the corporation's involvement in the initiative; enhancements to brand identity; and increases in customer loyalty, sales, traffic, and media exposures achieved through the initiative. Special efforts should be made to collect information on total levels of exposure created by corporate expenditures (e.g., total impressions achieved through paid media, publicity, material distribution, special events, and web site visits) and the monetary value associated with this. A cause promotion initiative, for example, that included a direct contribution of $35,000 for paid advertising may have actually received

$75,000 worth of media exposure due to qualifications by the charity for nonprofit rates, often at a 50 percent discount.

Methodologies associated with measuring these outcomes are often more complex and more expensive than those required for assessing outputs. Some of this information can come from internal records and existing tracking systems (e.g., sales data) and reports from external agencies (e.g., broadcast stations) and community partners (e.g., a charity who reports on the number of people who stopped by their booth sponsored by the corporation at a health fair). However, a majority of these factors will require custom consumer surveys, with sample sizes large enough to be representative and methodologies that can be replicated in the future. They may even require establishing a baseline measure, a measure at specific campaign milestones, and a post survey.

Once outcomes are quantified, attempts should be made to determine return on investment. As a simplistic example, a corporation that contributed $50,000 for promotional expenditures related to a charity walk that hypothetically generated 500,000 impressions in the marketplace would assess the cost for each impression at 10 cents, and then compare this cost with prior similar efforts. A cause-related marketing effort that generated 1,000 more product sales than in prior comparable years and increased awareness of the featured product by 25 percent among target markets would be evaluated against total contributions made to the initiative and, again, compared with prior similar efforts.

As noted earlier, this discipline is in its early stages. Managers are encouraged to become more rigorous in tracking, building historic databases, and creating metrics to guide evaluation and decision making.

4. Measure and Report Outcomes for the Cause, Based on Initiative Objectives and Goals.

As with outcomes for the corporation, of interest here are accomplishments relative to objectives and goals that were established earlier for the cause and/or charity, ones specifically supported by the corporation's involvement in the initiative. Basic measures may include one or more of the following, most often supported by cause promotions and cause-related marketing initiatives:

- Changes in awareness of the social issue.
- Changes in levels of concern for the social issue.

- Number of volunteers recruited by the initiative and associated hours.
- Amount of funds raised for the charity or issue.

In some cases, outcomes may be expressed in more tangible terms, such as outcomes associated more often with social marketing initiatives, corporate philanthropy, community volunteering, and socially responsible business practices. Examples that could be connected to a specific corporate initiative include the following:

- Number of children fed in after-school programs.
- Number of homeless people sheltered.
- Rises in test scores.
- Tons of waste diverted from landfills.
- Reduction in toxic emissions.
- Number of low-flow toilets installed.
- Number of computers recycled.
- Number of families provided a home away from home while their children were in hospitals.
- Increase in number of toddlers with life vests on a specific beach.
- Number of home owners who took recommended steps for fire prevention.

This measurement effort should be conducted in cooperation with cause partners. Ideally, the information is collected by others and then reported to the corporation. Corporate managers are encouraged to negotiate for this arrangement when establishing agreements with nonprofit and public agency partners.

5. Monitor Status of Social Issues That Initiatives Are Supporting.

Managers are encouraged to put systems in place to periodically check on the current status of the social conditions being supported by their initiatives (e.g., number of new cases of HIV in the past year). Most recognize that impact on social problems takes time and that many factors beyond a corporation's social initiative will contribute to alleviating problems. Given the ideal of a long-term commitment by the corporation to a social issue, however, it follows that a best practice would be to monitor changes and implications of these changes for future social investments.

6. Allocate Adequate Resources for Measurement and Reporting.

In the end, the major challenge associated with evaluation of corporate social initiatives and calculating returns on investments is an economic one. An ideal budgeting scenario would be to assess costs for evaluation efforts based on agreed-upon purposes and then to present this total as a proposed budget. In reality, this draft amount will likely be adjusted based on current financial considerations and priorities. Managers are then encouraged to explore less costly but still valuable methodologies, such as shared cost studies and ad hoc surveys.

Table 9.3 summarizes the strengths and concerns involved in the six types of corporate social initiatives we have outlined.

SUMMARY OF BEST PRACTICES

Choosing Social Issues to Support

1. Choose only a few social issues to support.
2. Choose those that are of concern in the communities where you do business.
3. Choose issues that have synergy with mission, values, products, and services.
4. Choose issues that have potential to support business goals: marketing, supplier relations, increased productivity, cost reductions.
5. Choose issues that are of concern to key constituent groups: employees, target markets, customers, investors, and corporate leaders.
6. Choose issues that can be supported over a long term.

Selecting Initiatives to Support Social Issues

7. Select initiatives that best meet business objectives and goals.
8. Select initiatives that meet priority needs for the cause.

9. Select multiple initiatives for a single cause, adding ones missing for current cause efforts.

10. Select initiatives representing the most potential for strong community partners.

11. Select initiatives where you have a history of experience.

12. Select initiatives that will leverage current abundant resources.

Developing and Implementing Program Plans

13. Form internal, cross-functional teams to develop plans.

14. Include community partners in plan development.

15. Establish clear objectives and measurable goals (outcomes) for the company.

16. Establish clear objectives and measurable goals (outcomes) for the cause.

17. Develop a communications plan.

18. Identify and plan for additional strategic elements.

19. Get senior management buy-in.

Evaluating Efforts

20. Determine purpose of evaluation.

21. Measure and report resource outputs.

22. Measure and report outcomes for the company, based on initiative objectives and goals.

23. Measure and report outcomes for the cause, based on initiative objectives and goals.

24. Monitor status of social issues that initiatives are supporting.

25. Allocate adequate resources for measurement and reporting.

SUMMARY COMMENTS FOR BEST PRACTICES

The final and perhaps most important advice offered by a vast majority of those we interviewed is to take time to develop a formal document that establishes written *corporate guidelines* for social initiatives,

Table 9.3 Summary of Strengths to Maximize and Concerns to Minimize

	Major Strengths to Maximize	*Major Concerns to Minimize*
Cause Promotions	• Builds corporate reputation • Attracts and retains a motivated workforce • Supports marketing objectives • Builds strong community relationships • Leverages current corporate social initiatives	• Visibility for corporate efforts can easily be lost. • Coordination with cause partners can be time consuming. • Staff time and involvement can be significant. • Promotional expenses can be significant. • Consumers may be skeptical of corporate motivations and commitment.
Cause-Related Marketing	• Supports marketing objectives • Builds strong community relationships • Leverages current corporate social initiatives	• Coordination with cause partners can be time consuming. • Staff time and involvement can be significant. • Promotional expenses can be significant. • Consumers may be skeptical of corporate motivations and commitment.
Social Marketing	• Builds corporate reputation • Contributes to general business goals • Attracts and retains a motivated workforce • Supports marketing objectives • Builds strong community relationships • Leverages current corporate social initiatives	• Coordination with cause partners can be time consuming. • Staff time and involvement can be significant. • Efforts may require external expertise. • Promotional expenses can be significant.

Philanthropy	• Builds corporate reputation • Attracts and retains a motivated workforce • Builds strong community relationships • Leverages current corporate social initiatives	• Visibility for corporate efforts can easily be lost. • Tracking resource expenditures and value can be difficult and expensive.
Community Volunteering	• Builds corporate reputation • Attracts and retains a motivated workforce • Builds strong community relationships • Leverages current corporate social initiatives	• Visibility for corporate efforts can easily be lost. • Staff time and involvement can be significant. • Tracking resource expenditures and value can be difficult and expensive.
Socially Responsible Business Practices	• Builds corporate reputation • Contributes to business goals • Attracts and retains a motivated workforce • Reduces operating costs • Reduces regulatory oversight • Builds strong community relationships • Leverages current corporate social initiatives lost	• Visibility for corporate efforts can easily be lost. • Efforts may require external expertise. • Consumers may be skeptical of corporate motivations and commitment.

guidelines that will inform and ease decision making regarding many of the twenty-five best practices presented in this chapter and will reflect the unique history, culture, goals, markets, and strategies for your company.

These guidelines should be developed (and updated at least every two to three years) by interdepartmental teams and should include sections describing most of the following decisions:

- Priority social issues to support.
- Desired business outcomes from support of social initiatives.
- Desired social and environmental outcomes from initiatives.
- Preferred types of initiatives.
- Guidelines for determining levels of contribution.
- Preferred types of giving (e.g., cash versus in-kind donations versus volunteering).
- Ideal community partners.
- Expectations regarding interdepartmental involvement in planning.
- A planning template, especially for developing internal and external communication plans.
- Philosophies regarding corporate visibility and recognition for efforts.
- Expectations and plans for tracking, evaluation, and reporting.
- Criteria for continued support.

This document, or at least components of it, can then be shared with potential community partners, helping to establish early on corporate priorities and expectations.

As always, executive management approval and enthusiasm for these guidelines will be critical to their usefulness. The ultimate scenario would be that they actually own the guidelines and embody a passion for doing the most good, as exemplified by the CEO of Kenneth Cole Productions:

What started organically as a personal effort and a contribution to the community as well as a business strategy has become our trademark. Our cause-related marketing is a process that starts with meetings at the beginning of every season, where we take inventory of what concerns us today and what we believe will still be important in a few months. . . . In the absence of therapy, I rant, I rave, I eventually exhaust myself, and then I listen to everyone else do the same thing. A quiet settles over the room as we ask ourselves how we can appropriately address what is on our minds.

Kenneth Cole[9]

A Marketing Approach to Winning Corporate Funding and Support for Social Initiatives: Ten Recommendations

If substantial financial resources are to be raised and sustained over a long period of time, it's essential that supportive partners, especially large corporate partners, get as well as give. To find the intersection of public interest and private interest that will work for your partners, begin by sitting down with them to learn about their needs before telling them about yours. What are their marketing and sales challenges? What specific public relations messages do they hope to convey? Who are their principal competitors and on what playing fields are they competing? How do they hope this partnership will be viewed by their employee workforce? Then go back and brainstorm so that you can return to the table with creative ideas for vehicles that will both raise money for and increase awareness of your cause, but will also meet the business needs of your partner.[1]

—Bill Shore, founder and CEO
of Share Our Strength

W e think Bill Shore's advice is right on, as it reflects a customer-oriented approach to the exchange process, one that has the best chance for securing corporate support for social initiatives. In fact, a synthesis of recommendations presented in this chapter is reminiscent of steps traditionally used in developing a marketing plan: a process that finds the best fit between an organization's mission, objectives, and capabilities and the needs and wants in the marketplace. It is a process that develops and executes product, pricing, distribution, and promotional strategies based on the unique profile of targeted audiences—a process built to win.

This final chapter is written for executives, administrators, and program managers of NGOs and public sector agencies seeking contributions from corporations for developing and implementing initiatives intended to support a social cause. Most often, these organizations are seeking financial support for promotional campaigns, program expansion, and outreach efforts. They may find, as we have learned, that corporations are sometimes even more willing to contribute nonmonetary resources, those they may consider they have in abundance (e.g., staff expertise, employee volunteers, idle equipment, space in promotional materials, and access to underutilized distribution channels). Although the guidelines presented here are most applicable to organizations initiating proposals to corporations, the fundamental principles also apply to those who have been approached by a corporation to assess a potential partnership.

The following 10 recommendations are based on what we have learned from corporate executives about benefits they are seeking from their contributions, concerns that can hold them back, circumstances that prompt their interest in participation, how they choose among social initiatives to support, how they evaluate potential proposals, and what they want and expect from their partners. Our focus now turns from the process of selection, development, and implementation of social initiatives to guidelines for approaching and securing corporate support. From this point forward, the corporate decision maker is in the customer seat and the cause agency is a marketer.[2]

RECOMMENDATION 1

Start by developing a list of social issues that your organization or agency is currently charged with supporting and that would benefit from additional resources. Be specific.

Most nonprofit organizations and many governmental agencies exist to support some social cause and, at any given point in time, are focused on programs and services that will advance their mission. Of interest here are those projects and initiatives that would benefit from additional funding or other resources in order to have a greater impact. Key at this initial step is to identify one or more specific issues that can then be put forth for consideration.

For example, at the mission level, the American Cancer Society works to eliminate cancer as a major health problem through efforts including research, education, advocacy, and service.[3] When considering needs for corporate support and involvement, this step would involve identifying specific priorities for campaigns or programs, such as one that encourages kids to get at least 60 minutes of moderate to vigorous physical activity five days a week or more, or one that urges women and men over 50 to get tested for colon and rectal cancer.

Similarly, the Nature Conservancy, which works to preserve plants, animals, and natural communities by protecting lands and waters, currently lists five priority conservation initiatives on its web site for focus, ones to address climate change, fire management, freshwater conservation, invasive species, and marine conservation.[4] This specific delineation will provide direction for identifying potential corporate partners.

Issues for the Boys & Girls Clubs of America, the Positive Place for Kids, range from wanting to help members develop basic computer skills to wanting to increase gang prevention and intervention efforts in the community, to wanting to provide family fun nights and single-parent support groups as a part of their family support initiative. As we can foresee, each of these social issues can eventually lead to the discovery of different natural partners in the corporate world—partners like Microsoft, which donated more than $100 million in software and cash, providing a comprehensive package of the latest Microsoft products to clubs throughout the country.[5]

Relative to a marketing model, we could think of these specific social issues as products (offerings) that the nonprofit organization or governmental agency wants to sell in the marketplace (e.g., physical activity, marine conservation, and computer skills), ones whose "sales volume" would benefit from increased financial and related support. And this is where potential corporate partners come in. In reality, these organizations and agencies are seeking corporate partners who will help design, package, produce, promote, and distribute products to a marketplace. Our first need, as recommended here, is to clarify and prioritize potential products.

RECOMMENDATION 2

Identify a short list of corporations that these social issues might have a connection with, something that relates to their business mission, products and services, customer base, employee passions, communities where they do business, and/or their corporate giving history.

We heard frequently from those interviewed for cases in this book that one of the first and most important criteria for selecting a social issue to support is that it has some connection to their business. And we saw examples of how this worked.

Inherent in a business *mission*, whether formally articulated or not, is the organization's purpose, what it is that they want to provide or accomplish in the larger environment. Given this, it seems logical for the University of North Carolina at Chapel Hill to have considered the New York Times Foundation for contributions to their School of Journalism. Likewise, it was natural for the American Red Cross, in need of cellular phones for workers to communicate with each other during times of disaster, to approach AT&T Wireless, a company that wants to connect people to information and things they "care about most."[6]

Potential connections to *products* are even easier. It seems an obvious fit for Yellowstone National Park to think of General Electric for better lighting to reduce the sky glow around Old Faithful; for the Lions Club to consider LensCrafters as a partner to collect old or unused eyeglasses; for an Arizona water coalition to think they had a good chance with a store like Home Depot as a corporate sponsor; and for a children's hospital to imagine that a local life vest manufacturer would be interested in having their brand name featured on drowning prevention program materials.

Some issues will appeal to the corporations because they appeal to their *customer base*. The Arthritis Foundation may have predicted Aleve would be interested in sponsoring their annual walk, and local humane societies probably thought they would be welcomed to conduct adoption fairs at PETsMART. Similarly, we know that corporations want to attract and retain a motivated workforce and are responsive to issues that their *employees* care about. Nonprofit agencies serving the homeless in the

Washington, D.C., area probably know that employees at Fannie Mae are eager to participate in activities to help them raise funds to support their programs.

We saw how passionate corporations can be about contributing to issues in their own back yard, as Habitat for Humanity in Detroit discovered with Ford, and local HIV/AIDS prevention organizations have found with the Coca-Cola Foundation and Coca-Cola bottlers in Africa.

Finally, the strongest connection to a social issue may be through a long corporate history of giving to a particular cause. Schools in Florida probably knew they could count on Washington Mutual to help get the word out about a town hall meeting on school issues, and local AIDS organizations probably know Kenneth Cole Productions will be open to ideas for campaigns to support the use of condoms.

These connections can be found using a variety of relatively simple research techniques, including reviewing corporate giving and citizenship statements on corporate web sites, in annual reports, in publications (e.g., *Chronicle of Philanthropy*, the *Foundation Center*, the *Federal Register*, and the *Council on Foundations*), and in press releases available online, and through discussions with board members and other community leaders involved in local businesses. It would, of course, be advantageous if the community agency has an existing or historical relationship with one of these companies on the short list.

As a final component of this activity, at the same time that a short list of ideal potential corporations is made, it is also important to identify corporations that your agency or organization does not consider a good match and/or activities that would not be acceptable (e.g., a state immunization coalition may have established partner guidelines that exclude certain corporate partners such as pharmaceuticals, or a public school may decide that it will limit activities from a soft drink sponsor to promotions of bottled water only).

RECOMMENDATION 3

Approach corporations and/or their communication agencies and find out more about their interests and experiences relative to supporting social initiatives.

In the ideal world, an initial contact would begin with a brief meeting or telephone conversation with the CEO of each of your targeted companies. It is this person's perspective that is invaluable at this phase of the process, providing more information about the company's interests, experiences, and preferences relative to supporting social causes, and about current business challenges and opportunities. Entering at this level might be made more likely if someone on the board of your agency, or a community leader associated with your agency or cause, is able to provide an introduction. The initial conversation could even be conducted by one of these VIPs, with a subsequent referral to others in the company.

However, it is more likely that initial contacts will be with department managers or their assistants. Relevant departments include those dealing with community affairs (e.g., Public Affairs, Corporate Social Responsibility, or Community Relations), corporate communications, marketing, and/or public relations. If the corporation has a foundation, initial meetings may include their representatives as well. If possible, try to arrange an initial meeting that includes one representative from their community affairs area and one from marketing. It is their combined perspectives and responsibilities that will provide the richest input.

Introductory comments should focus on positioning the meeting as an inquiry. You are exploring opportunities for community partnerships to support initiatives of interest to your organization. Your purpose is to learn more about their company's interests and needs and, if appropriate, come back with ideas on ways you might work together to benefit the cause, as well as meet some of their business goals. This is an interview, not a proposal. Let them know what research you have done on their company that has led you to them and how it aligns with your agency's mission.

Whether in one meeting or multiple meetings, some of the first questions you want to explore are those related to their interests regarding social issues and their experiences relative to social initiatives. Your questions could include the following:

- What social issues currently interest their organization the most and why? You can share what issues you are aware of that they supported in the past and ask why those issues were selected. If current issues differ from those that were of concern in the past, what brought about this change?

- What causes are their employees passionate about, if any? Is this a major consideration for them when they consider options for support and involvement?

- What causes are their target markets or customers passionate about? Again, is this a major consideration when they evaluate options?

- What forms of support interest them most? You could mention the various types of initiatives and ask, in general, which are the most and least appealing. Do they tend to like to work with community partners or prefer to handle things internally?

- What has worked well in the past? What outcomes did they value most?

- What hasn't worked well in the past? What lessons were learned?

RECOMMENDATION 4

Listen to their business needs.

Other initial topics to explore are those related to the company's business goals and objectives. Your interest is grounded in your perspective that social initiatives can and should support economic as well as social and environmental goals; that when corporations can demonstrate a return on their investment in social initiatives, they are more likely to develop long-term relationships with community partners and focus their giving programs on what is working. You think of them as a potential customer and want to understand what needs they have that a partnership with you might be able to fill. Your conversation will inspire your staff to consider options for initiatives with the best chance for winning their support.

Question areas should touch briefly on most aspects of the business, exploring corporate image, operations, human resources, community relations, public relations, and marketing issues. They might be framed as follows:

- Are there any aspects of your *visibility or reputation* in the community that you are interested in enhancing? It may be something that people don't know about you that you wish they did, or something they think about you that you wish they didn't.

- Are there any *key messages* about your company that you feel a sense of urgency to communicate?

- What about *operational issues*? Are there any guidelines from regulatory agencies that you are trying to meet that would benefit from public support? Are there any relationship issues with suppliers, franchise owners, and/or distributors that would be strengthened by involvement in social issues?

- Are you facing any major challenges relative to *attracting and retaining a motivated workforce* that might be supported by corporate involvement in the community or by volunteer opportunities?

- Are there any *consumer or business markets* that you are pursuing where involvement in a social cause might give you a competitive edge, or where a relationship with a strong community partner might be beneficial?

- In terms of *brand images*, are there any specific products that you are trying to position or reposition? Are there aggressive *sales goals* related to any of these products?

One example presented in this book that might help demonstrate the value of these questions is the case regarding Subway, described in Chapter 5. One could imagine that an interview such as the one outlined above, conducted by a representative from the American Heart Association, might have revealed Subway's interest in being perceived as a healthy fast-food option. The interview may also have shown that Subway wanted to support franchise owners with increased sales, to build pride for their products among employees, to differentiate themselves from others in the fast-food industry, and that they wanted their line of low-fat subs to capture a significant share of the healthy fast-food category, ideally to launch it. One can further imagine that the American Heart Association representative might be eager to return to the office, confident that he or she might have just found a major sponsor for the annual fundraising walk.

RECOMMENDATION 5

Share with them the social issues your organization supports, the initiatives you are considering or engaged in, and your strengths and resources. Find out which, if any, they find most appealing.

Social issues, as we are referring to them here, are the specific problems that your organization is interested in solving, ones that would benefit from additional financial and related support. We have suggested that these issues be considered products you want to sell in the marketplace. At some point in this getting-to-know-each-other process, this list should be shared. It should be limited to those that your research, hunches, and early discussions suggest might be of most interest to the corporation being approached and interviewed. This is also when you share your guidelines for acceptable activities.

The American Legacy Foundation's story of finding corporate support for one of its initiatives illustrates this process well. As background, the American Legacy Foundation was established in 1999, funded primarily by funds from the Master Settlement Agreement with the tobacco industry. The organization works to build a world where young people reject tobacco and anyone can quit smoking. Efforts are concentrated on providing grants, technical training and assistance, youth activism, strategic partnerships, countermarketing and grassroots marketing campaigns, and public relations. The organization has a special focus on helping communities disproportionately affected by the toll of tobacco, including African Americans, Hispanics, and Native Americans. One of the foundation's signature programs is "Circle of Friends: Uniting to Be Smoke-Free," a national grassroots social movement to highlight the importance of supporting smokers who want to quit, while also educating people about the toll of tobacco-related disease on women, their families, and communities.

Of interest for this illustration is one of the foundation's specific partnerships, designed to reach young women smokers ages 16 to 24. The foundation was seeking to help young women who want to quit smoking, but also to educate other young women in this age group so that they never start smoking. Match this interest with the knowledge that Avon, the global cosmetics giant, was planning to debut a new beauty business, called "mark," targeting the 300 million young women ages 16 to 24 in the United States, who have an estimated spending power of $250 billion, $75 billion of which is spent in the beauty and fashion sectors.[7] Picture Avon **mark** executives' reaction when the American Legacy Foundation explored a potential partnership with them. Recent compelling research findings had indicated that among the 25 percent of young women ages 16 to 24 who smoke, 65 percent wanted to quit, but only 3 percent succeeded for a least a year.[8]

The two organizations agreed to work together, through Circle of

Friends, to reach young women with healthy lifestyle messages around smoking. In a press release announcing the partnership, Deborah Fine, the president of Avon Future, commented: "Building upon Avon's more than 100-year legacy and leadership in the area of women's health, **mark** is privileged to continue this commitment with a new generation of women who are eager to make a difference."[9] The press release announced that **mark** would be promoting cessation messages, encouraging mark representatives to communicate with their peers about tobacco use, and donating all proceeds from the sale of the Circle of Friends Sunburst Pin to the American Legacy Foundation.

RECOMMENDATION 6

Prepare and submit a proposal to those corporations most interested in your social issues. Present several optional initiatives for potential support, ones that are the best match for their stated business and marketing needs.

At this point, you are hopefully rich with input. Ideally, you know the priority social issues the targeted company or companies are interested in and ones they consider a priority. You understand their current business goals and challenges and have identified ones that you might be able to support. You have a sense of what types of initiatives they prefer most and you have an inside track on what they value in a partnership— and what makes them leery. This should make it easy to take the next step, crafting a proposal.

A proposal should include a clear statement of *purpose*, highlighting the potential impact that proposed initiatives would have on a social issue of common concern. "This initiative is intended to help reduce oral disease among children by increasing access to dental care among low-income populations." It should make clear how this specific initiative would meet *priority needs for the cause*. "Your financial support will enable us to reach the vast majority of underserved youth enrolled in after-school programs at Boys & Girls Clubs across the country." You should also indicate your interest and commitment to help develop evaluation mechanisms to measure this impact.

Identify the *strengths and resources* you intend to bring to the table, including your technical and clinical expertise regarding the issue, staff time you intend to dedicate to the project, involvement of high-visibility board members or elected officials, and actual funds you intend to commit. Talk about your interest in a long-term partnership if at all feasible.

Outline *options for their contributions*, recalling their preferences for direct monetary contributions versus in-kind services or employee volunteering.

Highlight *potential benefits for the corporation*. Include mention of how you believe this new initiative will leverage their current and past efforts in the community. Suggest ways their employees might be involved. Point out the business and marketing goals you believe this may support, and express your interest in working with them to maximize these opportunities. Provide options for visibility for their contributions, remaining open to their preferences for tactical strategies such as logo placement and use of corporate colors. Mention any additional *strong community partners* that are currently involved or that you intend to approach, and what they will also be providing. Offer initial ideas about how you might publicly recognize their contributions, ones that reflect the corporation's business and marketing goals as well as its unique culture and style.

Using these principles, imagine how product managers at Dole might have responded to a proposal from the National Cancer Institute's "5 A Day for Better Health" program that outlined an opportunity to play a vital role in the national "5 A Day" initiative, which would include Dole's presence on nutritional education program materials that would likely reach over 30,000 schools and 100,000 elementary teachers in the United States and would provide multiple co-branding opportunities, including using the "5 A Day" logo stickers on a banana. "Where do I sign?"

RECOMMENDATION 7

Participate in developing an implementation plan.

Traditional components of an implementation plan will include setting objectives and goals (desired outcomes) for the company and the cause; selecting target audiences; identifying strategic activities; and determining roles, responsibilities, timelines, and budgets. As we heard from many corporate executives, involvement of cross-functional teams in this planning process (from the corporation as well as the NGO or public agency) is often key to a successful program and should be encouraged early on.

Initial plans should be considered a draft, as there will likely be needs for your agency, as well as the company, to review intended strategies with senior management and, in many cases, to test ideas with other key publics including customers of the corporation, donors to your agency, or citizens in a community. For example, a public agency interested in corporate support for a childhood immunization campaign may learn quickly, by conducting a couple of focus groups with parents, that a partnership that included a drugstore's name on the front of a brochure raised considerable concern with material content, but that by adding the phrase "Printing courtesy of" before the name and putting it on the back of the brochure, objections were assuaged. From the corporation's point of view, a quick test with customers in a retail store might reveal that cause promotional messages on grocery bags would not be noticed unless the checkout clerk also mentioned the promotion.

RECOMMENDATION 8

Offer to handle as much of the administrative legwork as possible.

Several initiatives—especially cause promotions, cause-related marketing, and social marketing ones—tend to involve more administrative time and effort than others, such as providing a cash grant or participating in a one-time employee volunteer event. In cases where these initiatives have been identified as ideal relative to desired outcomes, it may be important for the NGO or the public agency staff to facilitate the partnership by offering to take on a variety of administrative tasks, which may range from establishing record-keeping systems to editing copy to coordinating with printers and delivering materials.

Willingness to assume these responsibilities will do more than just relieve the corporate partner. It may make the difference in how much they are able to contribute to the campaign and its duration; it may also influence whether a company is willing to commit to a multiyear campaign or a one-time-only event. This then affects the possibility of exploring additional initiatives in the future.

Consider the partnership between *PARADE* magazine and Share Our Strength and others sponsors, where partners needed to track and then report on the numbers of people across the country that baked, bought, or sold goods during the Great American Bake Sale, and then distribute funds to qualifying organizations, in part according to geographic locations

where funds were raised. An offer by Share Our Strength and other partners to help make this happen may be key to the publisher's high level of
program participation.

RECOMMENDATION 9

Assist in measuring and reporting outcomes.

Agency managers should express in early discussions a commitment
to program evaluation. Corporate satisfaction and long-term commitment to a partnership may in fact rely significantly on this factor.

Once program goals and strategies have been established, a specific
evaluation plan can be developed to assess program processes as well as
outcomes. This should be a team effort, as it will be important to measure and report outcomes for the cause relative to established objectives
and goals, as well as for the company. This plan should include delineation of roles and responsibilities as well as fund requirements.

Evaluation efforts vary significantly by type of initiative, each presenting its own set of metrics, requirements, and challenges. Red Cross may
have simply reported back to AT&T Wireless the number of chapters that
received their donated phones, the numbers of times the phones were used,
and the types of emergency situations that were ameliorated by this improved access during times of disaster. The task for the water conservation
coalition and Home Depot in Arizona would be more daunting, with desired process measures including number of participants in workshops and
reach and frequency of advertising messages; and outcome measures would
need to attempt to monitor increases in sales of featured products as well as
changes in awareness of water conservation techniques and levels of water
usage in the region. The effort would clearly need more hands on deck.

RECOMMENDATION 10

**Provide recognition for the corporation's contribution, in ways pre-
ferred by the company.**

Although we found varying levels of enthusiasm for corporate recognition and a range of preferred forms for this recognition, one theme was
pervasive: Let the cause partner and those who benefited from the initiative tell the story.

Consider the power of American Legacy Foundation presenting Deborah Fine, president of Avon Future, the Corporate Leadership Award honoring "individuals committed to advancing the foundation's mission to build a world where young people reject tobacco."[10] And if you were a division manager for 7-Eleven in Texas, imagine your appreciation when the Texas Department of Transportation recognizes your efforts for influencing motorists to "stash their trash." What better acknowledgment could there be for Shell's contribution than for the Nature Conservancy to be the one to publicly applaud volunteer efforts to protect coastal habitats or for a school superintendent to include a thank-you to Washington Mutual in the district's newsletter? And imagine the satisfaction for Aleve to be publicly recognized by the Arthritis Foundation, for Pampers by the SIDS Foundation, for Wal-Mart by the Children's Miracle Network, for Subway by the American Heart Association, for Crest by the Surgeon General, for Dole by the National Cancer Institute, and for Lysol by Keep America Beautiful. Such kudos are about as good as it gets.

SUMMARY OF RECOMMENDATIONS FOR THOSE SEEKING CORPORATE SUPPORT

This chapter has presented guidelines and principles (listed together below) that we believe offer NGOs and public agencies the best chances for winning support from corporations for social initiatives.

1. Start by developing a list of social issues that your organization or agency is currently charged with supporting and that would benefit from additional resources. Be specific.

2. Identify a short list of corporations that these social issues might have a connection with, something that relates to their business mission, products and services, customer base, employee passions, communities where they do business, and/or their corporate giving history.

3. Approach corporations and/or their communication agencies and find out more about their interests and experiences relative to supporting social initiatives.

4. Listen to their business needs.

5. Share with them the social issues your organization supports, the initiatives you are considering or engaged in, and your strengths and resources. Find out which, if any, they find most appealing.

6. Prepare and submit a proposal to those corporations most interested in your social issues. Present several optional initiatives for potential support, ones that are the best match for their stated business and marketing needs.

7. Participate in developing an implementation plan.

8. Offer to handle as much of the administrative legwork as possible.

9. Assist in measuring and reporting outcomes.

10. Provide recognition for the corporation's contribution, in ways preferred by the company.

We recognize that few have the luxury, the time, the patience, or the perfect-world scenario that might be needed to following these recommended practices, particularly in a sequential order. We know that the reality looks more like "we need to get more funds to make this campaign work, and we need them soon, so let's apply for a grant from General Mills or ask one of our board members if they'd renew their company's annual commitment." We understand this is asking a lot—from the NGO, the public agency, and the potential corporate partner.

At a minimum, keep focused on an intention to develop a program that will do the most good for the cause as well as the company, and hold close a conviction that the public, nonprofit, and private sectors can and should work together to meet social and environmental goals as well as economic ones. In fact, all of our stakeholders and benefactors are counting on us to do just that.

NOTES

Chapter 1   *The Case for Doing at Least Some Good*

1. Carly Fiorina, keynote address, Business for Social Responsibility Annual Conference, Los Angeles, California, November 12, 2003, Hewlett-Packard Company, Copyright (November 2003) Hewlett-Packard Development Company, L.P.,http://www.hp.com/hpinfo /execteam/speeches/fiorina/ Speeches & Articles (accessed December 2, 2003).

2. World Business Council for Sustainable Development, "Corporate Social Responsibility," http://www.wbcsd.ch/templates/Template WBCSD1/layout.asp?type=p&MenuId=MzI3&d (accessed March 25, 2004).

3. Business for Social Responsibility, "Introduction," http://www.bsr.org /BSRResources/WhitePaperDetail.cfm?DocumentID=48809 (accessed March 25, 2004).

4. Association of Fundraising Professionals, http://afpnet.org/tier3_ print.cfm?folder_id=2345&content_item_id=2286 and http://www .aafrc.org/images/giving_usa_2003_sources_pie.jpg (accessed May 27, 2004).

5. Cone Inc., *2000 Cone/Roper Executive Study: Cause Initiatives from the Corporate Perspective*, http://www.coneinc.com/Pages/research .html (accessed October 6, 2003).

6. Cone Inc., *Our Research* (Boston: Cone Inc., 2000), http:// www.coneinc.com/Pages/research.html (accessed July 5, 2004).

7. Corporate Social Responsibility Newswire Service press release, "KPMG Survey: More Top U.S. Companies Reporting on Corporate Responsibility," KPMG, LLP., June 10, 2002, http://www .csrwire.com/print.cgi/1153.html (accessed March 25, 2004).

8. Starbucks Corporation, *Corporate Social Responsibility Annual Report for Fiscal 2002* (Seattle: Starbucks Corporation, 2002), 2.

9. American Express Company, *Philanthropy at American Express Report* (New York: American Express Company, 2004), http://home3.americanexpress.com/corp/philanthropy/fdnbro.asp (accessed March 25, 2004).

10. Corporate Social Responsibility Newswire Service press release, "Michael Dell Discusses Digital Inclusion at La Raza Conference: Executive Emphasizes Company's Commitment to Hispanic Consumers," Dell Computer Corporation, http://www.csrwire.com/print.cgi?sfArticleId=1978 (accessed March 25, 2004).

11. Franklin D. Raines, speech, Greenlining Institute Economic Development Summit, Los Angeles, California, April 10, 2003, Fannie Mae, http://www.fanniemae.com/media/speeches (accessed March 25, 2004).

12. Telephone interview with Andy Acho, worldwide director, Environmental Outreach & Strategy, Ford Motor Company, April 13, 2004.

13. Carlos M. Gutierrez, "Corporate Citizenship," Kellogg Company, http://www.kelloggs.com/kelloggco/corporate_citizenship/index.html (accessed March 25, 2004).

14. Carly Fiorina, speech, Business for Social Responsibility Annual Conference, Los Angeles, California, November 12, 2003, Hewlett-Packard Company, Copyright (November, 2003) Hewlett-Packard Development, L.P. http://www.hp.com/hpinfo/execteam/speeches/fiorina/bsr2003.html (accessed March 25, 2004).

15. CSRwire, Oak Brook, IL, "McDonald's Social Responsibility Report: One-Year Global Update 05/02/2003, http://www.csrwire.com/article.cgi/1799.html (accessed July 2004).

16. Nike Inc., *Nike 2001 Corporate Responsibility Report: Vision*, (Beaverton: Nike Inc., 2001), 4, http://www.nike.com/nikebiz/nikebiz.jhtml?page=29&item=fy01 (accessed March 25, 2004).

17. Craig Smith, "The New Corporate Philanthropy," *Harvard Business Review*, May–June 1994, 105–107.

18. Ibid., 108.

19. Ibid.

20. David Hess, Nikolai Rogovsky, and Thomas W. Dunfee, "The Next Wave of Corporate Community Involvement: Corporate

Social Initiatives," *California Management Review* 44, no. 2, Winter 2002, 114.

21. Business for Social Responsibility, "Introduction."
22. Cone Inc., "The Cone/Roper Study—A Benchmark Survey of Consumer Awareness and Attitudes Towards Cause Related Marketing, Cone Communications, 1993/94," http://www.msen.mb.ca/crm.html (accessed March 25, 2004).
23. Cone Inc., "Post-September 11th: Major Shift in American Attitudes Towards Companies Involved With Social Issues," http://www.coneinc.com/Pages/pr_8.html (accessed March 25, 2004).
24. Cone Inc.,"2002 Cone Corporate Citizenship: The Role of Cause Branding: Executive Summary," 4, http://www.coneinc.com/Pages /pr_13.html (accessed April 2, 2004).
25. Paul Bloom, Steve Hoeffler, Kevin Keller, and Carlos Basurto, "Consumer Responses to Social and Commercial Sponsorship," working paper, 2003.
26. Minette E. Drumwright, "Socially Responsible Organizational Buying: Environmental Concern as a Noneconomic Buying Criterion," *Journal of Marketing* 58 (July 1994):1–19.
27. Business for Social Responsibility, "Introduction."
28. Hamish Pringle and Marjorie Thompson, *Brand Spirit: How Cause Related Marketing Builds Brands* (London: Wiley, 2001), 5–9.
29. Ibid., xxi.
30. Ibid., xxii.
31. Bloom, Hoeffler, Keller, and Basurto, "Consumer Responses."
32. Council for Economic Priorities, *Shopping for a Better World: The Quick and Easy Guide to All Your Socially Responsible Shopping* (New York: Council for Economic Priorities, 1994).
33. *Fortune*.com, "2004 America's Most Admired Companies," http://www.fortune.com/fortune/mostadmired/subs/2004/keyattributes /0,19405,social_resp,00.html (accessed July 5, 2004).
34. William Baue, "April 29, 2002: *Business Ethics'* 100 Best Corporate Citizens Outperform S&P 500," SRI World Group, Inc., http://www.socialfunds.com/news/article.cgi/832.html (accessed March 25, 2004).
35. Business for Social Responsibility, "Introduction."
36. Ibid.

37. Hess, Rogovsky, and Dunfee, "Next Wave," 113–114.
38. Smith, "New Corporate Philanthropy," 109–110.
39. Cone Inc., *2002 Cone Corporate Citizenship Study: New National Survey Finds Americans Intend to Punish Corporate "Bad Guys," Reward Good Ones* (Boston: Cone Inc., 2002). http://www.conenet .com/Pages/pr_13.html (accessed April 2, 2004).
40. Ibid.
41. Business for Social Responsibility, "Introduction."
42. The Timberland Company, *Timberland Corporate Social Responsibility Report for the Year 2000* (Boston: The Timberland Company, 2000).
43. Cisco Systems, Inc., *Case Study: Energy Efficiency in Design and Construction—Cleaner Air and Millions in Savings* (San Jose: Cisco Systems, Inc., 2003), http://www.cisco.com/en/US/about /ac227/ac228/ac229/about_cisco_corp_citi_case_study.html (accessed April 2, 2004).
44. World Business Council for Sustainable Development web site, "Banking on a Good Reputation," as reported in the *Financial Times*, July 21, 2003, by Jane Fuller, http://www.wbcsd.ch/lugins /DocSearch/details.asp?type=DocDet&DocID=MTgzNQ (accessed July 21, 2003).
45. Ibid.
46. Praveen Sinha, Chekitan S. Dev, and Tania Salas, "The Relationship Between Corporate Social Responsibility and Profitability of Hospitality Firms: Do Firms That Do Good Also Do Well?" working paper, January 15, 2002, 4, Cornell School of Hospitality Management, http://www.hotelschool.cornell.edu/chr/research/working/ (accessed April 2, 2004).
47. Business for Social Responsibility, "Introduction."
48. NewCircle Communications, "Corporate Social Responsibility— A New Ethic for a New Economy," CSRWire, SRI World Group, Inc., http://www.csrwire.com/page.cgi/nc1.html (accessed April 2, 2004).
49. William Baue, "*Business Ethics'* 100 Best."
50. Susan Orenstein, "The Selling of Breast Cancer," *Business 2.0*, February 2003, http://www.business2.com/articles/mag/print /0,1643,046296,00.html (accessed October 6, 2003).
51. American Heart Association Inc,. "Tobacco Industry's Targeting of Youth, Minorities, and Women," American Heart Association Inc., http://www.americanheart.org/presenter.jhtml=identifier

=11226 (accessed March 25, 2004), and Philip Morris USA—Policies, Practices & Positions, "Youth Smoking Prevention," http://www.pmusa.com/policies_practices/ysp/communications.asp (accessed July 2004).

52. Sinha, Dev, and Salas, "Corporate Social Responsibility and Profitability."

53. McDonald's Corporation, *Social Responsibility Report 2002*, 11.

54. John Gourville and Kash Rangan, "Doing Well by Doing Good: Understanding and Valuing the Cause Maketing Relationship." Harvard Business School, working paper August 29, 2003.

55. Bloom, Hoeffler, Keller, and Basurto, "Consumer Responses."

Chapter 2   Corporate Social Initiatives

1. Washington Mutual, Inc., 2001 Community Annual Report (Seattle: Washington Mutual, Inc., 2001), http://publicsite.wamu.com/about/community/commitment/annualreport/summary.htm (accessed July 29, 2003).

2. Washington Mutual, Inc., 2002 Community Annual Report (Seattle: Washington Mutual, Inc., 2002), http://publicsite.wamu.com/about/community/commitment/annualreport/summary.htm (accessed March 25, 2004).

3. Washington Mutual, Inc. Giving Guidelines (Seattle: Washington Mutual, Inc., 2004), http://publicsite.wamu.com/about/community/support/givingguidelines/givingguidelines.htm (accessed March 25, 2004).

4. Washington Mutual, Inc., 2003 Community Annual Report, 12.

5. Washington Mutual, Inc., "WaMu & Education: Class Acts" http://publicsite.wamu.com/about/community/programs/wamueducation/wamueducation.htm (accessed March 25, 2004).

6. Ibid., 21.

7. Ibid., 17.

8. Washington Mutual, Inc., 2002 Community Annual Report, 2.

9. Dell Computer Corporation, "Michael Dell Discusses Digital Inclusion at The National Council of La Raza, Austin, Texas," Corporate Social Responsibility Newswire Service, July 16, 2003, http://www.csrwire.com/print.cgi?sfArticleId=1978 (accessed March 25, 2004).

10. Michael Dell, "Letter from the Chairman: Dell Corporate Vision," Dell Computer Corporation, http://www.dell.com/us/en/gen

/corporate/vision_print_ceo_environ.htm (accessed August 18, 2003).

11. Dell Computer Corporation, Dell Environmental Report: Fiscal Year 2003 in Review, (Austin: Dell Computer Corporation, 2003), 7, http://www1.us.dell.com/content/topics/global.aspx/corp/environment/en/index?c=us&l=en&s=corp (accessed March 25, 2004).

12. U.S. Environmental Protection Agency, "Resource Conservation Challenge," www.plugintorecycling.org (accessed March 25, 2004).

13. Dell Computer Corporation, Dell Environmental Report: Fiscal Year 2003 in Review, 27.

14. Dell Computer Corporation, Dell press release, December 19, 2001, Austin, Texas, http://www.dell.com/us/en/gen/corporate/press/press office_print_news_2001-12-19-aus-00 (accessed 8/21/2003).

15. Dell Computer Corporation, "Dell and the Environment," http://www1.us.dell.com/content/topics/global.aspx/corp/environment/en/index?c=us&cs=19&l=en&s=dhs (accessed March 25, 2004).

16. Dell Computer Corporation, Dell Environmental Report: Fiscal Year 2003 in Review, 7-15.

17. Ibid.

18. McDonald's Corporation, "Awards and Recognition," http://www.mcdonalds.com/corp/invest/pub/annual_rpt_archives/2001_annual.html (accessed March 25, 2004).

19. McDonald's Corporation, Social Responsibility Report 2002 (Long Island: McDonald's Corporation, 2002), 4, http://www.mcdonalds.com/corp/values/socialrespons/sr_report.html (accessed March 25, 2004).

20. McDonald's Corporation, Social Responsibility Report 2002, 2.

21. Ibid., 4.

22. Ibid., 16.

23. McDonald's Corporation, "Children's Day," http://www.mcdonalds.com/corporate/whatsnew/childrensday/children.html 8/18/2003 or http://www.mcdonalds.com/corp/values/wcd.html (accessed March 25, 2004).

24. Ibid.

25. McDonald's Corporation, "Celebrity Support," http://www.mcdonalds.com/countries/usa/whatsnew/pressrelease/2003/08052003/index.html or http://www.mcdonalds.com/corp/values/wcd/celebrity.html (accessed August 18, 2003).

26. McDonald's Corporation, Social Responsibility Report 2002, 14.
27. Ibid.
28. Ibid., 21.
29. Ibid., 20.

Chapter 3   *Corporate Cause Promotions*

1. Ben & Jerry's Homemade Holdings, Inc., "One Sweet Whirled: One Sweet Campaign to Fight Global Warming," http://www .onesweetwhirled.org (accessed April 2, 2004).
2. Ben & Jerry's Homemade Holdings, Inc., "Our Mission Statement," http://www.benjerry.com/our_company/our_mission (accessed March 27, 2004).
3. Ben & Jerry's Homemade Holdings, Inc., "One Sweet Whirled."
4. PETsMART, the bouncing ball, PETsMART Charities, and Just A Buck, Change Their Luck are trademarks of PETsMART Store Support Group, Inc., and may be federally registered or pending registration in the United States and other jurisdictions.
5. PETsMART Inc., "Happiness Is Saving a Pet's Life," http:// www.petsmart.com/adoptions/index.shtml (accessed March 27, 2004).
6. Ibid.
7. Ibid.
8. Arthritis Foundation, Arthritis Walk home page, http://www .arthritis.org/events/arthritiswalk/default.asp.
9. British Airways, Plc., "Change for Good," http://www.british airways.com/travel/crcfgood/public/en_gb (accessed March 27, 2004), and http://www.britishairways.com/responsibility.
10. U.S. Fund for UNICEF, "Change for Good," http://www.unicefusa .org/support/cfg.html (accessed October 9, 2003).
11. UNICEF, "Change for Good," http://www.unicef.org/noteworthy /changeforgood (accessed April 7, 2004).
12. Ibid.
13. Wal-Mart Stores Inc., "Wal-Mart: Good. Works.," http://www.walmart foundation.org (accessed October 9, 2003).
14. Ibid.
15. Wal-Mart Stores Inc., "Children's Miracle Network," http://www .cmn.org/web/sponsors/sponsorpages/wmart.htm (accessed March 30, 2004).

16. PARADE Publications, "Great American Bake Sale Media Center," http://www.greatamericanbakesale.org (accessed October 9, 2003).
17. PARADE Publications, "Facts on Parade," http://www.parade.com/mediarelations/press_releases/facts.html (accessed October 9, 2003).
18. David Oliver Relin, "Thanks a Million," *PARADE*, October 5, 2003, 18–20.
19. Nordstrom Inc., "Diversity Affairs," http://about.nordstrom.com/aboutus/diversity/diversity.asp (accessed October 9, 2003).
20. Ibid.
21. The Body Shop International, Plc., "The Body Shop: Our Values," http://www.thebodyshop.com/web/tbsgl/values_aat_issue.jsp (accessed on March 30, 2004)
22. The Body Shop International, Plc., "The Body Shop: Our Values," http://www.thebodyshop.com/web/tbsgl (accessed on March 30, 2004).
23. Johnson & Johnson Health Care Systems, "Healing the Crisis in Nursing: A Progress Report," http://www.jnj.com/news/jnj_news/20030506_100339.htm (accessed October 9, 2003).
24. Copyright © Johnson & Johnson Health Care Systems Inc., 2004.
25. Luxottica S.p.A., "LensCrafters: Give the Gift of Sight," www.givethegiftofsight.org (accessed April 2, 2004).
26. Michael Siegel and Lynne Doner, *Marketing Public Health: Strategies to Promote Social Change* (Gaithersburg, MD: Aspen, 1998), 321.

Chapter 4 *Cause-Related Marketing*

1. American Express Company, "2000 Report: Philanthropy at American Express," http://home3.americanexpress.com/corp/philanthropy/default.asp (accessed March 30, 2004).
2. Business for Social Responsibility, "Cause Related Marketing: Introduction," http://www.bsr.org/BSRResources/WhitePaperDetail.cfm/?DocumentID=215 (accessed March 30, 2004).
3. Windermere Real Estate Services Inc., "The Windermere Foundation:

Helping Homeless and Low-Income Families," www.windermere.com (accessed March 30, 2004).

4. Newman's Own, "Shameless Exploitation in Pursuit of the Common Good," Newman's Own, http://www.newmansown.com/125 million.htm (accessed March 30, 2004).

5. Libby Wells, "Emotional Appeal of Charging for Charity Rings Up the Donations for Favorite Causes," Bankrate Inc., http://www .bankrate.com/brm/news/cc/20000320.asp (accessed March 30, 2004).

6. L. Nicholas Deane, "Credit Cards and Donor Affinity," The NonprofitTimes, April 15 (2003). http://www.nptimes.com/fme/apr03 /fme_2.html (accessed March 30, 2004).

7. Ibid.

8. Working Assets, "Working Assets Mission, Donations, and Activism," http://www.workingassets.com/aboutwa.cfm (accessed November 11, 2003).

9. First USA, "World Wildlife Fund Platinum Card: Help the Wild Things Stay Wild," http://www.firstusa.com/cgi-bin/webcgi/web serve.cgi?partner_dir_name=world_wildlife_fund&page=cont& mkid=6T9N (accessed March 30, 2004).

10. American Lung Association, "When You Can't Breath Nothing Else Matters," http://www.thealacard.com/ (accessed April 14, 2004).

11. Hamish Pringle and Marjorie Thompson, *Brand Spirit: How Cause Related Marketing Builds Brands*, (London: John Wiley and Sons Ltd, 2001), 32.

12. Avon Foundation, "Avon Foundation Welcome: Help Make Us Obsolete—Support the Cause," http://www.avoncompany.com/women /avoncrusade/index.html (accessed March 30, 2004).

13. Ibid.

14. MMWR2003. Cigarette Smoking Among Adults—United States. 52(40): 953–956. CDC Annual Smoking Attributable Mortality, Years of Potential Life Lost and Economic Costs—United States, 1995–1996.

15. QVC Inc., "Corporate Facts," http://www.qvc.com/mainhqfact.html (accessed November 11,2003).

16. From print and appearing in *People* magazine 8/25/03, p. 39.

17. American Legacy Foundation, "Press Room."

18. Keep America Beautiful Inc., "Who We Are," http://www.kab .org/who1.cfm (accessed April 2, 2004).

19. Information provided by Alex Whitehouse, vice president of marketing, LYSOL Brand.

20. Target Corporation, press release, "Guests Help Target Award $13 Million to Schools Nationwide," September 29, 2003, http://biz.yahoo.com/prnews/030929/cgm048_l.html (accessed April 14, 2004).

21. Comcast Corporation, "About Comcast Corporation," http://comcast.com/About_Comcast/default.html?LinkID=80 (accessed November 3, 2003).

22. Louis Chunovic, "Liz Castells-Heard," Television Week, May 3, (2003), http://www.adcastells.com/castells-news/pdf/4.-TelevisionWeek-990F0.pdf (accessed April 2, 2004) and information from Liz Castells-Heard.

23. 2004 Twin Cities International Corporate Citizen Awards, April 20, 2004, presented by the International Leadership Institute in conjunction with the *Twin Cities Business Monthly*.

24. Newman's Own, "Shameless Exploitation."

Chapter 5   *Corporate Social Marketing*

1. Procter & Gamble Company, "Crest Healthy Smiles 2010 Program Fights the Nation's 'Silent Epidemic' In Oral Health," http://www.cresthealthysmiles.com/press_release/pr_2010_program.htm (accessed April 7, 2004).

2. Philip Kotler and G. Zaltman, "Social Marketing: An Approach to Planned Change," Journal of Marketing, Vol. 35: 3–12 (1971).

3. Philip Kotler, Ned Roberto, and Nancy Lee, *Social Marketing: Improving the Quality of Life* (Thousand Oaks, CA: SAGE Publications, 2002).

4. Philip Kotler and G. Armstrong, *Principles of Marketing* (Upper Saddle River: Prentice-Hall, 2001), 269.

5. Kotler, Roberto, and Lee, *Social Marketing*.

6. BSR "Introduction," http://www.bsr.org/BSRResources/WhitePaperDetail.cfm?DocumentID=48809 (accessed March 25, 2004).

7. National Institute of Child Health and Human Development, "Health Information & Media—SIDS: 'Back to Sleep' Campaign," http://www.nichd.nih.gov/sids/pampers.htm (accessed April 7, 2004).

8. Ibid.

9. Ibid.

10. Tools of Change, "Back to Sleep—Health Canada SIDS Social Marketing Campaign," http://www.toolsofchange.com/English/Case studies/default.asp?ID=161 (accessed April 7, 2004).

11. RadioShack Corporation, "StreetSentz: Common Sentz Tips For Safer Kidz," RadioShack Corporation, http://www.radioshack corporation.com/cr/community_relations.shtml (accessed August 14, 2003).

12. Best Buy Company, Inc., "Best Buy Electronics Recycling Program," http://www.e4partners.com/best_buy_consumer_electronics_recycling .htm (accessed April 7, 2004).

13. Best Buy Company, Inc., "Best Buy Announces Electronics Recycling Program," http://www.crra.com/ewaste/articles/bestbuys.html (accessed April 7, 2004).

14. Ibid.

15. Kotler, Roberto, and Lee, *Social Marketing*, 56.

16. Premera Blue Cross, "New Premera Blue Cross/UW Analysis May Help Doctors Reduce Health Threats From Drug-Resistant Bacteria," https://www.premera.com/stellent/groups/public/documents /xcpproject/newsroom_press_releases.asp#TopOfPage (accessed April 7, 2004).

17. National Cancer Institute, "Dole Vice President Accepts Position as Director of NCI 5 A Day Program," http://www.5aday.gov /whats_new101901.shtml (accessed April 7, 2004).

18. Dole Food Company, Inc., "Dole 5 A Day Program Overview," http://www.dole5aday.com/Media/Press/M_ProgramOverview.jsp? topmenu=5 (accessed April 7, 2004).

19. Ibid.

20. Dole Food Company, Inc., "Dole 5 A Day," http://www.dole5 aday.com (accessed October 8, 2003).

21. Tuerff-Davis EnviroMedia Inc, "'Don't Mess with Texas' Litter Prevention Campaign," http://www.enviromedia.com/study4.php (accessed August 25, 2003).

22. 7-Eleven Inc., "7-Eleven Tells Customers: 'Dine on the Dash but Stash Your Trash",) http://www.7-eleven.com/newsroom/articles.asp ?p=2052 (accessed August 25, 2003).

23. Ibid.

24. Safeco Corporation, "About Us," http://www.safeco.com/safeco /about/ (accessed April 7, 2004).

25. The Home Depot Inc., "Social Responsibility Report," http://www
.homedepot.com/HDUS/EN_US/corporate/corp_respon/social_
respon.shtml (accessed April 7, 2004).
26. Ibid.
27. "Water—Use It Wisely" and the "100 Ways in 30 Days to Save
Water" promotion are registered trademarks of Park and Company
Marketing Communications, Inc.
28. Kotler, Roberto, and Lee, *Social Marketing*.

Chapter 6   *Corporate Philanthropy*

1. Ronald Paul Hill, Debra Stephens, and Iain Smith, "Corporate Social Responsibility: An Examination of Individual Firm Behavior,"
Business and Society Review, 108:3 (2003), 339–364.
2. Business for Social Responsibility, "Issue Brief: Philanthropy,"
http://www.bsr.org/BSRResources/IssueBriefsList.cfm?area=all
(accessed April 14, 2004).
3. Ibid.
4. Ari Weinberg, "America's Most Generous Corporations," Forbes Inc.,
http://moneycentral.msn.com/content/invest/forbes/P64835.asp?
Printer (accessed April 14, 2004).
5. Michael Porter and Mark Kramer, "The Competitive Advantage
of Corporate Philanthropy," Harvard Business Review, December 2002, http://www.isc.hbs.edu/HBR_Dec2002_Corporate_
Philanthropy.htm http://www.corphilanthropy.org/ (accessed April
14, 2004).
6. ConAgra Foods, Inc., news release, "New Program Will Fight
Hunger Among Pocatello Children," Pocatello, Idaho, October 14,
2003, http://www.conagra.com/media/news.jsp?ID=20031016 (accessed April 14, 2004) and *ConAgra Foods 2003 Annual Report*
(Omaha: ConAgra Foods, Inc., 2003), http://www.conagra.com
/investors/index.jsp (accessed April 14, 2004).
7. ConAgra Foods, "New Program."
8. ConAgra Foods, Inc., news release, "Amarillo's First Kids Café Site
to Hold Grand Opening at the North Branch YMCA," Amarillo,
Texas, August 15, 2003, http://www.conagra.com/media/news.jsp
?ID=20030815 (accessed April 14, 2004).

9. ConAgra Foods, Inc., "Feeding Children Better," http://www
   .conagrafoods.com/leadership/community_children.jsp (accessed April
   14, 2004).
10. Ibid.
11. ConAgra Foods 2003 Annual Report, 26.
12. Author interview with manager, Global Communications &
   PR, GE Consumer & Industrial Products, via e-mail, September
   2003.
13. The New York Times Company Foundation, "The New York
   Times Company Foundation 2002 Annual Report," http://www.
   nytco.com/pdf-reports/2001_Annual_Report_Shareholder_Info.pdf
   (accessed April 14, 2004).
14. The New York Times Company Foundation, news release 475, "The
   New York Times Co. Foundation to Give $100,000 to School of Jour-
   nalism and Mass Communication," July 11, 1997, http://www.unc
   .edu/news/newsserv/archives/jul97/nytimes.html (accessed April 14,
   2004).
15. Emory University, "Emory University Kenneth Cole Fellowship
   in Community Building and Social Change," http://oucp.emory
   .edu/Info/KCole.html (accessed November 11, 2003).
16. Robin Givhan, "Polishing an Image: Kenneth Cole Brings Social
   Activism to Fashion Industry," Washington Post, August, 2003, M2.
17. Ibid.
18. Bill Shore, *The Cathedral Within: Transforming Your Life by Giving
   Something Back*, (New York: Random House, 1999), 91.
19. Author interview with Chris Shea, president of the General Mills
   Foundation and SVP General Mills.
20. General Motors, "Corporate Responsibility and Sustainability
   Report for 2001–2002," http://www.gm.com/company/gmability
   /sustainability/reports/02/500_product/560_responsible/562_safe
   _driving.html (accessed April 14, 2004).
21. General Motors, "Key Partners: Community Involvement Partners,"
   http://www.gm.com/company/gmability/community/partners/index
   .html (accessed April 14, 2004).
22. Microsoft Corporation, "Microsoft's New Unlimited Potential Initiative Seeks to Bridge Global Technology Skills Gap," Microsoft
   Corporation, http://www.microsoft.com/presspass/press/2003/sep03
   /09-04UPGrantsPR.asp (accessed April 14, 2004).

23. Costco Wholesale, "Opportunities," http://company.monster.com /costco12/ (accessed April 14, 2004).

24. Committee to Encourage Corporate Philanthropy, The New Century Philanthropy, volume III, no. 4 (Spring 2003), http://www .corphilanthropy.org/ (accessed April 14, 2004).

Chapter 7 *Corporate Community Volunteering*

1. The Timberland Company, press release, "The Timberland Company Launches Community Builders Tour to Support and Celebrate Communities," September 2, 2003, http://www.timberland.com /cgibin/timberland/timberland/corporate/tim_press_release.jsp?ID=P R000055 (accessed April 14, 2004).

2. Bill Shore, *Revolution of the Heart* (New York: Riverhead Books, 1995), 64.

3. Ibid., 8.

4. Ibid., xix.

5. Ford Motor Company, "Community Relations Committees," http:// www2.ford.com/en/goodWorks/fundingAndGrants/fordMotor CompanyFund/2001Report/communityRelationsCommitees .htm (accessed December 10, 2003).

6. Ford Motor Company, "Ford Motor Company Continues to Invest in Rebuilding Detroit Communities," http://www.autointell.com /news-2000-2/August-29-00-p3.htm (accessed April 14, 2004).

7. Ibid.

8. Ford Motor Company, news release, "Ford Volunteers Collected 2 tons of Greeting Cards for St. Judes," Dearborn, Michigan, February 11, 2003.

9. Carly Fiorina, "Keynote Address: Business for Social Responsibility Annual Conference," November 12, 2003, Los Angeles, Copyright (November, 2003) Hewlett-Packard Development Company, L.P. http://www.hp.com/hpinfo/execteam/speeches/fiorina/Speeches & Articles (accessed December 2, 2003)

10. Hewlett-Packard Development Company, L.P., "HP Philanthropy," http://www.hp.com/cgi-bin/pf-new.cgi?IN=http://grants.hp.com /index.html (accessed April 14, 2004).

11. Carly Fiorina, "Keynote Address."

12. Ibid.
13. Ibid.
14. Cone Inc., News Release November 11, 2001 "Post-September 11th: Major Shift in American Attitudes Towards Companies Involved with Social Issues."
15. Cone Inc., "2002 Cone Corporate Citizenship: The Role of Cause Branding: Executive Summary," http://www.coneinc.com/Pages /pr_13.html (accessed April 2, 2004).
16. FedEx Corp., "Our People: Community," http://www.fedex.com /us/about/overview/people/community/index.html?link=4 (accessed April 14, 2004).
17. FedEx Corp., "About FedEx: FedEx Community," http://www .fedex.com/us/about/responsibility/community/ (accessed April 14, 2004).
18. Fannie Mae Foundation, "We Are Volunteer Employees (WAVE)," http://www.fanniemaefoundation.org/about/wave.shtml (accessed April 14, 2004).
19. Ibid.
20. Fannie Mae Foundation, "We Walk Together. A Report on the First 15 Years of Fannie Mae Foundation's Help the Homeless Program," http://www.fanniemaefoundation.org/publications/pdf/Catalog OfPublications.pdf
21. Ibid.
22. Fannie Mae Foundation, "We Are Volunteer Employees (WAVE)."
23. Australian Government Department of the Environment and Heritage, "Environment Australia: Envirobusiness Update," Environment Australia 2001, Issue 6 (April 2001), http://www.deh.gov.au /industry/publications/ebu/ebu6/yourenv.html (accessed April 22, 2004).
24. Shell Oil Company, "Shell Coastal Volunteers," http://www.conser vationvolunteers.com.au/shell/ (accessed April 23, 2004).
25. Peter Duncan, "Can Australia Play a Leading Role in the Corporate Responsibility Debate?" BHERT News, Issue 9 (November 2000), 2.
26. AT&T Wireless, "About Us: Overview, Our Vision," http://www .attws.com/our_company/ (accessed April 15, 2004).
27. American Red Cross, "Press Room: AT&T Wireless and American Red Cross Team Up to Make Communities Safer," http://www .redcross.org/press/disaster/ds_pr/020826awe.html (accessed April 15, 2004).

28. Celina Adams, manager of corporate contributions, Timberland's Social Enterprise Department, e-mail survey message to author, November 2003.

29. Stanley Litow, vice president of corporate community relations and president of IBM International Foundation, e-mail survey message to author, June 2004.

30. Stuart Burden, director of community affairs—the America's, Levi Strauss & Co., e-mail survey message to author, July 2003.

Chapter 8 *Socially Responsible Business Practices*

1. Motorola Inc., "Motorola and the Environment: Motorola's Environmental Vision," http://www.motorola.com/EHS/environment/ (accessed April 15, 2004).

2. Business for Social Responsibility Education Fund, Corporate Social Responsibility: A Guide to Better Business Practices, (San Francisco: Business for Socially Responsible Education Fund, 2000), 179.

3. Ibid., 112.

4. Cisco Systems, Inc., "Energy Conservation—Case Study: Energy Efficiency in Design and Construction," http://www.cisco.com /en/US/about/ac227/ac228/ac229/about_cisco_corp_citi_case_study. html (accessed April 16, 2004).

5. Avert, "Avert.org: HIV and AIDS Statistics for Sub-Saharan Africa," http://www.avert.org/subaadults.htm (accessed April 16, 2004).

6. The Coca-Cola Company, "HIV/AIDS program," http://www2 .coca-cola.com/citizenship/africa_employee_program.html (accessed April 16, 2004).

7. Ibid.

8. Business for Social Responsibility Education Fund, Corporate Social Responsibility, 4.

9. Motorola Inc., "Motorola: Leadership Programs to Protect the Environment," http://www.motorola.com/EHS/environment/leadership/ (accessed April 16, 2004).

10. Ibid.

11. Ibid.

12. Ibid.

13. Intel Corporation, "Intel: Environmental, Health, and Safety 2002 Report," http://www.intel.com/intel/other/ehs/prevention/prevent.htm (accessed April 16, 2004).
14. Ibid.
15. Ibid.
16. White Wave, Inc., "Press Releases 2003: White Wave Invests in Wind to Fuel Soy Manufacturing," http://www.silkissoy.com /index.php?id=108&pid=27 (accessed April 16, 2004).
17. Sue Mecklenburg, vice president of corporate business practices, interview with author, October 2003.
18. GreenMoney Journal, "Starbucks and Conservation International Partnership Recognized in Top Global Sustainable Development Partnership Category at World Summit in Johannesburg," http://www.greenmoneyjournal.com/article.mpl?newsletterid=22& articleid=219
19. Penny Bonda and Katie Sosnowchik, green@work magazine, July/ August 2003.
20. Sara Silver, "Inside Track," Financial Times (London), December 2, 2002, Monday London Edition 1, 14.

Chapter 9 *Twenty-five Best Practices for Doing the Most Good for the Company and the Cause*

1. Michael E. Porter and Mark R. Kramer, "The Competitive Advantage of Corporate Philanthropy," Harvard Business Review, December 2002, 5.
2. Ibid.
3. Philip Kotler and Nancy Lee, "Best of Breed: When It Comes to Gaining a Market Edge While Supporting a Social Cause, 'Corporate Social Marketing' Leads the Pack," Stanford Social Innovation Review, 1, no. 4 (2004): 18.
4. Philip Kotler and Gary Armstrong, *Principles of Marketing*, 9th Edition (Upper Saddle River: Prentice Hall, 2001), 514–515.
5. Ben & Jerry's News Release, August 1, 2002 (Newstream), Ben & Jerry's and Native Energy Partner to Fight Global Warming: Ice Cream Maker to Help Cool Planet with Wind http://www.ben jerry.com/our_company/press_center/press/native_energy08012002 .html (accessed July 15, 2004)

6. Fannie Mae Foundation, We Walk Together: A Report on the First 15 Years of Fannie Mae Foundation's Help The Homeless Program, 2003, Foreword.

7. Curt Weeden, *Corporate Social Investing* (San Francisco: Berrett-Koehler Publishers, Inc., 1998), 68.

8. Committee to Encourage Corporate Philanthropy, "The Corporate Giving Standard: A Measurement Model for Corporate Philanthropy" http://www.givingstandard.com/ (accessed April 21, 2004).

9. *Kenneth Cole, Footnotes* (New York: Simon and Schuster, 2003), 162–163.

Chapter 10   A *Marketing Approach to Winning Corporate Funding and Support for Social Initiatives: Ten Recommendations*

1. Bill Shore, *Revolution of the Heart*, (New York: Riverhead Books, 1995), 118.

2. Samantha Coker, "Corporate/NGO Alliances: Engaging Corporations in Corporate Social Responsibility Initiatives" Seattle University, Summary Project, 2003.

3. American Cancer Society, "ACS Mission Statement," http://www.cancer.org/docroot/AA/content/AA_1_1_ACS_Mission_Statements.asp (accessed April 21, 2004).

4. The Nature Conservancy, "How We Work: Initiatives," http://nature.org/initiatives/ (accessed April 21, 2004).

5. Boys & Girls Club of America, "Programs: Specialized Initiatives," http://www.bgca.org/programs/specialized.asp (accessed April 21, 2004).

6. AT&T Wireless, "Media Relations: About Us," http://www.attws.com/our_company/ (accessed April 21, 2004).

7. Avon Products, Inc., "Mark: Makeup You Can Buy And Sell," http://pr.meetmark.com/PRSuite/about/pressroom.jsp?ArtID=PRESSRELEASE2&page=1 (accessed April 21, 2004).

8. American Legacy Foundation, "Press Release July 16, 2003: New Research on Young Women and Smoking: Two-thirds Want to Quit, but Only Three Percent Succeed." (Preliminary data as of January

2003.) http://www.americanlegacy.org/AmericanLegacy/skins/alf/display.aspx?moduleid=8cde2e88-3052-448c-893d-d0b4b14b31c4&mode=User&action=display_page&ObjectID=8f356b23-f3e2-4cde-925d-63656772acb5 (accessed April 21, 2004).

9. Ibid.

10. Town Topics® Princeton's Weekly Community Newspaper since 1946, December 3, 2003, http://www.towntopics.com/dec0303/people.html (accessed July 16, 2004).

INDEX